TEACHING & SUPPORTING CHILDREN WITH
SPECIAL EDUCATIONAL
NEEDS & DISABILITIES
IN PRIMARY SCHOOLS

SAGE was founded in 1965 by Sara Miller McCune to support the dissemination of usable knowledge by publishing innovative and high-quality research and teaching content. Today, we publish more than 750 journals, including those of more than 300 learned societies, more than 800 new books per year, and a growing range of library products including archives, data, case studies, reports, conference highlights, and video. SAGE remains majority-owned by our founder, and after Sara's lifetime will become owned by a charitable trust that secures our continued independence.

Los Angeles | London | Washington DC | New Delhi | Singapore

2nd Edition

TEACHING & SUPPORTING CHILDREN WITH
SPECIAL EDUCATIONAL
NEEDS & DISABILITIES
IN PRIMARY SCHOOLS

JONATHAN GLAZZARD, JANE STOKOE, ALISON HUGHES, ANNETTE NETHERWOOD
and LESLEY NEVE

SAGE | LearningMatters

Los Angeles | London | New Delhi
Singapore | Washington DC | Boston

Learning Matters
An imprint of SAGE Publications Ltd
1 Oliver's Yard
55 City Road
London EC1Y 1SP

SAGE Publications Inc.
2455 Teller Road
Thousand Oaks, California 91320

SAGE Publications India Pvt Ltd
B 1/I 1 Mohan Cooperative Industrial Area
Mathura Road
New Delhi 110 044

SAGE Publications Asia-Pacific Pte Ltd
3 Church Street
#10-04 Samsung Hub
Singapore 049483

© 2015 Jonathan Glazzard, Jane Stokoe, Alison Hughes, Annette Netherwood, Lesley Neve

First published as *Teaching Primary Special Needs* in 2010 by Learning Matters Ltd. Reprinted in 2011. Second edition published in 2015.

Editor: Amy Thornton
Production controller: Chris Marke
Project management: Deer Park Productions, Tavistock, Devon
Marketing manager: Catherine Slinn
Cover design: Wendy Scott
Typeset by: C&M Digitals (P) Ltd, Chennai, India
Printed in Great Britain by Henry Ling Limited at The Dorset Press, Dorchester, DT1 1HD

Library of Congress Control Number: 2014958165

British Library Cataloguing in Publication Data

A catalogue record for this book is available from the British Library

ISBN 978-1-4739-1248-9 (pbk)
ISBN 978-1-4739-1247-2

At SAGE we take sustainability seriously. Most of our products are printed in the UK using FSC papers and boards. When we print overseas we ensure sustainable papers are used as measured by the Egmont grading system. We undertake an annual audit to monitor our sustainability.

Contents

About the authors

Jonathan Glazzard has overall responsibility for Initial Teacher Training in Primary Education at the University of Huddersfield. He is course leader for the Primary QTS route and also teaches on the MA programme. Jonathan has worked at the University of Huddersfield since 2005. Prior to this, he worked as a primary school teacher and Assistant Head Teacher in Barnsley for 10 years. During his time in schools, Jonathan was responsible for the co-ordination of special educational needs. In addition to leading the Primary QTS course at Huddersfield, Jonathan teaches special and inclusive education at the university. He is currently using narrative approaches to research inclusive education for his doctoral thesis.

Jane Stokoe is a primary teacher with over 30 years' teaching experience across all phases of primary education. In more recent years she has specialised in working within the Foundation Stage and Key Stage 1, and is now enjoying the challenges of combining the role of Assistant Head with the role of SENCO in a primary school in Barnsley. She works in partnership with the University of Huddersfield to support trainee teachers, a role she greatly values. Additional experiences include working with and supporting a range of Early Years settings in the implementation of effective practice in the delivery of synthetic phonics. Jane has worked throughout her career to develop appropriate inclusive practices for all children and is committed to developing strategies to support the needs of learners with special educational needs.

Alison Hughes became a Senior Lecturer at the University of Huddersfield on the BA(Hons) Early Primary Education course following a successful teaching career lasting 34 years. She has now retired from the university. She was a teaching head of a primary school for 11 years, during which time she worked with colleague heads on a number of collaborative partnerships and was a facilitator for the National College for School Leadership Leading Small Primary Schools programme. She has had a wide range of other teaching experiences which include working with Reception, Key Stage 1 and Key Stage 2 children. She has a strong interest in special educational needs and spent some time as Teacher-in-Charge of a hearing impaired unit. Earlier in her career she also worked in secondary education in Bradford, Inner London and Bedford.

Annette Netherwood has had extensive experience of teaching special educational needs pupils, in both mainstream and special schools, and has also delivered lectures on special needs and initial professional development to QTS trainees at the University of Huddersfield. She obtained her MA in Action Research through exploring effective teaching and learning methods for SEN pupils. She has contributed to the Institute for Citizenship's work on the teaching of citizenship to SEN pupils, and has also been a research associate for the National College for School Leadership, leading to the publication of research which explored innovative curriculum design. She has recently retired from teaching and is currently studying for her Education Doctorate at the University of Sheffield.

Lesley Neve has now retired as Senior Lecturer at the University of Huddersfield. She has long experience of teaching across all phases of education. In more recent years she has specialised in working in teacher training both within the Foundation Stage and Key

Stage 1 and also for the Lifelong Learning sector. In addition to working with trainees at Huddersfield, Lesley also placed the students on a special needs placement. Her interests include accessibility and integrating technology into mainstream settings. A sufferer from dyslexia herself, Lesley has also previously worked as a SENCO.

1

What do we mean by 'special educational needs and disabilities' in primary schools?

Chapter objectives

This chapter covers:

- the history of the special educational needs (SEN) system in England;
- the statutory duties on schools and LAs;
- the key aspects of the 2014 Code of Practice.

Teachers' Standards

This chapter addresses the following Teachers' Standards:

Part 2: Teachers must have an understanding of, and always act within, the statutory frameworks which set out their professional duties and responsibilities.

Introduction

This chapter will introduce students briefly to the historical development of inclusive education. It will examine the current policy context in relation to SEN and it will discuss the new Code of Practice for SEN (DfE, 2014).

History

The 1972 Education Act gave all children the right to an education; however, severe their disabilities. Following this Act many local education authorities struggled, without guidance, to provide school education for children with SEN and most of the education took place in special schools (Warnock, 2005). In 1974 Margaret Thatcher, then the Secretary of State for Education, commissioned the Committee of Inquiry into the Education of Handicapped Children and Young People to review the education of pupils with SEN.

Mary Warnock led the inquiry and the recommendations from this were published in the Warnock Report in 1978 (DES/Warnock, 1978). The report introduced the terminology of *special educational needs* and made the recommendation that, where possible, children with SEN should be educated in mainstream schools. The concept of *integration* was born which focused largely on the assimilation of pupils with SEN into mainstream schools. Integration placed little or no onus on the school to make adaptations or adjustment to meet the specific needs of learners. Instead learners with SEN were expected to adapt to a system of education which was largely unchanged.

The recommendations of the Warnock Report formed the basis of the 1981 Education Act which introduced a financial safety net to support the most vulnerable children in mainstream provision. This was to be known as the *statement* of SEN. However, the 1981 Education Act made no provision for any additional funding to be allocated to local education authorities to implement the new procedures (Warnock, 2005). The effect of this was that parents fought with cash-strapped local education authorities to gain statements for their children (Warnock, 2005). Tribunals were established in the 1990s to adjudicate in the disputes. Warnock has more recently stated that she personally felt that she held 'a degree of responsibility for what turned out to be not a very bright idea' (Warnock, 2005: 27) when making specific reference to the statementing process.

The signing of the Salamanca Agreement (UNESCO, 1994) signalled a policy shift from integration to *inclusion* and marked an international commitment to the principle of inclusive education. Nations signed up to the principle that ordinary schools should accommodate all children, regardless of their physical, intellectual, social, emotional, linguistic or other conditions. This was an important policy development because the agreement placed an onus on schools to be more proactive in meeting the needs of learners with disabilities.

The late 1980s and the 1990s saw the growth of the competitive market in which schools had to operate. The Education Reform Act of 1988 resulted in the introduction of the National Curriculum and this was accompanied with the introduction of statutory assessment tests (SATs) in primary and secondary schools and the publication of these results in the form of league tables. Additionally, a system of rigorous school inspections was established during the 1990s and failing schools were named and shamed. Under-performing schools were placed in 'special measures' and subjected to a process of re-inspection and threat of closure unless results improved. It could be argued that the marketisation of education was largely unconducive to the development of inclusive practices in schools and many academic commentators have argued that that the implementation of inclusive education policies within a discourse of raising standards resulted in policy agendas which were largely incompatible (Warnock, 1996; Armstrong, 1998; Barton, 1998).

Despite the climate of competition the Labour government continued the raising standards agenda when they came to power in 1997 at the same time as advancing an agenda for inclusive education. Through policy documents (DfEE, 1997; DfES, 2004), disability discrimination legislation and agendas such as *Every Child Matters* (HMSO, 2003) there was an emphasis on the need for schools to plan more proactively to meet the diverse needs of different learners and a clear expectation that schools should become increasingly inclusive.

However, according to Goodley:

> *Educational environments, curricula content, teacher identities are all normatively associated with environments, standards and achievements that are at odds with*

the quirkiness of disabled learners. Schools continue to exclude children by virtue of their inaccessibility. Curricula promote standards that some with (or without) impairments will never reach ... Teachers are assessed in ways that celebrate high achievement over the valuing of difference ... disabled students continue to be singled out for specialized attention, are segregated from non-disabled peers through the presence of non-disabled adult supporters and remain unrepresented in images of schooling and educational attainment.

(Goodley, 2007: 319)

Therefore for children with SEN it is important to reflect on the extent to which current curricula and approaches to assessment marginalise and therefore exclude children with disabilities.

Voice of a Special Educational Needs Co-Ordinator (SENCO)

'Inclusion' ... one short word. It is a word, however, that I struggle to define despite its prominence in my current professional role. Should I be asked to substitute this with an alternative my response would be 'belonging'. Immediately other words spring to mind, including 'acceptance'. It is profoundly evident that I have no clear understanding of the word 'inclusion' and that despite my strong beliefs that I wish to 'include' all children in my teaching I am unable to offer an explanation as to the meanings of my practices. I offer no apologies for my poor understanding of this educational term. Through copious discussions with friends and colleagues, as well as my own readings, it has become evident that this one word, in reality, has several meanings. It is a word with several meanings to different individuals who may at the same time be working to enable and support its principles. There is little wonder that, despite working in an 'inclusive' environment, I continue to find it a frustrating and challenging experience.

There are aspects of some interpretations of 'inclusion' that I embrace wholeheartedly. To include children is to ensure that they are not simply a physical presence. I strive to make adaptations to my practices to ensure that all children can access all aspects of their education. I view the classroom as 'ours'. It is a space which belongs to all of us, a space in which we can all grow and develop, and a space where we can all enjoy a strong sense of belonging. To simply belong, however, is inadequate in terms of explaining inclusion. 'Acceptance' is of course another term which will have different meanings for different people. It is, I now acknowledge, acceptance that is central to my own interpretation of 'inclusion'. I believe that we are all capable of great things and that equally we all find some aspects of life and learning more challenging. The current agenda relating to inclusion does not, in my opinion, support acceptance. There is a strong force to drive all children towards a narrow measure of success, so narrow that it cannot be fully attained by all children. I truly strive to accept the differences between children.

REFLECTIVE TASK

Discuss the following questions with a colleague on your course.

- Is the current emphasis on English, mathematics and age-related expectations in the National Curriculum instrumentally failing certain groups of learners and allowing other learners to excel?

- How can assessment systems in schools be modified to broaden out what is meant by success and achievement?

Current policy context

Current SEN policy focuses on achieving better outcomes for pupils with SEND. Outcomes include achievement, access to further and higher education, access to employment and independent living in adult life. There is a clear focus within policy on the need for schools to close the achievement gap between pupils with and without SEND and there is a clear emphasis on schools and teachers demonstrating higher expectations of learners with SEND.

The White Paper, 2010

The government's White Paper *The Importance of Teaching* (DfE, 2010) set out the coalition government's strategy on education. In relation to pupils with SEND the White Paper promised to:

- ensure that school inspections focus more on the education of pupils with SEND;
- ensure that school inspections focus more on the progress that pupils make from their starting points;
- improve initial teacher training, with specific reference to training in SEND;
- address the culture of low expectations for disadvantaged groups.

Ofsted review of SEND, 2010

Ofsted reviewed educational provision for pupils with SEND in 2010 (Ofsted, 2010). Key points raised in the report are stated below:

- The Ofsted review found evidence that the way the system is currently designed contributed to widespread weaknesses in the quality of provision for children with SEN.
- Some schools and other organisations were working well together and focusing on the *outcomes* for the young person.
- Rigorous monitoring of progress, with quick intervention and thorough evaluation of its impact was critical to successful outcomes for children.
- High aspirations and a determination to enable young people to be as independent as possible led most reliably to the best educational achievement.
- The need for a continuing focus on, and the highest expectations for, disabled children and young people and those with SEN is not just an issue for schools and colleges, or even for all local services, but also for national bodies, including Ofsted itself.

The Green Paper, 2011

The government's Green Paper on SEND (DfE, 2011) stated that:

- The current system of SEN support is too complicated, identifies issues too late, has too much duplication, and does not focus sufficiently on outcomes for pupils with SEND.
- Parents find the current system too bureaucratic and complain that their voices are not listened to.
- SEN can sometimes be 'unhelpfully conflated' with falling behind, and this may have contributed to the growing number of pupils who have been identified as having SEND.
- With the right support and high quality teaching children with SEND can be supported to achieve good outcomes.

Current legislation

All educational institutions must be compliant with the Equality Act 2010 which identifies disability as a protected characteristic. The implications are that schools and other educational institutions must be able to demonstrate that they have taken steps to ensure that learners with disabilities are not subjected to either direct or indirect discrimination. Additionally, educational institutions must be able to demonstrate that they have taken steps to promote positive relationships between different groups of learners. They will also need to demonstrate that they have made reasonable adjustments to the educational provision to ensure that learners with disabilities are provided with equality of opportunity.

Code of Practice

The new Code of Practice for Special Educational Needs and Disabilities (DfE, 2014) replaces the previous Code of Practice (DfES, 2001). Within the new Code there is a stronger focus on supporting learners into adult life, thus the Code offers protection and support from birth to the age of 25. There is also a stronger focus on strengthening participation of parents and pupils and fostering effective collaboration between external agencies. The following sections will briefly summarise the key aspects of the new Code of Practice.

Definition

The new Code of Practice (DfE, 2014) has not changed the definition of SEN:

- A child and young person has SEN if they have a learning difficulty or disability which calls for special educational provision to be made.
- A child of compulsory school age or a young person has a learning difficulty or disability if they have significantly greater difficulty in learning than the majority of others of the same age or has a disability which prevents or hinders them from making use of facilities of a kind generally provided for others of the same age in mainstream schools.

Key principles

The key principles of the Code of Practice (DfE, 2014) are:

- participation of children, their parents and young people in decision making;
- early identification of children and young people's needs and early intervention to support them;
- greater choice and control for young people and parents over support;
- collaboration between education, health and social care services to provide support;
- high quality provision to meet the needs of children and young people with SEN;
- a focus on inclusive practice and removing barriers to learning;
- successful preparation for adulthood, including independent living and employment.

Participation in decision making

Supporting and involving children and young people and their parents in decisions about support means having regard to:

- the views, wishes and feelings of the child and his or her parent, or the young person;
- the importance of the child and his or her parent, or the young person, participating as fully as possible in decisions relating identification of needs, needs assessments, LA and school provision, reviews of progress and Education, Health and Care Plans (EHC);
- the importance of the child and his or her parent, or the young person, being provided with the information and support necessary to enable them to participate in the decision-making process;
- the need to provide the child and his or her parent, or the young person, with complete and accessible information.

Articles 12 and 13 of the United Nations Convention on the Rights of the Child (United Nations, 1989) state that children and young people have the right to express their opinions and to have these taken into account in relation to all matters which affect them. Their views should be given due weight according to their age, maturity and capability. Schools will need to consider how to support those pupils without verbal communication to enable them to participate in decision-making processes and to express their views.

Schools are now required to publish on their websites the mechanisms that they have established to enable parents, children and young people to express their views and participate in decision-making processes. Schools should also encourage parents to share their knowledge of the child or young person. The Code of Practice (DfE, 2014) explicitly states that the views of parents must not be used as a proxy for the views of children and young people. The Children and Families Act 2014 places a duty on LAs to engage directly with the young person rather than their parents when they have reached the end of compulsory schooling. The Code of Practice (DfE, 2014) acknowledges that some pupils and parents will lack the mental capacity to make decisions and express their views and in these cases LAs and schools should consider how advocates might be able to support them to get their voices heard.

SEN support

SEN support replaces School Action/School Action Plus. It is the category of support for children with SEN who are not on EHC plans.

- It focuses on the impact of the provision for children and young people and places emphasis on a *graduated approach* to addressing needs.
- The aim is to improve the quality of the educational experience and outcomes of school for all pupils ensuring high quality teaching and learning.

The Code of Practice (DfE, 2014) emphasises that differentiated and personalised provision will meet the needs of the majority of pupils. However, there is an acknowledgement within the Code that *some pupils* will require provision which is additional to or different from the provision which meets the needs of the majority. The Code stresses that high quality SEN provision is underpinned by:

- high quality teaching;
- high ambitions for children and young people with SEND;
- stretching/challenging targets for children and young people with SEND;
- clear systems for tracking progress towards these targets;
- continual reviewing of provision;
- a clear relentless focus on approaches which impact on pupil progress;
- a focus on promoting positive outcomes in personal, social and emotional development.

Schools are required to publish a SEN Information Report which details admission arrangements and the processes in place for identifying SEN and mechanisms which have been established to enable children, young people and parents to participate fully in the processes. Additionally, this report needs to provide details of the provision available in the school to support pupils with SEND.

Schools must support pupils with a wide range of SEN and make reasonable adjustments to their provision to enable pupils with SEND to participate fully in the opportunities which are available to all pupils. Under the Equality Act 2010 schools have a duty to prevent discrimination, promote equality of opportunity and foster good relations. There is a clear emphasis in the Code on teachers setting high expectations for all pupils, irrespective of their prior achievement and if teaching is high quality fewer children will require special educational provision.

Schools are required to assess the attainment and skills of each pupil on entry. The Code is explicit that effective planning will enable pupils with SEND to study the full national curriculum. Schools need to ensure that all teachers have the knowledge and skills to be able to identify pupils who are making less than expected progress, taking into account their individual circumstances. The first response from schools is to ensure that high quality teaching is specifically targeted at the area of weakness. Schools must not delay in putting into place additional teaching and intervention for pupils who are making less than expected progress. However, the Code explicitly states that:

- Low attainment and slow progress does not necessarily mean that a child has SEN.
- Attainment in line with chronological age does not mean that a child has no learning difficulties.
- Persistent and disruptive or withdrawn behaviour does not necessarily mean that a child has SEN.
- Difficulties solely related to limitations in English are not SEN.

Schools must have in place a clear approach for identifying and responding to SEN. These mechanisms should enable schools to identify needs at the earliest point. Four broad areas of need are identified in the Code of Practice:

- Communication and interaction needs: these include pupils with autistic spectrum disorder (ASD) and those with speech, language and communication needs (SLCN).
- Cognition and learning needs: these include moderate learning difficulties (MLD), severe learning difficulties (SLD), profound and multiple learning difficulties (PMLD) and specific learning difficulties (SpLD) which include dyslexia, dyscalculia and dyspraxia.
- Social, emotional and mental health difficulties: these include attention deficit disorder (ADD), attention deficit hyperactivity disorder (ADHD) and attachment disorder.
- Sensory and physical difficulties: these include visual impairment, hearing impairment and multisensory impairment.

Need can fall into one of these broad categories or cut across categories. Teacher training institutions should ensure that trainee teachers have the knowledge and skills to identify needs and understand how to support pupils in overcoming barriers to learning, participation and achievement in each of the above areas. SENCOs should ensure that all teachers have access to continuing professional development in relation to SEND and SENCOs should regularly undertake professional development to update their knowledge and skills.

The Code of Practice (DfE, 2014) explicitly states that additional intervention and support cannot compensate for lack of good quality teaching. SENCOs in conjunction with other school leaders play a pivotal role in monitoring the quality of teaching and learning for pupils with SEND. Before pupils are identified as having SEND school leaders need to be absolutely certain that pupils have been exposed to consistently high quality teaching. Where pupils have been identified as having SEND schools are required to adopt a graduated response to address their needs. SENCOs should ensure that there is a clear provision map which identifies what specific interventions and support are available for pupils with SEND across the school and this provision should be managed carefully. This means that interventions which do not have an impact on the progress of learners with SEND should be discontinued and replaced by more effective interventions which target effectively specific areas of need.

Graduated response

In adopting a graduated response for pupils on SEN Support teachers and SENCOs need to use the following process:

- Assess: assessments should draw on analysis of the pupil's needs, teacher assessment and observations. Views of parents and pupils should be sought along with the views of other professionals who may have involvement with the child.
- Plan: parents must be informed if a decision is taken to provide SEN support for the child. This decision should be recorded on the school information system and parents should be made aware of the planned support and interventions.
- Do: the class teacher retains responsibility for the pupil, even in cases where the child is working with a teaching assistant (TA) on a one-to-one basis or as part of a group for some of the time. The chosen interventions should be selected on the basis of how successful they have been in addressing outcomes for pupils.
- Review: the impact of the intervention should be identified and parents and pupils should be involved in the review. Targets should be identified and parents and pupils should be involved fully in the target setting process.

A decision about whether or not to involve external specialists should be based on whether a pupil continues to make less than expected progress despite intervention. The involvement of specific specialists will largely be dependent upon the area of need but specialists may include educational psychologists, child and adolescent mental health services (CAMHS), speech and language therapists, advisory and other specialist teachers, occupational therapists, physiotherapists and behaviour support. The progress of pupils with SEND should be reviewed regularly but at least three times per year and reviews of progress should involve the child or young person and the parent or an advocate where this is deemed necessary.

PRACTICAL TASK PRACTICAL TASK PRACTICAL TASK PRACTICAL TASK PRACTICAL TASK

During your school-based placement identify opportunities to further your understanding of the roles and responsibilities of different professionals in supporting children with SEN. These may include educational psychologists, the SENCO, speech and language therapists, behaviour specialists, physiotherapists, visual and hearing-impaired specialists or professionals from a communication and interaction team. This is not an exhaustive list. Some of these professionals may well be supporting children and practitioners in your placement setting. It would be useful to arrange a mutually convenient time to discuss their roles. Additionally you may wish to 'shadow' them as they work with children and other professionals in your school. Following your experience of shadowing multi-agency professionals, carefully consider the ways in which this expertise is disseminated to school-based professionals and the ways in which reasonable adjustments are made to adopt the advice given.

The Code of Practice states that pupils without EHC plans must be educated in mainstream schools (except in specific circumstances). There is a clear commitment in the Code to the principles of inclusive education and removing barriers to learning and participation for pupils in mainstream schools. The Children and Families Act 2014 secures the general presumption that children with SEND will be educated in mainstream schools. Schools are not allowed to refuse to admit a pupil receiving SEN Support on the basis that they do not feel able to support the child's needs or because they do not have an EHC plan. The Equality Act 2010 prohibits schools from discriminating against pupils with disabilities in relation to admission arrangements.

Schools must establish a culture of high expectations for pupils with SEND under the new system. Pupils with SEND must be included in opportunities which are available to pupils without SEND and schools need to be able to demonstrate that they have made reasonable adjustments to their provision to address the specific needs of pupils with SEND. Special schools continue to have an important role to play in working collaboratively with mainstream schools to support them in addressing the needs of pupils with SEND.

Education, Health and Care plans (EHC)

The EHC plans replace the statements which have supported pupils with the most severe needs for more than 30 years. Pupils who are currently entitled to a statement of SEN will be transferred onto EHC plans. The purpose of the EHC plans is to make special educational provision to meet the needs of pupils whose needs cannot be met by SEN Support. The LA will carry out a needs assessment to review the education, health and care needs of the child. A needs assessment will not automatically lead to a plan. The assessment will review all available evidence including information about the pupil's progress and attainment, their personal, social and emotional development, the nature, extent and context of the special educational need and the impact of the actions which have been taken to date to address the need. Children, young people and parents should be fully involved in the assessment process and should be consulted about the intention to ask for a needs assessment. Requests for assessments can arise from parents, young people over the age of 16 but under 25, a person acting on behalf of a school, foster carers, health and social care professionals, early years practitioners, youth offending teams and probation services. Under the Children and Families Act, 2014 anyone can bring a child or young person who they believe has SEND to the attention of the LA.

Plans should be:

- clear, concise, readable and accessible to parents, children, young people and practitioners;
- specific on special educational needs, outcomes and special educational, health and care provision needed, with clearly identified sections;
- supportive of preparation for key transition points; and
- portable.

Parents can request a specific school or college to be named as the preferred choice of educational institution in the EHC plan because one of the key principles of the new Code of Practice is to give parents and carers more choice. Additionally parents and children on EHC plans have the right to request a place in a special school.

Personal budgets

Young people and parents of children with EHC plans have a right to request a personal budget. Personal budgets may include elements of education, social care and health funding, dependent upon the needs of the child or young person. Joint commissioning arrangements should be established to enable partner organisations to make arrangements for agreeing personal budgets and there must be a clear locally agreed policy for personal budgets. Families or young people can receive direct payments or funding may be held by the school/college or by a third party.

- A personal budget is a specific amount of funding identified to deliver parts of the provision set out in an EHC plan.
- Families can request a personal budget as part of the planning process when EHC plans are drawn up or during Annual Reviews of the EHC plan.
- Personal budgets can include funding from education, health and social care – in education, funding for personal budgets will be for more specialist or individualised provision rather than services the school is expected to provide as part of the local offer.
- A LA must secure a school's agreement where any provision, bought by the parent/young person using a direct payment, will be provided on the school's premises.

Reviewing progress

Classroom or subject teachers working with the SENCO should assess where a child is not making adequate progress, despite high quality teaching targeted at an area of weakness. They should draw on evidence from a clear analysis of the pupil's need such as:

- teacher's assessment and experience of the pupil;
- information on pupil progress, attainment, and behaviour;
- individual's development in comparison to their peers;
- the views and experience of parents;
- the child's own views; and
- advice from external support services.

Reviews of progress will determine what kind of support a child needs i.e., whether SEN Support is appropriate or whether it is necessary to request a needs assessment for an EHC plan. For children and young people with EHC plans reviews of progress will determine the appropriateness of the plan and identify future targets.

Legal duties on schools

The main legal duties on schools will not change, but the way they will be met may change. Schools must continue to:

- meet their Equality Act duties for pupils with disabilities;
- use their 'best endeavours' to meet pupils' SEN – this means doing everything they can to meet children and young people's SEN;

- inform parents when pupils receive support for SEN and involve them in reviews of progress;
- admit a young person, where the school is named in an EHC plan;
- co-operate with the LA in developing the local offer; and
- have regard to the new 0–25 SEND Code of Practice.

The Code of Practice (para 9.79) states that schools named on EHC plans have a duty to admit those pupils unless:

- it would be unsuitable for the age, ability, aptitude or SEN of the child or young person; or
- the attendance of the child or young person there would be incompatible with the efficient education of others, or the efficient use of resources.

New duties require schools to:

- produce and publish online a School SEN Information Report;
- appoint a suitably qualified or experienced member of staff as SENCO;
- make arrangements to support pupils with medical conditions and schools must have regard to statutory guidance supporting pupils at school with medical conditions.

Para 6.85 of the Code states that:

> The SENCO **must** be a qualified teacher working at the school. A newly appointed SENCO **must** be a qualified teacher and, where they have not previously been the SENCO at that or any other relevant school for a total period of more than twelve months, they **must** achieve a National Award in Special Educational Needs Co-ordination within three years of appointment.
>
> (DfE, 2014: 97)

Implications for school governors

School governors:

- must have regard to the SEND Code of Practice and should oversee the implementation of the reform and provide strategic support to the head teacher;
- must publish information about the school's SEND policy on the school's website;
- must ensure that there is a qualified teacher designated as SENCO;
- must co-operate generally with the LA including in developing the local offer and when the school is being named in an EHC plan;
- must ensure that arrangements are in place in schools to support pupils at school with medical conditions;
- must also publish information about the arrangements for the admission of disabled pupils, the steps taken to prevent disabled children being treated less favourably than others, the facilities provided to assist access of disabled children, and their accessibility plans.

Implications for head teachers

All head teachers:

- should take overall responsibility for implementing the SEND;
- ensure that the SENCO is a member of the leadership team;
- ensure that all teachers, TAs, governors and parents understand the implications of the reforms;
- put in place arrangements to ensure parents are able to participate fully in decision-making processes and reviews of their child's progress;
- establish processes to enable children and young people to participate in decision making and discussions about their progress;

- ensure a process is in place to review SEND provision on a regular basis;
- develop clear policies to support children in the process of transition to secondary education.

Implications for SENCOs

The SENCO role is a strategic one working with the senior leadership to develop policies in relation to SEND. The SENCO and leadership team must ensure that provision is in place to support identified needs. The role involves:

- overseeing day-to-day operation of the school's SEN policy;
- co-ordinating provision for children with SEN;
- liaising with the designated teacher where a looked after child has SEN;
- advising colleagues on graduated approach to SEN Support;
- advising on use of delegated SEN budget/other resources;
- liaising with parents of children with SEN;
- links with other education settings and professionals from other agencies;
- liaising with other schools to plan smooth transitions for pupils who transfer to new schools;
- working strategically with the head teacher and governors to ensure that provision is fully compliant with the Equality Act and is fully compliant with all duties specified in the Code;
- monitoring the quality of teaching and learning for pupils with SEND as part of whole school monitoring;
- monitoring progress and attainment data of pupils with SEND as part of whole school monitoring;
- ensuring that SEN records are stored safely and kept up to date.

Implications for school nurses

Where schools have nurses, they can be part of the integral part of the whole school approach to SEND in that they can:

- support effective communication with all professionals, children, young people and families in relation to health and educational outcomes;
- provide clear information and actions to be taken in relation to health needs;
- identify specific training requirements around health needs for TAs;
- take part in reviewing the EHC plan;
- clarify roles and responsibilities of key health workers; and
- support plans for transition to adult services/colleges.

Implications for maintained nurseries

Providers are required to:

- follow the standards set out in the Early Years Foundation Stage framework, which includes supporting children with SEND;
- use their best endeavours to make sure that a child with SEN gets the support they need, ensuring that children with SEN engage in the activities of the school alongside those who do not have SEN;
- adopt the new SEN Support approach – they are no longer required to record on early years action/early years action plus;
- work in partnership with parents/carers to develop a plan of support;
- admit a child, where the nursery is named in their EHC plan;
- co-operate with the LA in developing the local offer; and
- have a qualified teacher designated as a SENCO.

Your statutory responsibilities: teachers

Classroom and subject teachers are at the heart of the new SEN Support system. They are responsible for driving the movement around the four stages (assess, plan, do, review) of action with the support guidance of the SENCO and other specialist staff. The classroom teacher should:

- take responsibility for all children including those with SEND;
- take a lead in planning for pupils with SEND;
- focus on outcomes for the child;
- be responsible for meeting SEN, harnessing strategically the support of the SENCO to support the quality of teaching.
- evaluate the quality of interventions and other educational provision regularly;
- have high aspirations for every pupil: set clear and challenging progress targets for pupils;
- involve parents and pupils in planning and reviewing progress: seek their views and provide regular updates on progress.

The role of learning support assistance

- Learning support assistants (LSAs)/TAs are part of the whole school approach to SEN, working in partnership with the classroom/subject teacher and the SENCO to accelerate pupil progress and narrow gaps in performance.
- It is for schools to decide how they deploy TAs depending on their level of experience. To be most effective the support they give should be focused on the achievement of specific outcomes within the graduated approach to SEN support agreed with parents in the context of high quality teaching overall.
- LSAs/TAs can be part of a package of support for the individual child but should never be a substitute for the teacher's involvement with that child.

Support for pupils with medical difficulties

- The reforms place a duty on governing bodies to ensure that arrangements are in place in schools to support pupils at school with medical conditions. These arrangements should show an understanding of how medical conditions impact on a child's ability to learn, as well as increase their confidence and promote self-care.
- Governing bodies should ensure that school leaders consult health and social care professionals, pupils and parents to ensure that the needs of children with medical conditions are effectively supported; staff should be properly trained to provide the support that their pupils need.
- Governing bodies should ensure that the appropriate level of insurance is in place and appropriately reflects the level of risk.
- These changes should give parents and pupils confidence in the school's ability to properly support pupils with medical conditions so that they have full access to education, including school trips and physical education.

The Local Offer

The Local Offer is published by the LA. It sets out the provision of services across education, health and social care including the provision available for pupils receiving SEN Support (i.e. those not on EHC plans). The Local Offer should provide clear, comprehensive, accessible information about the provision available and how parents and young people can access these services. Information about how to request a needs assessment, how needs will be identified and assessed, alternative educational provision and the provision of local services including online and blended learning should be included in the Local Offer.

- The Local Offer should be co-produced. Parents, children and young people should participate in contributing to the Local Offer and the full range of partner organisations that support SEND services within a LA must collaborate to produce the final agreed offer.
- Specific information, support and advice on how to manage personal budgets should also be included.
- The duty on schools to co-operate with the LA in developing the local offer is aligned to the requirement on schools to publish SEN information, which gives details about their individual approach to identifying and supporting children with SEN.
- The Local Offer must include information on services across education, health and social care and from birth to 25; how to access specialist support; how decisions are made including eligibility criteria for accessing services where appropriate; and how to complain or appeal.
- The Local Offer should provide information about what the agreed protocols are for sharing information across education, health and social care services. It must address issues of confidentiality, consent and security of information. LAs are required to discuss with parents, children or young people any information they wish to share about them with other agencies.

SEN information report

Schools are required to publish an information report on the school website which provides parents with clear information about the school admissions policy and details on how SEN will be identified, information on assessment processes and the provision available in the school. It is effectively the school's 'local' offer to parents and children.

Schools should ensure that the information is easily accessible by young people and parents and is set out in clear, straightforward language. It should include information on the school's SEN policy and named contacts within the school for situations where young people or parents have concerns. It should also give details of the school's contribution to the Local Offer and must include information on where the LA's Local Offer is published. Parents, children and young people should have opportunities to contribute to the school's 'local offer'.

School admissions

The Code of Practice does not change existing duties on schools and LAs about admissions.

- It maintains the general principle, that children and young people with SEN should be educated in mainstream settings.
- Schools including Academies must admit a child named on an EHC plan unless special circumstances prevent this.
- Parents and young people can request for a school to be named in an EHC plan – the LA must comply with their wish except in exceptional circumstances.

Joint commissioning

The principle which underpins joint commissioning is that of collaboration. Education, health and social care services should work together to ensure that the right support is available for pupils with SEND. Different services or agencies must agree formally how they will work together to provide personalised and integrated support to meet the needs of pupils with SEND. The agreement must cover the full range of services for children and young people aged from 0 to 25 and include those with and without EHC plans.

Joint commissioning involves joint understanding, joint planning and delivery of services and joint review of provision. A strategic body (The Health and Wellbeing Board) must be established within the LA to promote integrated partnership working. Each partner needs to understand precisely who is responsible for what and there must be clearly agreed protocols which set out how partners will work together effectively to raise outcomes for children with SEND.

- Joint commissioning is how partners agree how they will work together to deliver joint outcomes for children and young people with SEND.
- Schools should be involved in the commissioning process to influence decisions about commissioning provision for children with SEND generally and will need to be involved directly in commissioning provision for individual pupils.
- The commissioning of services is based on need. Partners may draw their data from a number of sources and should ensure they take account of all children and young people, not just those with EHC plans or registered disabled.

Preparation for adulthood

Support needs to start early and should centre around the child or young person's own aspirations, interests and needs to enable children and young people to achieve their ambitions in relation to:

- higher education and/or employment – including exploring different employment options, such as support for becoming self-employed and help from supported employment agencies;
- independent living – enabling people to have choice and control over their lives and the support they receive and their accommodation and living arrangements, including supported living;
- participating in society – including having friends and supportive relationships, and participating in, and contributing to, the local community; and
- being as healthy as possible in adult life.

Implications for parents

A core principle of the reforms is that parents of children with SEN and young people with SEN should participate in decision making.

- Parents should know what they can reasonably expect their local school, college, LA and local services to provide.
- Schools and LAs should work with parents and carers to plan what services their children need.
- LAs have a duty to provide information, advice and support on SEN to children and young people directly, as well as to parents; this has been extended to include children and young people with disabilities (even if they don't have SEN) and their parents.

Schools engaging with parents

Schools need to:

- reassure parents that, just because the system is changing, that does not mean that children who have SEN will not get the support they need;
- explain the new system to parents so they understand what is changing and what is not changing in their school;

- be clear when changes are being made and what impact they will have – ensure parents understand how the school determines 'outcomes';
- clarify what role parents and pupils will have to influence the changes;
- ensure parents are involved in on-going planning, progress reporting and decision making;
- signpost parents to further information and support;
- LAs will need to ensure that there is sufficient support and advice available for children, young people and parents/carers.

LAs

- LAs will work with schools to ensure there is appropriate provision in place to support children with SEND.
- Through the local offer schools will be able to access information about provisions and services available in their area.
- For children with more complex needs, the LA will work with schools to conduct an assessment for EHC needs.
- Joint commissioning arrangements should enable partners to make best use of all the resources available in an area to improve outcomes for children and young people in the most efficient, effective, equitable and sustainable way.

Funding arrangements

- Funding for schools is provided by central government to LAs through the Dedicated Schools Grant. LAs distribute this to schools by using a local funding formula.
- Additional funds are allocated to schools by LAs to support pupils with SEND and the amount allocated will depend on the number of pupils with SEND and the severity of their needs.
- Schools are able to apply for access to additional top-up funding if the expenditure on a pupil exceeds the allocated amount.

Ofsted inspection framework for schools

The Ofsted framework for school inspections (Ofsted, 2014) places a responsibility on school inspectors to judge how well pupils make progress from their starting points. Inspectors will focus on the quality of teaching for all pupils and this will be evaluated on the basis of pupils' achievements from their starting points. Inspectors will focus on:

- the extent to which teachers have high aspirations for all students, including those who have SEN;
- whether those pupils with the greatest needs receive the most expert support;
- the extent to which pupils with SEND make the best possible progress and are independent so that they are well prepared for their futures;
- the extent to which school leaders ask challenging questions about the progress and attainment of every pupil or young person; the extent to which they use whatever information is available to compare the progress of their pupils against that of other pupils who started at the same level, at the same age, across the country; whether they do not make excuses for lower rates of progress; whether they focus on ensuring teaching is strong, that staff meet the needs of all pupils, and provide well targeted challenges in lessons;
- the extent to which schools make use of the community in which the children live as well as the one in which they are educated in order to meet the needs of pupils with challenging social and emotional difficulties.

REFLECTIVE TASK
REFLECTIVE TASK

Discuss the following questions with a colleague.

- Do you agree with the new requirements of the Code of Practice?
- What challenges might the requirements of the new Code of Practice present to schools?
- What are the challenges of developing effective pupil participation?
- What are the challenges of developing effective parental participation?
- What are the challenges of developing effective multi-agency collaboration?
- What do you think about the introduction of personal budgets for parents? What are the arguments for and against these?

PRACTICAL TASK   PRACTICAL TASK   PRACTICAL TASK   PRACTICAL TASK   PRACTICAL TASK

During your next placement set up a meeting with the SENCO. Discuss how the school has addressed the requirements of the new Code of Practice.

CASE STUDY

John was ten years old when he attended an autistic resource base, which was attached to a mainstream school. He had previously been excluded from several mainstream primary schools for presenting challenging behaviour and terrorising other pupils and staff. Even though John had no official diagnosis of autistic spectrum disorder, his previous school indicated that this was a possibility.

John's parents had found his behaviour at home very difficult to deal with. He regularly bullied his younger brother and he often attacked his parents. He frequently used abusive language and often refused to comply with parental expectations. Over a period of several years this had placed pressure on the family, particularly on his mother. He would display manipulative behaviour and would go to great lengths to 'get his own way'.

John had not responded well to his early mainstream education. He had been permanently excluded from two schools on account of his behaviour and the LA appeared to be running out of options. A decision was made that resulted in John attending the autistic resource base at the research school, despite the fact that there had been no official diagnosis of autism. A review meeting confirmed that he would be partially included in the mainstream school on a 'trial' basis.

Very soon after John started in the resource base he began to terrorise the other children and attack the staff. Within weeks of him starting, he was given several fixed-term exclusions for his behaviour. After a month of him being at the resource base a medical diagnosis confirmed that John was not autistic but in fact had a pathological personality disorder known as 'Pathological Demand Avoidance'. This is a rare condition. As a result of this diagnosis, John was moved out of the resource base.

The medical professionals explained that the disorder had caused John to develop a sense of paranoia. He distrusted everyone. This paranoia resulted in him placing a padlock on his school lunch box so that no one could steal his food. John also developed several obsessions. One such obsession was that

John did not want people to say specific words on particular days of the week. He stated what the 'forbidden' words were and if they were used, he would scream and tantrum, was very manipulative and was extremely good at instigating arguments that he was determined to 'win'.

The LA had no suitable placement for John and no other local school wanted to admit him. The head teacher of the research school, eventually agreed to admit John on a temporary full-time basis, conditional on the LA promising to fund two part-time teachers and two part-time support assistants. In addition to this the Head asked the LA to fund cover for a lunchtime supervisor who would 'oversee' John during this part of the day. The staff that were employed to educate and supervise John were not experienced in working with children who had this condition.

Another barrier to effective inclusion was also established before the placement started. In view of John's behaviour, Sally, the class teacher, refused outright to teach John. She was concerned that his behaviour would present too many challenges and she argued that she had not had the necessary training to deal with it. She also expressed concern that John would impede the progress of the rest of the pupils. This was a particular worry for her, given the fact that the class were due to take their statutory tests at the end of the year.

John was not given a chance to prove himself. The Head supported Sally and an agreement was made that John would be taught in his own room. His part-time teachers and his support staff would support him in a room next to Sally's room.

John started his placement in the research school. The classroom that he was placed in was not 'set up' as a classroom. Initially John used the whole room. However, over a period of weeks he gradually withdrew into the carpet area of the classroom and this became 'John's den'. He barricaded the carpet area off with cupboards and screens and he insisted that all his lessons were to take place in this part of the room. He placed a table within his 'den' and a set of drawers and this is where he 'worked' for the majority of the day. John would not allow other staff into his 'den'. The only people who were privileged enough to be allowed access were the people who were responsible for supervising him. Initially, he did eat his lunch with the other children but very quickly he retreated into eating it within his 'den'.

It became apparent that no structures were put into place for John. His teachers did not plan lessons for him. He was allowed to decide which activities to engage in and sometimes it was clear that he was not taking part in any educational activity at all. Initially he had visited the youngest children's classrooms and he enjoyed 'helping' them. However, after he had established his 'den', he no longer wanted to do this and he stopped visiting. He had also initially taken part in playtimes with other children. However, his constant swearing had resulted in them complaining and a decision was taken that John would have his own playtimes, supervised by his teachers and support staff.

One of John's teachers frequently had rows with him. She seemed to be confrontational and this made him worse. His lunchtime supervisor took on the role of 'doting' grandma, which John exploited by manipulating her. One day John had returned into his 'den' from an individual playtime to find that some art work had been left in his space. He responded by ripping up all the work. He suffered consequences for this and was publicly humiliated by the Head, the deputy and one of his support teachers in front of the whole school. John's response to this was to retaliate and shout back at the Head. In John's eyes his space had been violated and not respected.

After a review meeting to discuss transfer to secondary provision it was decided that John would attend a local special school for pupils with severe behaviour problems. At his transition meeting the Head of the research school recommended that John would be best educated in his own classroom, with his own teachers. He was described as a severely disruptive child who needed to be kept apart from the other children for their own safety. The special school accepted this advice and set up a classroom where John would be educated on his own. John is still at the research school and awaiting transfer to the special school.

Reflect on this case study.

- What were the barriers to John's inclusion?
- How was John's voice marginalised?
- How might the situation have been handled differently?

REFLECTIVE TASK

REFLECTIVE TASK

Discuss the following questions with a colleague.

- Should all learners with SEND be included in mainstream schools?
- What are the arguments for and against special schools?
- What are the arguments for and against including pupils with SEND in mainstream schools?

PRACTICAL TASK   PRACTICAL TASK   **PRACTICAL TASK**   PRACTICAL TASK   **PRACTICAL TASK**

During your school-based placement ask if you can be a silent observer during a review meeting for a specific child. This might be a meeting to review the child's progress or an annual review meeting. This will present you with a valuable opportunity to observe the way in which professionals from different agencies work collaboratively. After the meeting consider the way in which the meeting was structured and the ways in which the contributions of different agencies and other stakeholders acknowledged the child's achievements and identified the areas for future support.

Individual education plans

Although the new Code of Practice (DfE, 2014) makes no explicit reference to individual education plans (IEP), anecdotal evidence suggests that many schools will continue to use these to support pupils with SEN. The IEP is a tool for recording:

- the child's short-term targets;
- the teaching strategies to be used;
- the provision to be put in place (intervention);
- when the plan is to be reviewed;
- the success/exit criteria for measuring whether the target(s) have been met;
- the outcomes. (DfES, 2001: 5, 50, 54)

Essentially the IEP should record provision that is *additional to* and *different from* normal differentiated provision. Teachers should record three or four individual targets and these should be focused and measurable. Teachers should always involve parents or carers and pupils in setting and reviewing targets. Targets should be reviewed regularly. The views of parents should be sought at the review point and the SENCO should be involved in the monitoring and review process.

According to Skidmore the IEP 'owes much to an objectives-based model of teaching inspired ultimately by theories of learning derived from behavioural psychology'. He emphasises that individualised approaches such as these 'may act as a straightjacket upon more creative, innovative approaches to provision...' (Skidmore, 2004: 16).

The implications of Skidmore's critique are worthy of consideration. Teachers need to embrace creative pedagogical approaches for all children. Innovative approaches to teaching and learning are more likely to motivate all learners. Intervention programmes to support learning are often identified on IEPs as strategies for raising attainment. Teachers and trainee teachers should critically examine these carefully to check that they are relevant and sufficiently engaging for learners' special educational needs.

CASE STUDY

Ben entered his nursery setting at the age of three. The practitioners in the setting noticed that Ben had some communication problems. Ben's communication was limited and he communicated through pointing and the use of isolated words. It was noted that Ben's parents responded to his pointing and use of isolated words and his needs were usually met immediately. Observations had also indicated that Ben also had a low self-concept. He quickly became upset if he was asked to complete new activities. The practitioners in the nursery were concerned about Ben's communication development.

The parents were invited into the setting for a meeting. Their views, experiences and observations of Ben in his home setting were discussed to form a holistic assessment of Ben's achievements and needs. Ben's parents confirmed that they also had concerns related to some aspects of Ben's communication. At the meeting strategies were discussed and shared to address the immediate concerns. One of the targets agreed at the meeting for Ben's IEP was that Ben's use of pointing and isolated words should be followed by a modelled simple caption or sentence, which conveyed the same meaning. For example, Ben pointed and said 'cat'. The adult modelled this by saying 'there's a cat'. The parents were encouraged to share this strategy with immediate family members and all adults who had regular contact with Ben.

- Why was it important for Ben's parents to contribute to his IEP?
- How would you ensure that the parents continued to have a voice?
- What additional targets would have been appropriate support Ben's development?

A SUMMARY OF **KEY POINTS**

➢ Historically, policy discourse has moved from policies of exclusion to integration to inclusion.

➢ The policy of inclusive education has been implemented within an overarching policy of raising standards which some academics have argued has resulted in policies which are incompatible.

➢ The new Code of Practice (DfE, 2014) focuses on supporting learners with SEND into adult life, raising outcomes for these learners, increasing pupil and parent participation and strengthening multi-agency collaboration.

RESEARCH SUMMARY RESEARCH SUMMARY **RESEARCH SUMMARY** RESEARCH SUMMARY

Glazzard (2013) has produced research which demonstrates the negative impact that specialist provision for pupils with autism within a mainstream primary school can have on overall notions of school effectiveness. Whilst the provision brought significant advantages to the school in terms of the development of inclusive values amongst the pupils, the research also demonstrates that the provision had a negative impact on overall achievement data.

MOVING *ON* > > > > > > MOVING *ON* > > > > > > MOVING *ON*

Now that you understand the principles of the Code of Practice, you now need to become confident with using pupils' IEP targets to inform the planning process. When you are next on placement it will be useful if you can collect copies of the IEPs for children in your class. Discuss the targets with your mentor and discuss ways in which you can take account of these targets when planning lessons.

REFERENCES REFERENCES **REFERENCES** REFERENCES **REFERENCES** REFERENCES

Armstrong, D. (1998) 'Changing faces, changing places: Policy routes to inclusion', in P. Clough and L. Barton (eds), *Managing Inclusive Education: From Policy to Experience*, London: Paul Chapman Publishing, pp. 31–47.

Barton, L. (1998) 'Markets, managerialism and inclusive education', in P. Clough and L. Barton (eds) *Managing Inclusive Education: From Policy to Experience*, London: Paul Chapman Publishing, pp. 78–91.

Department of Education and Science (DES)/Warnock, M. (1978) *Special Educational Needs, Report of the Committee of Enquiry into the Education of Handicapped Children and Young People*, London: HMSO.

Department for Education (DfE) (2010) *The Importance of Teaching: The Schools White Paper*, Norwich: The Stationery Office.

Department for Education (DfE) (2011) *Support and Aspiration: A New Approach to Special Educational Needs and Disability: A Consultation*, Norwich: The Stationery Office.

Department for Education (DfE) (2014) *Special Educational Needs and Disability Code of Practice: 0 to 25 Years: Statutory Guidance for Organisations Who Work With and Support Children and Young People with Special Educational Needs and Disabilities*, London: DfE.

Department for Education and Employment (DfEE) (1997) *Excellence in Schools*, London: DfEE.

Department for Education and Skills (DfES) (2001) *Special Educational Needs Code of Practice*, Nottingham: DfES.

Department for Education and Skills (DfES) (2004) *Removing Barriers to Achievement: The Government Strategy for SEN*, Nottingham: DfES.

Glazzard, J. (2013) 'Resourced provision: the impact of inclusive practices on a mainstream primary school', *Support for Learning: British Journal of Learning Support*, 28(3), 92–6.

Goodley, D. (2007) 'Towards socially just pedagogies: Deleuzoguattarian critical disability studies', *International Journal of Inclusive Education*, 11(3), 319–34.

Her Majesty´s Stationery Office (HMSO) (2003) *Every Child Matters*, Norwich: The Stationery Office.

Office for Standards in Education, Children's Services and Skills (Ofsted) (2010) *The Special Educational Needs and Disability Review: A Statement is Not Enough*, Manchester: Ofsted.

Office for Standards in Education, Children's Services and Skills (Ofsted) (2014) *The Framework for School Inspection*, Manchester: Ofsted.

Skidmore, D. (2004) *Inclusion: The Dynamic of School Development*, Berkshire: Open University Press.

United Nations (1989) *The UN Convention on the Rights of the Child*, London: UNICEF.

United Nations Educational, Scientific and Cultural Organisation (UNESCO) (1994) *World Conference on Special Needs Education: Access and Quality*, Paris: UNESCO.

Warnock, M. (1996) 'The work of the Warnock Committee', in P. Mittler and V. Sinason (eds) *Changing Policy and Practice for People with Learning Difficulties*, London: Cassell, pp. 19–32.

Warnock, M. (2005) 'Special educational needs: a new look', *Impact*, 11, Salisbury: Philosophy of Education Society of Great Britain.

FURTHER READING FURTHER READING **FURTHER READING** FURTHER READING

Frederickson, N. and Cline, T. (2009) *Special Educational Needs, Inclusion and Diversity*, (2nd edn), Berkshire: Open University Press.

USEFUL WEBSITES USEFUL WEBSITES **USEFUL WEBSITES** USEFUL WEBSITES

http://www.nasen.org.uk

PART 2
THEORY

2
Inclusive education:
theoretical perspectives

Chapter objectives

After reading this chapter you will:

- **know and understand the different perspectives on inclusion;**
- **know and understand theories of disability;**
- **begin to understand interpretations of inclusion;**
- **become aware of tensions within the field of inclusive education;**
- **start to consider the implications of these perspectives and theories for your own professional practice.**

Teachers' Standards

This chapter addresses the following Teachers' Standards:

Part 2: Teachers must have an understanding of, and always act within, the statutory frameworks which set out their professional duties and responsibilities.

Introduction

This chapter examines inclusion from a number of different perspectives. Research and other academic writings on special education and inclusion adopt various perspectives of inclusion and meanings of inclusion are often vague, not clearly articulated and vary according to the vested interests of individuals, groups, cultures and societies. Ultimately as a teacher and even as a trainee teacher you will need to develop a view of what inclusion means to you. This may change over time as you encounter new situations but you need a set of values, beliefs and principles upon which to base your practice. This chapter will help you to begin this process of reflection.

What is inclusion?

According to Corbett and Slee:

> *Inclusive education is an unabashed announcement, a public and political declaration and celebration of difference. It requires continual proactive responsiveness to foster an inclusive education culture.*

> (2000: 134)

According to Carrington and Elkins, 'above all, inclusion is about a philosophy of acceptance where all pupils are valued and treated with respect' (2005: 86). Although inclusion is often associated with the concept of *mainstreaming* Warnock has emphasised that inclusion is about the quality of the educational experience rather than the location of it:

> *Inclusion is not a matter of where you are geographically, but of where you feel you belong. There are many children, and especially adolescents, identified as having special educational needs, who can never feel that they belong in a large mainstream school.*

> (2005: 38)

The main difficulty in relation to defining inclusion is that it means different things to different people with different vested interests. Government policy documents continue to stress the need for schools to close the achievement gap between learners with and without SEND. There is an explicit focus in the Code of Practice (DfE, 2014) on improving outcomes for pupils with SEND and this includes: accelerating achievement, increasing independence of learners, increasing employment rates and enabling more learners with SEND to access further and higher education. While the focus on outcomes is admirable, Barbara Cole's (2005) research has demonstrated that to parents of pupils with SEND what matters the most is whether their children are cared for, treated with dignity and whether teachers demonstrate a willingness to try different approaches to advance an agenda for social justice. These parental interpretations of inclusion contrast sharply with the policy documents which emphasise the language of academic performance. To add further complexity, it is worth noting that inclusion often means different things to people within and across organisations and cultures and the link between special educational needs and inclusion has been challenged by some academics (Thomas and Loxley, 2007).

Biological perspectives

Special education has historically been dominated by the use of medical vocabulary. Words such as *syndrome*, *symptoms* and *disorder* have been included into the lexicon and the focus has been on locating the source of the difficulty within the body. In adopting a biological perspective on special education the contribution of the wider context (for example, access to high quality teaching) and its role in creating learning difficulties is effectively ignored. Within a biological paradigm the person's impaired biological make-up is identified as the source of the problem.

Thomas and Loxley (2001, 2007) argue that biological perspectives on impairment and disability place insufficient emphasis on the wider environment in which learning occurs. The medical model adopts a therapeutic discourse in that biological difficulties are diagnosed and cured by medical professionals who provide appropriate 'treatment'. At he turn of the twentieth century science as a discipline was held in high esteem and scientific processes such as testing and measurement were aligned with the growth of positivism as a research paradigm.

The legacy of special education is that teachers gave their faith to experts and specialists who were trusted to carry out assessments on pupils. Their specialist knowledge was held in high esteem and it was assumed that some pupils required specialist teaching from teachers with specialist qualifications. The biological model thrived particularly due to the esteemed disciplines of science and psychology which privileged quantification, measurement and biology. Thomas and Loxley (2001, 2007) make the point that this focus on specialist pedagogy made general classroom teachers think that special children required special teachers and a special curriculum when in reality all that really matters in education is that pupils need to be taught by teachers who are enthusiastic, patient and sensitive.

PRACTICAL TASK   PRACTICAL TASK   PRACTICAL TASK   PRACTICAL TASK   PRACTICAL TASK

This is a group task. Work together and study closely one section from the Code of Practice (DfE, 2014). Can you find examples of language which reflects a medical model of disability in the code?

Sociological perspectives

During the latter half of the twentieth century, sociological theories started to pose a direct challenge to scientific paradigms. The growth of disability theory in particular started to introduce the idea that disability is a product of an oppressive and exclusive society rather than arising from a biological impairment (Avramidis and Norwich, 2012). The social model denies that impairments have any implications for disability (Avramidis and Norwich, 2012) and emphasises that disability is socially created through physical, social, cultural, political and economic barriers which have disabling effects. The disability movement started to focus on the rights of people with disabilities.

A sociological perspective of inclusion emphasises equality, respect, participation in decision making, rights, democracy, social justice and collective belonging. It has a set of principles distinct to the biological model which emphasises 'needs', diagnosis, intervention and cure. Roaf and Bines (1989) argued that a focus on 'needs' detracts from an emphasis on 'rights'. The sociological perspective on inclusion moves away from notions of 'learning difficulties' to notions of 'rights'. These might include:

- the right to a good education;
- the right to be accepted;
- the right to belong;
- the right to be respected;
- the right to be equal but different;
- the right to express personal views, to be listened to and for those views to be acted upon;
- the right to participate;
- the right to protection;
- the right to information;
- the right to privacy;
- the right to have freedom of thought;
- the right to survive.

These are not listed in hierarchical order and are not exhaustive. Many of them are also stated as rights in the United Nations Convention on the Rights of the Child (United Nations, 1989). These rights reflect the values of inclusion and are distinct from the values of special education which emphasise *need*, *correction* and *cure*.

CASE STUDY

A primary school wanted to demonstrate a visible commitment to children's rights. The senior leaders decided to consult all pupils to collect their perspectives on the rights to which they felt they had an entitlement. Children's views were collected from all classes on large mind maps. Teachers then worked collaboratively to identify ten rights which were recurrent themes on the mind maps. The rights were then published on the school website and displayed in all classrooms and around the school. For example, a sign displaying 'you have a right to privacy' was displayed on all toilet doors.

REFLECTIVE TASK

Rights are not unproblematic. For example, the rights of a pupil with severe social, emotional and behavioural difficulties to be accepted into a local community school have to be balanced against the rights of all children to an uninterrupted education.

- Can you think of other situations where rights have to be balanced?

A sociological perspective on inclusion emphasises the role of external factors in creating learning difficulties rather than biological deficits within the body. These external factors include but are not limited to:

- language;
- family/parenting;
- culture;
- gender;
- ethnicity;
- the social environment of the school;
- the physical environment of the school.

A sociological perspective on disability places a responsibility on society for the creation of disablement, exclusion, marginalisation and oppression. It has a distinct set of values which, when combined together, aim to create a better, fairer and more socially just society. It also examines inclusion from a broader perspective by incorporating aspects such as race, gender, sexuality, disability and religion into the melting pot and it interrogates fundamental factors within society (including housing, employment, poverty, financial) which can result in social exclusion and marginalisation.

Philosophical perspectives

Philosophical perspectives of inclusion present challenging questions about inclusion as a philosophical concept. These include but are not restricted to:

- Can we include everyone?
- Is there a limit to inclusion?
- Is inclusion a logical concept in the first place?

Hodkinson (2012) asks whether inclusion, with its associated notions of equality and social justice, can co-exist within an education system based on neo-liberalist principles of marketisation and competition. Additionally, philosophical debates (Wilson, 1999; Hansen, 2012) have been useful in emphasising that there are limits to inclusion in that communities and institutions will always feel that they need to exclude individuals in order to ensure their own existence.

Philosophical frameworks (for example, Foucault, 1977) have been used to analyse the role of power and surveillance in analysing the experiences of pupils with special needs in mainstream schools. Julie Allan's work (1996, 2008) provides an excellent analysis of the positioning of pupils with special needs as objects of power and surveillance drawing on Foucault's (1977) conceptual framework of surveillance. Additionally Goodley (2007) draws on the theoretical work of Deleuze and Guattari (1987) to propose a more socially just model upon which to base pedagogy. Allan's (2008) work on inclusion provides a superb analysis of how the work of key philosophers can be applied to inclusion. All of this work is complex and challenging and beyond the scope of this book. However, some students may wish to look more closely at the relationship between inclusion and philosophy and this work will be a useful starting point.

REFLECTIVE TASK

Are there limits to inclusion? Can everyone be included? Can we have schools which cater for all children?

Political perspectives

A political perspective on inclusion necessitates a critical interrogation of current policy texts in order to identify what current and recent governments mean or have meant by the term *inclusion*. While a caring discourse of inclusion (Corbett, 1992) emphasises treating children with respect and dignity, the language within policy texts (DfE, 2010, 2011, 2014) focuses on raising standards for pupils with special needs and closing the achievement gap between pupils with special needs and those without. Policy texts (DfE, 2010) also emphasise the language of exclusion particularly in relation to pupils with behavioural difficulties who pose a threat to the standards attained by the majority. In using words such as 'disruptive' and 'challenging' these pupils are effectively 'othered' out of existence by being isolated in alternative provision. Policy texts fail to interrogate critically why pupils might display behaviour which is construed as challenging or why pupils might be underachieving. They adopt a medical model which blames the child by locating the source of the problem within the child. The texts fail to deconstruct how aspects of the schooling system including the curriculum, assessment processes, the nature and quality of teaching or the attitudes of teachers might be responsible for creating student disengagement, resistance and low achievement.

Policy texts emphasise a particular version of inclusion which adheres to the principles of neo-liberalism. Pupils are expected to be able, productive, skilled, independent and enterprising and pupils who find any of these challenging are effectively marginalised by an education system which fails to meet their needs. Academic literature consistently emphasises the plurality of inclusion. Inclusion means different things to different groups and individuals with different vested interests. For the government the position of the country in the global economy remains a critical priority. Politicians need an education system which produces a highly knowledgeable and skilled workforce. In short, they require an able workforce which will be able to ensure that the economy can effectively compete against other countries worldwide. These economic motivations subvert inclusion because inclusion is then used as a disciplinary, normalising force (Armstrong, 2005) which eradicates diversity by its focus on closing gaps.

The medical model of disability

Special education has traditionally been situated within a psycho-medical paradigm (Skidmore, 2004) or medical model which locates the impairment within the individual. It is otherwise known as a personal tragedy model. The individual/impairment is viewed as needing to be cured by medical and other professionals (Avramidis and Norwich, 2012) and this justifies treatment which can take a variety of forms. The model has partly survived due to the prominence of psychology as a discipline. The model is biological in that it situates impairment within a person's biological make-up and is in direct contrast to the social model which views disablement as a result of society's failure to accommodate the needs of people with impairments (Avramidis and Norwich, 2012). With its focus on biological deficits the model is tragic in the sense that it is victim-blaming and places no responsibility on the door of society for its failure to make adaptations and adjustments to accommodate people with disabilities. Within this model the intervention takes place at the level of the individual because the 'problem' is located within a person's biological make-up. Therefore the onus is on perfecting and normalising the individual in order to eradicate the impairment rather than celebrating an individual's uniqueness. The model does not raise critical questions about barriers in society which may have contributed to disability. Instead, it focuses on curing the individual so that they can function within a normalising society.

The tragedy model of disability and impairment is dominant through media representations of people with disabilities, language, culture, research, policy and professional practice (Swain and French, 2003). As such it is deeply engrained within society and perpetuates the view that impairment and disability are negative aspects of a person's identity and that people with disabilities want to reject their disabled identities to be 'normal' (Swain and French, 2003). The model subjects people with disabilities to disabling expectations – to be independent, normal and to adjust to a normalising society (Swain and French, 2003).

Categorisations of disability reflect the medical model. According to Dunne (2009), varying 'disorders' have been introduced into the lexicon of special needs, each with its own symptoms and disease-like characteristics, creating spectacle, fear and revulsion. Within the medical model educators are positioned as 'police' (Dunne, 2009), charged with hunting down abnormalities and correcting them through early identification processes. Through naming disability, individuals are then known and categorised and marked in particular ways. According to Billington:

> *Western culture seems fascinated by frozen, atomised 'photographs', mistaking pictures of individual characteristics, contextually isolated, with life itself... Through constantly attempting to 'freeze the frame', we construct fragmented snapshots which unerringly omit an 'other', and effectively restrict the possibility of change.* (2000: 90)

The medical model uses processes such as the examination to diagnose specific impairments. For example the educational psychologist may carry out a series of assessments or tests to diagnose dyslexia. A medical professional may diagnose autism or attention deficit hyperactivity disorder (ADHD). The model reflects the doctor/patient model in which the patient is examined by the doctor and is then prescribed a 'cure'. Within the medical model the medical professional may diagnose a specific disability and then offer a course of treatment to cure the symptoms (for example, Ritalin may be prescribed following a diagnosis of ADHD). The 'problem' is viewed as being situated within the child and the intervention takes place at that level. It could be argued that the techniques of diagnosis, intervention and surveillance categorise children by their differences and are rooted in a psycho-medical paradigm which 'conceptualizes difficulties in learning as arising from deficits in the neurological or psychological make-up of the child' (Skidmore, 2004: 2).

The problem with labels, as Billington has highlighted above, is that they skew the way in which people think about those who own the labels. Individuals become known on the basis of their label rather than for their individuality. This can, in some instances, result in the same 'treatments' or interventions being applied to a group of individuals who share a label. However, in reality the label may mask a person's individuality and children with the same label may well respond differently to a specific intervention or even require different interventions. Labels can also be disempowering; those with them may display *learned helplessness* (Peterson *et al.*, 1995) because they may feel like they will never overcome the deficit.

In contrast research has demonstrated how labels can actually empower individuals by providing them with a means to understand their difficulties (Glazzard, 2010). Labels can also provide access to additional funding or support to help the individual to make further progress. Despite this there is the issue that labels are social constructs. They are assigned on the basis of the extent of deviation from artificially constructed social norms. Individuals who transgress the prescribed limits of these norms are assigned a label by others in more powerful positions. This positions them as subjects and objects of power and draws attention to the fact that they have an 'abnormality' which is in need of correction. It has been argued that the diagnosis, intervention and remediation processes result in 'the entrapment of the child in a cocoon of professional help' (Thomas and Loxley, 2007: 55) which conceals the vested professional interests of 'expert' professionals under the rhetoric of humanitarianism (Tomlinson, 1985). Thomas and Loxley (2001, 2007) have highlighted how the problem with labels is that they transfer the need from the school onto the child. Through using the example of the label 'emotional and behavioural difficulties' the authors argue that the needs of the school to maintain discipline and order are transferred onto the child when pupils fail to respond to gentle sanctions, which are generally successful. It is then when children are reconceptualised from being unpunctual, lazy, rude or untidy (Thomas and Loxley, 2001) to having emotional and behavioural difficulties. They are then 'diverted along a new path ... to an alternative set [of practices] governed by ... psychologists, counsellors, social workers, psychiatrists – who listen, analyse and understand' (Thomas and Loxley, 2001: 53). They are then not trusted, viewed as deviants and in need of correction. The only solution is for them to accept their deviance (Thomas and Loxley, 2001) and to change fundamentally their identity.

The medical model places the responsibility for correction at the level of the individual. Consequently, pupils with social, emotional and behaviour difficulties are placed on behaviour plans and given targets for which they must take responsibility. Those with cognitive impairments are placed on individual education plans and given targets to act upon resulting in 'a highly individualised approach' (Skidmore, 2004: 15). These are monitored and reviewed on a regular basis and more targets are subsequently set. The aim is to normalise, correct and perfect the deficiencies within the child, thus negating aspects of diversity. Within this process the child is positioned as an object of power. They are given a voice and consulted (DfE, 2014) but the aim is to homogenise rather than to embrace heterogeneity. Such practices, which serve to negate diversity, are justified because they are viewed as benevolent responses to need (Graham, 2006). They serve as disciplinary forces which regulate the lives of individuals (Armstrong, 2005).

The social model of disability

The social model of disability (Oliver, 1990; Barnes, 1991) locates the problem of disability squarely within society (Oliver, 1996). The model assumes that disability 'is an artificial and exclusionary social construction that penalises those people with impairments who do not conform to mainstream expectations of appearance, behaviour and/or economic performance' (Tregaskis, 2002: 457). The underlying assumption of the social model is that disablement is socially created rather than being part of a person's biological make-up. The model fundamentally distinguishes between 'impairment' and 'disability'. Impairment can be physical, cognitive or sensory and is of biological origin. However, disability is a loss or limitation of *opportunities* to participate on an equal level with others due to physical or social barriers (Barnes, 1991). It then follows that impairments do not need to become disabling if the right adaptations and adjustments are made in society to enable individuals with impairments to enjoy the same opportunities that are afforded to those without impairments. The model assumes that disability is the product of disabling barriers within society rather than a product of a person's pathology.

The social model originated out of the experiences of disabled people as a direct challenge to the psycho-medical individual tragedy model. It assumes that disability is caused by the oppression of people with impairments in a disabling society. Whilst the model rejects the notion of disability as a personal tragedy it does not remove tragedy from the lives of people with disabilities and impairments (Swain and French, 2003). Although the model locates the cause of disability within the disabling barriers in society, disability itself is seen as a tragedy rather than an aspect of a collective or person's identity which is positive and liberating.

It has been argued that the social model has been an emancipatory force in the lives of many people with disabilities (Tregaskis, 2002). The responsibility for exclusion is placed at the door of a normalising society (Tregaskis, 2002) rather than placing responsibility for disablement on the individual with impairment. The social model offers hope to people with impairments that they can lead fulfilling lives and access the same opportunities that are enjoyed by those without impairments. The model was developed by disabled people as a response to the prevailing medical model which placed responsibility on people with disabilities to adapt to and fit in with mainstream society. Around that time the Union of the Physically Impaired Against Segregation defined disability as:

> *The disadvantage or restriction of activity caused by a contemporary social organisation which takes no or little account of people who have physical impairments and thus excludes them from the mainstream of social activities.* (UPIAS, 1976: 3–4)

This definition of disability challenged the victim-blaming medical model by drawing attention to the contribution that society makes towards creating disability. The social model re-defined disability from being a biological construct to being a social, cultural, political and economic construct. It re-positioned people with disabilities as people with rights (Humphrey, 2000) and highlighted the contribution that disabling environments make towards creating disablement.

As early as 1997 Shakespeare and Watson pointed out that the social model had brought major benefits to the lives of disabled people. It enabled disability to become a powerful influential force in social policy (Dewsbury *et al.*, 2004). From a social model perspective disability is caused by lack of access to the same goods or services that those without impairments are able to access. Disabling barriers include but may not be restricted to:

- **Physical barriers**: examples include access to lifts or ramps to access buildings.
- **Attitudinal barriers**: negative attitudes towards people solely because of their impairments. Attitudes can be shaped by various factors including a person's culture, social group, family and the media.
- **Political barriers**: lack of legislation which protects people with impairments from unfair treatment (discrimination) directly or indirectly.
- **Economic/financial barriers**: lack of financial assistance to enable people with impairments to access goods and services or lack of opportunity to access paid employment.

If these barriers are removed then people with impairments can access services and goods such as education, housing and employment and they are able to enjoy the opportunities enjoyed by those without impairments. Disabled activists have focused on how physical environments have in the past been designed by non-disabled people and how politics and research have been dominated by those who have no experience of disability (Humphrey, 2000).

The social model has influenced social policy and legislation to improve opportunities for those with impairments. For example disability discrimination legislation has been introduced to protect people with disabilities from direct and indirect forms of discrimination. The Equality Act 2010 identifies nine protected groups which educational institutions, employment and other organisations are prevented from discriminating against on the basis of:

- age;
- being or becoming a transsexual person;
- being married or in a civil partnership;
- being pregnant or having a child;
- disability;

- race including colour, nationality, ethnic or national origin;
- religion, belief or lack of religion/belief;
- sex;
- sexual orientation.

Thus, organisations need to be able to demonstrate that they have made adaptations and adjustments to remove barriers to participation. In terms of education an example of this could be the provision of additional, targeted support to enable learners with disabilities to achieve their full educational potential. In the case of employment, employers could provide disabled employees with a supported employment programme to support their transition into the workplace. The most obvious adjustments that are now evident in most schools, workplaces and other public buildings include the provision of lifts and ramps to enable individuals with disabilities opportunities to access the goods and services inside the organisation. However, the legislation also places an onus on all organisations to review their policies and practices on a regular basis to ensure that they are free from discrimination.

However, the social model has not escaped criticism. Dewsbury *et al.* (2004) highlighted how the everyday experiences and realities of being disabled are underplayed in social model accounts and that sociological accounts of disability provide an incomplete version of the experience of impairment. Whether or not impairment alone can be responsible for disablement is a point for debate and will surely depend on the severity of the impairment itself but it is worth noting that pupils with profoundly severe impairments can be educated if they are provided with a highly personalised and appropriate education which meets their needs. It has been argued that the social model focuses insufficiently on people's experiences of chronic illness and pain (Swain and French, 2003) and that personal struggles related to impairment may still exist even when disabling barriers no longer exist (Crow, 2003).

Despite these criticisms of the social model it could be argued that concentrating on impairment may be viewed as counter-productive to disabled people. Oliver states that:

> *There is a danger of emphasising the personal at the expense of the political because most of the world still thinks of disability as an individual, intensely personal problem. And many of those who once made a good living espousing this view would be only too glad to come out of the woodwork and say that they were right all along.*

> (1996: 5)

As Shakespeare puts it:

> *The achievement of the disability movement has been to break the link between our bodies and our social situation and to focus on the real cause of disability i.e. discrimination and prejudice. To mention biology, to admit pain, to confront our impairments has been to risk the oppressive seizing of evidence that disability is 'really' about physical limitations after all.*

> (1992: 40)

Goodley (2001) argued that whilst the social model rightly provides people with physical impairments with a socio-historical position, *learning difficulties* are often conceived as biological deficits, particularly in relation to people with severe learning difficulties where the deficit is viewed as static and irreversible. Goodley (2001) emphasises that it is necessary to view learning difficulties as a cultural, social, political, historical, discursive and relational phenomenon rather than a biological construct. Indeed, one only has to consider the extent to which the education system, with its associated curricula and assessment processes, is responsible for the creation of learning difficulties. It has been argued that paradoxically, the National Curriculum, whilst claiming to offer breadth of experiences, failed to address the breadth of education necessary to meet learners' diverse needs (Wedell, 2008). The functionalist model of education uncritically assumes that the norms and values being inculcated are beneficial to all (Roulstone and Prideaux, 2008). Thus, neoliberalist policies which emphasise academic achievement and education for employment are problematic for children with disabilities who 'might never be capable of (nor interested in) such achievements' (Goodley, 2007: 322) and who may never be able to lead an entrepreneurial life (Goodley, 2007; Goodley and Runswick-Cole, 2011).

Despite its criticisms, the social model presents educators with exciting possibilities. The model assumes that all learners can benefit from access to an education system which strives to reduce barriers to their participation and achievements. With access to appropriate pedagogy, adaptations, adjustments, positive attitudes and differentiated provision learners with physical, social, emotional, mental health, sensory, cognitive, communication or physical impairments can achieve. The principle that all can achieve regardless of need has its origins in the social model and is a key principle of inclusive education. This is largely uncontroversial and is embedded in school cultures. However, debate about the nature of this achievement is arguably more contentious given that current educational discourse emphasises the importance of all pupils demonstrating achievement in relation to a narrow set of performance indicators (DfE, 2010, 2013). Whilst the social model emphasises the importance of removing disabling barriers, thus enabling access and participation, the provision of a 'one size fits all' model erects rather than eradicates barriers to access, participation and achievement. This leads to the further marginalisation and oppression of those learners who are unable to access the dominant versions of success (Lloyd, 2008). Some learners will inevitably achieve the narrow performance indicators prescribed by the government. However, not all will and it is this minority who are then failed by an education system which has not met their needs.

The social model provides educators with theoretical underpinning upon which to base their practice. Firstly, teachers need to reflect upon and interrogate their practice to identify whether there are any barriers to access, participation and achievement for learners with specific impairments. Secondly, once disabling barriers have been identified teachers then need to remove these so that these learners can be fully included. Examples of removing barriers to achievement include:

- providing access to an electronic spell checker for a learner with dyslexia;
- providing access to a computer for a pupil who struggles with handwriting due to motor control difficulties;
- providing a pupil with dyslexia with access to a multi-sensory phonics intervention programme;
- providing a visual timetable for a child with autistic spectrum disorder;
- providing pre-teaching of skills before a lesson for pupils with cognitive impairment;
- providing access to a disabled toilet and electronic doors for a pupil with a physical impairment;
- providing access to enlarged text for a pupil with a visual impairment.

This is not an exhaustive list but nevertheless it does illustrate the practical application of a theoretical idea. Some disabling barriers within schools can be addressed through training staff rather than through purchasing physical resources. An example of this is a teacher who has negative attitudes towards pupils with social, emotional and behavioural difficulties. The teacher's attitudes in this case could be responsible for creating pupil disengagement and hence is disabling because this will affect participation and achievement. Through continuing professional development the teacher's attitudes can be shaped in positive ways so that they learn to be more empathetic, more supportive, have higher expectations for pupils and how to communicate with pupils in more positive ways. Further training could help the teacher to improve their teaching so that pupils are more likely to engage in lessons. These changes should help to increase participation which should ultimately increase pupils' achievements. The social model embraces a 'can-do' ethos which assumes that with correct adaptations and adjustments all pupils with impairments can achieve their full educational potential. These might include changes to:

- pedagogical approaches;
- the learning environment;
- attitudes;
- amount of support;
- daily timetables;
- curricula;
- assessment processes.

A social model perspective demands that educators reflect regularly and deeply on their practices in order to identify potential barriers to learning. It also necessitates that educators are flexible in their approaches, values, beliefs and attitudes. What works well for one child may not work for another and teachers continually engage in cycles of action research in which

- barriers to learning are identified;
- these are shared and discussed amongst colleagues and strategies and solutions are offered;
- strategies and solutions are then implemented;
- these are evaluated after a specified period of time;
- new barriers to learning are identified and the cycle is repeated.

Above all, teachers who adopt a social model perspective understand that pupils' opportunities are not limited as a result of biological impairments. Through access to good quality teaching and effective learning environments all pupils can achieve their full potential. The barriers to learning rather become teaching problems and blame for lack of achievement is never apportioned onto the child. In these cases the problem then becomes the teacher's or the school's problem rather than the child's problem. It is addressed through modifying and transforming pedagogy rather than through placing an onus on the child to correct or rectify the problem. The problem is investigated by investigating the 'deficiencies in the school rather than the deficits of the child' (Skidmore, 2004: 15).

PRACTICAL TASK PRACTICAL TASK PRACTICAL TASK PRACTICAL TASK PRACTICAL TASK

Arrange to visit a special school to carry out this task. Ask if it is possible for you to walk round the school and to spend some time working in classrooms for several days. Note down examples of how the social model has been applied in practice by interrogating:

- the physical environment;
- pedagogy and pedagogical approaches;
- attitudes of people;
- the curriculum and assessment processes;
- other aspects of the school.

The affirmative model of disability

The affirmative model of disability is succinctly explained by Swain and French:

It is essentially a non-tragic view of disability and impairment which encompasses positive social identities, both individual and collective, for disabled people grounded in the benefits of lifestyle and life experiences of being impaired and disabled.

(2003: 150)

The model essentially views disability as a positive, personal and collective identity. It emphasises that people with disabilities should feel positive and proud about their disability and impairments and that people with disabilities can ultimately lead full and satisfying lives. Swain and French (2003) highlight some of the positive aspects of being disabled. These include the right to give up paid employment and the ability to pursue personal hobbies and interests. These aspects can be life-enhancing rather than life-limiting. It can be liberating not having to conform to the expectations of a normalising society and the model focuses on the right to be equal but also the right to be different.

Swain and French (2003) argue that whilst many non-disabled people readily accept the social model, many remain challenged by the affirmative model because they find it difficult to accept that a disabled or impaired person could feel pleased or proud of their disabled identity. The authors cite several examples in their work of disabled people who are rightly proud of their disabled identities such that they would not want to be non-disabled and lose aspects of their identity which they have come to value so much. The affirmative model rejects the medical model but builds on the social model by re-defining disability as a valid and enriching lifestyle. The disability arts movement has embraced this model and has projected a positive disabled identity through a range of media including cabaret, song and visual arts.

The affirmative model celebrates difference not only in relation to impairment but also in relation to race, sexual preference, gender, age and social class. People with impairments and disabilities also fit into these categories and therefore the model is fully inclusive and is not limited to one specific category. It views diversity as a positive, enriching, energising and fulfilling force in people's lives. The challenge for educators is to harness diversity and to educate pupils about the benefits of being different. This can have a transformative effect by shaping or changing the values of children and young people, some of whom will already have started to form negative views about people who are different. These are perpetuated by language, social and cultural groups and media representations. Some of the messages that are communicated in school may directly challenge the values that children internalise from their home and social environments, their peer group and their culture. However, teaching is not just about communicating subject-specific knowledge and skills. The role of a teacher is to shape attitudes, value-systems and beliefs by advancing an agenda for social justice.

CASE STUDY

One primary school decided to demonstrate a visible commitment to diversity by hosting a diversity week. People were invited into school to talk to pupils and to carry out various projects with classes. Speakers included: a successful author with dyslexia, a teacher who uses a wheelchair, a university lecturer with Asperger's, a female plumber, a male child minder, an African drama/dance group and an LGBT youth group. Activities during the week included talks, drama, dance, music, film and poster making. The week focused on celebrating diversity and being proud.

- What are the benefits of diversity weeks?
- What issues might result from a diversity week?

Interpretations of inclusion

This section explores the meaning of inclusion. However, it has been argued that inclusion 'is not a simple, unambiguous concept' (Lindsay, 2003: 6). Indeed, Avramidis *et al.* have noted that inclusion 'is a bewildering concept which can have a variety of interpretations and applications' (2002: 158). As such it has become an elusive and empty term (Gabel, 2010) and Barbara Cole (2005) argues that it is better to explore *meanings* rather than the *meaning* of inclusion. Understandings of inclusion are not 'shared between, within and across individuals, groups … and larger collectives (Sikes *et al.*, 2007: 357). Thus, inclusion can be interpreted variously across people within a single school and between schools, cultures or societies. Thus, it is neither possible nor desirable to pin inclusion down to a single entity.

Inclusion has been reflected metaphorically in the literature as a *journey* (Ainscow, 2000; Allan, 2000; Nind, 2005; Azzopardi, 2010) or a *state of becoming* (Nutbrown *et al.*, 2013). Julie Allan's humorous reference to the term 'inconclusive education' (2000: 43) serves as a reminder that inclusion is always in process and never complete. In this respect inclusion challenges schools to develop continually their capacities to reach out to a diversity of learners (Ainscow, 2000) by developing socially just pedagogies which connect individual learners with their own ways of learning (Corbett, 2001). Inclusion therefore represents a proactive response on the part of schools and other educational institutions to embrace diversity (Azzopardi, 2009) in positive ways. According to Booth:

> *Inclusive education is the process of increasing the participation of learners within, and reducing their exclusion from the cultures, curricula and communities of neighbourhood centres of learning.*

> (2000: 63)

It has been argued that inclusion can exist in varying degrees from surface level to a level where it is deeply embedded into the value systems, rituals, routines and culture of schools and other institutions (Corbett and Slee, 2000). Thus, inclusion is deeply intertwined with personal and institutional value systems which reflect a commitment to various principles. These include but are not restricted to:

- democracy and freedom of speech;
- social justice;
- acceptance, respect and equality of opportunity (Thomas and Loxley, 2001);
- collaboration and participation;
- an agenda of rights (Roaf, 1988) rather than focusing on individual deficits or needs;
- anti-discriminatory practice.

The concept of 'need' is highly problematic in that it reinforces notions of *deficit* and *disadvantage* (Thomas and Loxley, 2007). Thus, to suggest that an individual has a 'need' implies that there is a deficit within a person which must be corrected through processes of intervention and remediation. Such processes serve normalising functions which eradicate undesirable aspects of diversity. Lloyd emphasises how processes within education are 'all concerned with normalization and ... standardization, of groups and individuals rather than contributing to the *denormalization* of the institutions ...' (2008: 228) which is so central to the development of inclusion. Lloyd calls for a reconceptualisation of *achievement* and the 'denormalization of institutions, systems and rules which comprise education and schooling' (2008: 228).

According to Dunne, inclusion has become an unquestionably 'potentially normalising, hegemonic discourse' (2009: 44). Armstrong *et al.* have emphasised that 'While social policy is dominated by the rhetoric of inclusion, the reality for many remains one of exclusion and the panacea of "inclusion" masks many sins' (2011: 30). It could be argued that the current education system and the curricula and assessment structures which underpin it serve to construct rather than eradicate barriers to participation and achievement. Thus, although some scholars have emphasised the role of teachers as change agents (O'Hanlon, 2003; Skidmore, 2004; Nind, 2005), inclusion can only be realised through a deep change to school culture, pedagogy (Graham and Harwood, 2011) *and* a reconceptualisation of the structures which underpin education (Lloyd, 2008).

Evidently it would seem that the notion of inclusion as a *transformation* of the education system coupled with the transformation of pedagogy is critical to understanding what inclusion means. Nutbrown *et al.* (2013) refer to inclusion as a *radical task* as well an attitude of mind. However, changing schools and school systems is problematic because 'there is not a perfect system awaiting us on the shelf' (Nind *et al.*, 2003). Changing people's values is also no easy task. According to Roger Slee (2011) until inclusion is disentangled from neoliberal values of governance practitioners will be restricted in the extent to which they are able to develop socially just pedagogies in their schools and classrooms. Inclusive education must be disassociated from special educational needs so that it is able, as a policy discourse, to articulate its distinct values (Slee, 2011). This involves a departure from the traditional labelling paradigm (Graham and Slee, 2008) which can result in further marginalisation, oppression and disadvantage.

According to Giroux (2003), educators should reject forms of schooling that marginalise students and capitalise instead on factors such as gender, social class, race and sexual orientation in transformative ways as resources to enable learning. Thus, a school's commitment to inclusion goes beyond a commitment to special educational needs and disability. Inclusion therefore necessitates a commitment on the part of schools and other educational organisations to challenge all forms of marginalisation which result in the oppression and systemic failure of certain groups of learners. Azzopardi (2009, 2010) has argued that the term 'inclusive education' is little more than a cliché: 'a politically correct term that is used for speeches and policy-makers to silence all woes' (2009: 21). The dissonance between the rhetoric of policy texts and the realities of day-to-day practice results in inclusion becoming a term which is devoid of meaning.

Diversity and threats to school performance

Although a commitment to inclusion and diversity go hand in hand within current educational discourse, diversity becomes a negative term used to categorise a minority of learners who are unable 'to access dominant versions of success' (Benjamin, 2002: 320). Discourses of performativity emphasise the eradication of diversity through the mantras of raising standards and closing the achievement gap. According to Ball 'performativity is a technology, a culture and a mode of regulation that employs judgements, comparisons and displays as means of incentive, control, attrition and change…' (2003: 216). Within a discourse of performativity teachers are unlikely to invest seriously in pupils with special educational needs where gains are likely to be marginal in relation to school performance indicators (Ball, 2003).

VOICE OF A SENCO

Throughout my teaching career I have always been acutely aware of an overwhelming desire to accept and support the very individual and diverse personalities I have had the pleasure of meeting and educating over many years. In the early years of my career I was aware of many teachers who labelled children who were unable to follow the rulebook. The term 'naughty' seemed to be splattered around like paint. 'Naughty' was applied to children who disrupted classes with their challenging behaviour. It was, however, also applied to children who were shy and did not respond to questions, or those who struggled to complete tasks. It was the labelling of the latter group which disturbed me the most. I would find myself trying to relate to these children, knowing how they were feeling, knowing that the more they felt pressurised and undermined the more their self-confidence and self-esteem would be damaged. My views have not changed and my empathy for such children is as strong today as it was then. Deep in my memory I have always realised that I was more able and ready to relate to these children. Many of them were a mirror image of me. I have, until now, acknowledged, only to myself and a few close friends, that certain aspects of my life have influenced both my views and practices. I have recalled isolated incidents, but in a very dismissive manner. In my own thoughts I have often revisited them. I have never wanted to dwell publicly on my past. The past was gone, the present and the future were my focus. In reality I was afraid of revisiting it, unsure of the feelings I would experience by doing so. Agreeing to share and discuss my life experiences has enabled me to understand more fully and deconstruct my own meanings of inclusion. I have lived and worked through the transition from integration to inclusion. The impact of current political agendas is not totally at odds with my practices and beliefs. I do believe that we should do the very best we possibly can for all children and enjoy supporting children to move forward in their learning, although I find the current performance culture frustrating. I continue to strive to support the whole child. Until recent years I was able to celebrate openly each and every development and I do so to this day. In the current wilderness of the standards agenda the children and I frequently celebrate alone.

REFLECTIVE TASK

- To what extent can personal experiences shape the development of teacher identity, particularly in relation to inclusion?
- What are the tensions between the standards agenda and the inclusion agenda?

Cole (2005) argues that inclusion presents itself as a risk on different levels when performance indicators are the overriding concern and this is a view to which we subscribe. She acknowledges the risks but argues that the risks are worth taking 'in the cause of equity and social justice' (Cole, 2005: 342). She argues that:

Policies of inclusion have to exist within the context of the broader, general education policy but this is not going to be an easy relationship and it is one that many argue is incompatible … In such a relationship there will be winners and losers and it is suggested that the losers will be the children who are deemed as having special educational needs.

(2005: 334)

REFLECTIVE TASK

Within schooling structures diversity is often viewed as a negative characteristic which threatens the status quo as well as school performance indicators. Rather than viewing diversity as an enriching and energising force and harnessing it to improve education for social justice, schools tend to stifle diversity by expecting pupils to conform to specific rules. Pupils are expected to wear school uniforms which serve to eradicate individuality. Pupils are expected to behave in a certain way and non-conventional behavioural characteristics are viewed as forms of resistance rather than as forms of expression. Teachers are usually encouraged to wear conservative forms of dress as a mark of 'professionalism'. Timetables and bells mean that pupils move through school at specific times in specific ways. Individual handwriting styles are constrained so that pupils' writing looks the same.

- Consider other ways in which schools constrain diversity rather than promoting it.
- Is this a good thing?

A SUMMARY OF **KEY POINTS**

➤ The medical model of disability locates the problem within the child and focuses on correction.

➤ The social model separates impairment and disability and assumes that disability is socially constructed through disabling barriers in society.

➤ The affirmative model celebrates disability and seeks to promote a proud disabled identity.

➤ There is no single meaning of inclusion. Interpretations vary across and between groups, societies, cultures and individuals and are influenced by vested interests.

RESEARCH SUMMARY RESEARCH SUMMARY **RESEARCH SUMMARY** RESEARCH SUMMARY

Read the following article:

Ainscow, M., Booth, T. and Dyson, A. (2006) 'Inclusion and the standards agenda: negotiating policy pressures in England', *International Journal of Inclusive Education*, 10(4/5), 295–308.

Despite the overwhelming strength of research evidence which suggests that the inclusion agenda and the standards agenda work in opposition, this research found that the standards agenda, whilst subverting inclusion, could actually promote schools to use more inclusive pedagogical approaches.

MOVING *ON* > > > > > > MOVING *ON* > > > > > > MOVING *ON*

Now that you are aware of the affirmative model of disability start to build up a bank of resources (story books, DVDs, posters, photographs, artefacts) which will enable you to teach pupils about the positive aspects of a disabled identity.

REFERENCES REFERENCES **REFERENCES** REFERENCES REFERENCES REFERENCES

Ainscow, M. (2000) 'Profile', in P. Clough and J. Corbett (eds) *Theories of Inclusive Education: A Students' Guide*, London: Paul Chapman Publishing, pp. 39–42.

Allan, J. (1996) 'Foucault and special educational needs: A "box of tools" for analysing children's experiences of mainstreaming', *Disability and Society*, 11(2), 219–33.

Allan, J. (2000) 'Reflection: inconclusive education? Towards settled uncertainty', in P. Clough and J. Corbett (eds) *Theories of Inclusive Education: A Students' Guide*, London: Paul Chapman Publishing, pp. 43–6.

Allan, J. (2008) *Rethinking Inclusive Education: The Philosophers of Difference in Practice*, Dordrecht: Springer.

Armstrong, D. (2005) 'Reinventing "inclusion": New Labour and the cultural politics of special education', *Oxford Review of Education*, 31(1), 135–51.

Armstrong, D., Armstrong, A.C. and Spandagou, I. (2011) 'Inclusion: by choice or chance?', *International Journal of Inclusive Education*, 15(1), 29–39.

Avramidis, E. and Norwich, B. (2012) 'The state of the research – compromise, consensus or disarray', in L. Per and G. Reid (eds) *Special Educational Needs: A Guide for Inclusive Practice*, London: Sage, pp. 24–34.

Avramidis, E., Bayliss, P. and Burden, R. (2002) 'Inclusion in action: an in-depth case study of an effective inclusive secondary school in the south-west of England', *International Journal of Inclusive Education*, 6(2), 143–63.

Azzopardi, A. (2009) *Reading Stories of Inclusion: Engaging with Different Perspectives Towards an Agenda for Inclusion*, Saarbruken: VDM Verlag Dr. Muller.

Azzopardi, A. (2010) *Making Sense of Inclusive Education: Where Everyone Belongs*, Saarbrucken: VDM.

Ball, S.J. (2003) 'The teacher's soul and the terrors of performativity', *Journal of Education Policy*, 18(2), 215–28.

Barnes, C. (1991) *Disabled People in Britain and Discrimination: A Case for Anti-discrimination Legislation*, London: Hurst and Co.

Benjamin, S. (2002) 'Valuing diversity: a cliché for the 21st century?', *International Journal of Inclusive Education*, 6(4), 309–23.

Billington, T. (2000) *Separating, Losing and Excluding Children: Narratives of Difference*, London: Routledge Falmer.

Booth, T. (2000) 'Reflection', in P. Clough and J. Corbett (eds) *Theories of Inclusive Education: A Students' Guide*, London: Paul Chapman Publishing, pp. 59–64.

Carrington, S. and Elkins, J. (2005) 'Comparisons of a traditional and an inclusive secondary school culture', in J. Rix, K. Simmons, M. Nind and K. Sheehy (eds) *Policy and Power in Inclusive Education: Values into Practice*, London: Routledge Falmer/Open University Press, pp. 85–95.

Cole, B. (2005) 'Good faith and effort? Perspectives on educational inclusion', *Disability and Society*, 20(3), 331–44.

Corbett, J. (1992) 'Careful teaching: researching a special career', *British Educational Research Journal*, 18(3), 235–43.

Corbett, J. (2001), 'Teaching approaches which support inclusive education: a connective pedagogy', *British Journal of Special Education*, 28(2), 55–9.

Corbett, J. and Slee, R. (2000) 'An international conversation on inclusive education', in F. Armstrong, D. Armstrong and L. Barton (eds) *Inclusive Education: Policy Contexts and Comparative Perspectives*, London: David Fulton, pp. 133–46.

Crow, L. (2003) 'Including all of our lives: renewing the social model of disability', in M. Nind, J. Rix, K. Sheehy and K. Simmons (eds) *Inclusive Education: Diverse Perspectives*, London: David Fulton, pp. 135–49.

Deleuze, G. and Guattari, F. (1987) *A Thousand Plateaus: Capitalism and Schizophrenia*, London: Continuum.

Department for Education (DfE) (2010) *The Importance of Teaching: The Schools White Paper*, Norwich: The Stationery Office.

Department for Education (DfE) (2011) *Support and Aspiration: A New Approach to Special Educational Needs and Disability: a Consultation*, Norwich: The Stationery Office.

Department for Education (DfE) (2013) *The National Curriculum in England: Key Stages 1 and 2 Framework Document*, London: DfE.

Department for Education (DfE) (2014) *Special Educational Needs and Disability Code of Practice: 0 to 25 Years: Statutory Guidance for Organisations Who Work With and Support Children and Young People with Special Educational Needs and Disabilities*, London: DfE.

Dewsbury, G., Clarke, K., Randall, D., Rouncefield, M. and Sommerville, I. (2004) 'The anti–social model of disability', *Disability and Society*, 19(2), 145–58.

Dunne, L. (2009) 'Discourses of inclusion: a critique', *Power and Education*, 1(1), 42–56.

Foucault, M. (1977), *Discipline and Punish: The Birth of the Prison*, Harmondsworth: Penguin.

Gabel, S.L. (2010) 'Forward: disability and equity in education and special education', in A. Azzopardi (ed.) *Making Sense of Inclusive Education: Where Everyone Belongs*, Saarbrucken: VDM, pp. 9–10.

Giroux, H.A. (2003) 'Public pedagogy and the politics of resistance: notes on a critical theory of educational struggle', *Educational Philosophy and Theory*, 35(1), 5–16.

Glazzard, J. (2010) 'The impact of dyslexia on pupils' self–esteem', *Support for Learning*, 25(2), 63–9.

Goodley, D. (2001) '"Learning Difficulties"', the social model of disability and impairment: challenging epistemologies', *Disability and Society*, 16(2), 207–31.

Goodley, D. (2007), 'Towards socially just pedagogies: Deleuzoguattarian critical disability studies', *International Journal of Inclusive Education*, 11(3), 317–34.

Goodley, D. and Runswick–Cole, K. (2011) 'Problematising policy: conceptions of "child", "disabled" and "parents" in social policy in England', *International Journal of Inclusive Education*, 15(1), 71–85.

Graham, L.J. (2006) 'Caught in the net: a Foucaultian interrogation of the incidental effects of limited notions of inclusion', *International Journal of Inclusive Education*, 10(1), 3–25.

Graham, L.J. and Harwood, V. (2011) 'Developing capabilities for social inclusion: engaging diversity through inclusive school communities', *International Journal of Inclusive Education*, 15(1), 135–52.

Graham, L.J and Slee, R. (2008) 'An illusory interiority: interrogating the discourse/s of inclusion', *Educational Philosophy and Theory*, 40(2), 247–60.

Hansen, J.H. (2012) 'Limits to inclusion', *International Journal of Inclusive Education*, 16(1), 89–98.

Hodkinson, A. (2012) '"All present and correct?" Exclusionary inclusion within the English education system', *Disability and Society*, 27(5), 675–88.

Humphrey, J.C. (2000) 'Researching disability politics, or, some problems with the social model in practice', *Disability and Society*, 15(1), 63–85.

Lindsay, G. (2003) 'Inclusive education: a critical perspective', *British Journal of Special Education*, 30(1), 3–12.

Lloyd, C. (2008) 'Removing barriers to achievement: a strategy for inclusion or exclusion?', *International Journal of Inclusive Education*, 12(2), 221–36.

Nind, M. (2005) 'Inclusive education: discourse and action', *British Educational Research Journal*, 31(2), 269–75.

Nind, M., Rix, J., Sheehy, K. and Simmons, K. (2003) *Inclusive Education: Diverse Perspectives*, London: David Fulton.

Nutbrown, C., Clough, P. and Atherton, F. (2013), *Inclusion in the Early Years*, London: Sage.

O'Hanlon, C. (2003) *Educational Inclusion as Action Research: An Interpretive Discourse*, Maidenhead: Open University Press.

Oliver, M. (1990) *The Politics of Disablement*, Basingstoke: Macmillan.

Oliver, M. (1996) *Understanding Disability*, Basingstoke: Macmillan

Peterson, C., Maier, S.F. and Seligman, M.E.P. (1995) *Learned Helplessness: A Theory for the Age of Personal Control*, Oxford: Oxford University Press.

Roaf, C. (1988) 'The concept of a whole school approach to special needs', in O. Robinson and G. Thomas (eds), *Tackling Learning Difficulties,* London: Hodder and Stoughton.

Roaf, C. and Bines, H. (1989) 'Needs, rights and opportunities in special education', in C. Roaf and H. Bines (eds) *Needs, Rights and Opportunities: Developing Approaches to Special Education*, London: Falmer.

Roulstone, A. and Prideaux, S. (2008) 'More policies, greater inclusion? Exploring the contradictions of New Labour Inclusive Education Policy', *International Studies in Sociology of Education*, 18(1), 15–29.

Shakespeare, T. and Watson, N. (1997) 'Defending the social model', *Disability and Society*, 12(2), 293–300.

Shakespeare, T.W. (1992) 'A reply to Liz Crow', *Coalition*, September, 40.

Sikes, P., Lawson, H. and Parker, M. (2007) 'Voices on: teachers and teaching assistants talk about inclusion', *International Journal of Inclusive Education*, 11(3), 355–70.

Skidmore, D. (2004) *Inclusion: The Dynamic of School Development*, Berkshire: Open University Press.

Slee, R. (2011) *The Irregular School: Exclusion, Schooling and Inclusive Education*, London: Routledge.

Swain, J. and French, S. (2003) 'Towards an affirmation model of disability', in M. Nind, J. Rix, K. Sheehy and K. Simmons (eds) *Inclusive Education: Diverse Perspectives*, London: David Fulton, pp. 150–64.

Thomas, G. and Loxley, A. (2001) *Deconstructing Special Education and Constructing Inclusion*, Buckingham: Open University Press.

Thomas, G. and Loxley, A. (2007) *Deconstructing Special Education and Constructing Inclusion*, Berkshire: Open University Press.

Tomlinson, S. (1985) 'The expansion of special education', *Oxford Review of Education*, 11(2), 157–65.

Tregaskis, C. (2002) 'Social Model Theory: the story so far ...', *Disability and Society*, 17(4), 457–70.

Union of the Physically Impaired Against Segregation (UPAIS) (1976) *Fundamental Principles of Disability*, London: UPIAS.

United Nations (1989) *The UN Convention on the Rights of the Child*, London: UNICEF.

Warnock, M. (2005) 'Special educational needs: a new look', *Impact*, 11, Salisbury: Philosophy of Education Society of Great Britain.

Wedell, K. (2008) 'Confusion about inclusion: patching up or system change?', *British Journal of Special Education*, 35(3), 127–35.

Wilson, J. (1999) 'Some conceptual difficulties about "inclusion"', *Support for Learning*, 14(3), 110–12.

FURTHER READING   FURTHER READING   **FURTHER READING**   FURTHER READING

Norwich, B. (2008) *Dilemmas of Difference, Inclusion and Disability*, London: Routledge.

USEFUL WEBSITES   USEFUL WEBSITES   **USEFUL WEBSITES**   USEFUL WEBSITES

http://www.csie.org.uk/inclusion/

http://www.nasen.org.uk/

PART 3
SUPPORTING CHILDREN WITH BEHAVIOURAL, EMOTIONAL AND SOCIAL DIFFICULTIES

3
Understanding behavioural, emotional and social difficulties

Chapter objectives

By the end of this chapter you should:

- understand the complexities of social, emotional and behavioural difficulties;
- understand how these complexities affect teaching and learning;
- be able to implement some strategies in order to support these pupils;
- be aware of the support from outside agencies.

Teachers' Standards

This chapter addresses the following Teachers' Standards:

TS7: Manage behaviour effectively to ensure a good and safe learning environment

- have clear rules and routines for behaviour in classrooms, and take responsibility for promoting good and courteous behaviour both in classrooms and around the school, in accordance with the school's behaviour policy
- have high expectations of behaviour, and establish a framework for discipline with a range of strategies, using praise, sanctions, and rewards consistently and fairly

Introduction

Children do not come to school as 'empty vessels'. Irrespective of their background all children are shaped by their social environment, and while for most this has a positive impact on their learning within school, for some it can sadly be a barrier.

It is often argued that social, emotional and behavioural problems have their roots in 'nurture' rather than 'nature', but irrespective of the cause as a trainee teacher you have to support these pupils while maximising their educational potential.

Emotional

Short term – minor – minimal effect e.g. goldfish dying

Long term – major – far reaching effects e.g. family crisis

A child's emotional state can severely affect their learning and while the actual emotion may be relatively easy to pin point for example, tears or withdrawal, the causes are not. Children often find emotions very difficult to deal with, as do many adults, and may actually be scared of their strength of feelings. It is often believed that emotion is not something to be shared and that we should assume a 'stiff upper lip' – further contributing to existing problems!

Social

As an adult you have your own norms and values and possibly a strong sense of what you consider to be right and wrong! However, as a teacher you will come into contact with many things that radically challenge these beliefs and it is imperative that these in no way 'cloud' your judgement when involved with a child with social, emotional and behavioural difficulties. What is considered the norm in some families may raise cause for concern from other parties, but this does not necessarily indicate that a child's problems are a direct result of family values.

Maslow's hierarchy of needs (1954) conclude that all human behaviour has a meaning and is a response to a drive to have needs met. The first and baseline need in this hierarchy is 'physiological or survival needs': these are the basic needs of food, warmth and shelter. However, it is an unfortunate fact that not all pupils you come into contact with will have these needs met on a regular basis, and as such will find it very difficult to move to the next level of need.

The next level, 'safety needs', can again be a challenge for some pupils as they do not always experience environments that make them feel physically and emotionally secure.

The third level, 'love, affection and belonging', is another aspect that can be lacking in pupils' lives and which can severely affect the next level which is 'self-esteem'.

The final level, 'self-actualisation', is when we can be motivated to realise our potential, an aspect we strive for in all our pupils but which can be difficult to achieve due to previous needs not being met.

At every level some pupils may feel challenged and possibly powerless to change their circumstances and it is often this aspect which manifests itself in challenging behaviour. As teachers we need to be aware of the possible lack of basic needs and address these to the best of our ability within an educational setting through creating secure environments and working areas, giving positive and supportive feedback, and giving all pupils the chance to be creative and autonomous. Many schools have now developed breakfast clubs and snack tables to ensure that pupils' basic physiological needs are met.

However, on a final note, do remember that we all have limitations and that you can only be expected to do your best! However, you have a responsibility to support all pupils and not to give up on them if they display challenging behaviour.

Behavioural

It cannot be assumed that children will arrive in school with a developed understanding of how to behave. How many times have you heard a child referred to as naughty? Yet, when you have had time to get to know them you begin to realise there is more to it than a 'naughty' streak! Behaviour manifests itself in many ways and can severely disrupt the learning of the child concerned and their classmates. It can be a result of social and emotional problems or of an underlying special educational need. Whatever the cause, the behaviour has a *function* for that child, and this will be discussed later in the chapter.

School policies

A clear vision for managing pupils' behaviour is based on establishing clear boundaries and rules and should be underpinned by positive behaviour strategies (Shelton and Brownhill, 2008). A consistent and coherent approach is underpinned by an agreed philosophy (Shelton and Brownhill, 2008).

Within your placement schools you will have the opportunity to view policies relating to many aspects of school organisation and curriculum. The behaviour policy may be a stand-alone document which encompasses all aspects, for example the school's policy on sanctions and rewards, or there may be several policies relating to different aspects. It is well worth asking to see these policies in order to familiarise yourself with the school's arrangements prior to classroom experience.

Medical implications

For some pupils behavioural difficulties can be linked to medical problems and in some cases the medication that is used to treat them. These problems can be both physical, such as epilepsy, or emotional, for example depression, and in these cases the intervention and support of medical professionals are vital. Data collection by type of SEN states:

> *Pupils with a range of difficulties, including emotional disorders such as depression and eating disorders; conduct disorders such as oppositional defiance disorder (ODD); hyperkinetic disorders including attention deficit disorder (ADD) or attention deficit hyperactivity disorder (ADHD); and syndromes such as Tourette's should be recorded as behavioural, emotional, or social difficulties (BESD) if additional or different educational arrangements are being made to support them.*
>
> (DfES, 2005: 8)

Behaviour that is medically based can be difficult to modify. However, it is still in the pupil's best interest to instigate whatever measures are possible in order to minimise the effects of the behaviour and to give the pupil the opportunity to achieve their potential.

Behaviour management or behaviour modification?

It goes without saying that teaching a child with behavioural difficulties can be very hard work. It often involves extra planning, making changes in the physical environment and liaising with others to name but a few – and availability of time can play a big part in this. While behaviour management can be time consuming, behaviour modification is usually considered to be more so, and so poses even further demands on the teacher. However, the rewards of modification are usually more positive and so become more beneficial in the long term.

When we talk about managing behaviour we usually mean just that: within the confines of school an individual's behaviour is managed through agreed strategies, sometimes involving praise for good behaviour, physical intervention, exclusion from the group and modified tasks and activities. While this method can often minimise disruption and allow teaching and learning to continue, it does not attempt to investigate the underlying causes and so seek a solution.

As mentioned previously all behaviour has a *function*. In simple terms this means that the behaviour is fulfilling some need or function for the child in question; unfortunately the child does not always recognise this for him or herself.

Functional analysis

This involves the participation of as many individuals as possible who are involved with the child including parents/carers, medical professionals and social workers. This group consider aspects of the child's life that are both positive and negative, and through shared and open discussion begin to link behaviours to life experiences. This can often be a long and in some cases a painful experience for those involved, but it can provide a starting point for modifying behaviour. A case study best illustrates this method.

CASE STUDY

Although Simon was often quiet and withdrawn in school his behaviour gave no cause for concern. He found it difficult to concentrate and ongoing assessment identified possible learning difficulties. However successive teachers were very positive about Simon as he was making progress.

When Simon entered Year 6 his behaviour changed dramatically; he was loud and abusive and would often attempt to hurt classmates for no apparent reason. Exclusion from the group, differentiated tasks and 'time out' had little or no effect and the problem was escalating.

A group meeting was called but his parents were very reticent to attend, although after reassurance from the school they agreed. All seemed to be very positive in Simon's life and it was becoming increasingly difficult to explain his behaviour. It was decided to reconvene the meeting at a later date.

In the interim period his parents contacted the school wishing to share information and were invited to speak to the head teacher as they felt unable to share with a larger group. They were obviously upset and the father explained that as an 11-year-old boy he had transferred to secondary education (the school where Simon was to go) where he was bullied to the extent that he felt it was still affecting his life. He had never shared this with anyone or received help, and hadn't realised that Simon had overheard arguments when aspects had been discussed.

It therefore seemed apparent that to Simon, Year 6 signalled the fast approaching transfer to a school of which the only knowledge he had was inadvertently from his father. It was felt that he was unable to share this with anyone as he felt a loyalty to his dad and his mechanism for coping was his inappropriate behaviour.

Subsequently Simon was able to undertake many very positive visits to the school, some even with his father, and as a result he became much more confident and self-assured about the transfer. The behaviour he displayed also began to diminish, and at the point of transfer he showed none of his previous problems.

Also on a positive note his father received support in order to resolve his own problems.

This was a very positive outcome and one that was arrived at relatively easily. This, however, is not always the case, as the 'answer' to the behaviour problem can be very difficult and sometimes impossible to source. However, whenever possible this method is extremely beneficial, and one which ultimately will enhance your teaching.

Attention deficit hyperactivity disorder (ADHD)

O'Regan (2002) states that there will be one or two pupils with ADHD in every classroom, with approximately 5% of school-aged children having ADHD. The ADHD diagnosis should not be applied to a child who appears 'naughty' or displays behavioural difficulties. In most cases the pupils who do have ADHD genuinely do not set out to be disruptive or defiant and are often distressed by their own behaviour.

A multi-disciplinary approach needs to be adopted with these pupils as professionals such as speech and language therapists and doctors can be hugely beneficial in supporting these pupils both at home and at school.

The ABC model

This method is also beneficial in ascertaining why a pupil may be behaving in a certain way, and so offers a way forward with a solution.

- **A** Antecedents – What is the context of the behaviour?
- **B** Behaviour
- **C** Consequences – What happens afterwards?

Antecedents

- What was the task? Why might the pupil find this challenging?
- What environment is the pupil working in? Can this cause a challenge? For example, some pupils find confined spaces a problem.
- Who is the pupil working with? Both staff and peers? Are there any recorded incidents involving these individuals?
- Are the work/resources presented differentiated appropriately in order that the pupil can achieve?
- What happened immediately before the behaviour? Was there a trigger? Did the pupil come into school from home in an anxious state?

Behaviour

- What exactly is the behaviour that is causing concern? Is there more than one type of behaviour? Are all behaviours linked or could they have different triggers?
- What are the reactions displayed by the pupil? Are these reactions observed in different contexts?

Consequences

- What happens when the behaviour ends? Does it actually end or does different behaviour take its place?
- Does the pupil appreciate that there has been a change in their own behaviour? Do they have the opportunity to discuss this with anyone?
- Do they have an understanding of why they display such behaviour?
- What reactions do they get from adults and peers? Does this reaction actually help or does it inflame the situation, for example peers who make fun of actions or behaviour. Consider that some other pupils might actually find the pupil's behaviour to be positive – it may draw the teacher's attention away from them or distract the class from having to complete their work!

What happens next? But most importantly what as a teacher do you do next? The ABC model needs to be more than a paper exercise that is completed after the event. It needs to be used as a tool to build an accurate picture of behaviour, in order to seek a solution. As with functional analysis this is not always an easy or straightforward process, but it is worth the time invested in it if a solution towards supporting a pupil can be found.

REFLECTIVE TASK

Consider a pupil with behaviour difficulties you have had experience of on your placement. Use the ABC method to analyse their behaviour. Talk to other staff who have worked with the pupil – do they agree with your findings?

The teacher's behaviour

Howarth and Fisher (2005) suggest that pupils with EBD will often believe that a teacher's irritation is personally directed towards them and as a result of this they may quickly start to create difficulties. It is often stated that children learn by example, and as such a teacher can be a very influential role model. It therefore goes without saying that a teacher should be a positive influence, especially when dealing with pupils with social, emotional and behavioural difficulties.

The language that a teacher uses can have a significant effect on pupils, sometimes resulting in them being labelled. Negative language does not support or enhance self-esteem, and by only slightly modifying what we say we can turn a negative statement into a positive one.

Social and emotional difficulties

While social and emotional problems can have a significant impact on both a child's ability to learn and their behaviour, it is an aspect that is often best addressed by other professionals. This does not, however, negate your responsibility to a child with social and emotional difficulties and it is imperative that you are able to support these pupils by understanding the role of others.

You may have already encountered pupils on your placements that for whatever reason are negatively affected by their social circumstances and or their emotional state, and no matter how strongly this affects you, in common with many other teachers, you can feel that your 'hands are tied'.

Therefore on any placement you must be made aware of the school's Safeguarding Officer, their role within school, and the school's procedure for reporting incidents including those of a social and or emotional nature. This designated person will, if necessary, be able to alert other professionals, for example, social workers and medical professionals to the case and deal with it in an appropriate manner.

However, it is still the class teacher who will ultimately have to deal with the pupil on a day-to-day basis, and as mentioned earlier a non-judgemental approach needs to be taken. Children with social/emotional problems often lack structure and boundaries in their lives and by creating these in the classroom the child can feel more secure and so able to learn. These children will also often confide in you as a trusted person in their lives, and once again it is vital that you are aware of the school's policy for reporting disclosures.

Schools are well aware that pupils need a very broad curriculum in order to enhance their social and emotional skills, and as a teacher this can become an integral and enjoyable part of everyday teaching.

PRACTICAL TASK   PRACTICAL TASK   PRACTICAL TASK   PRACTICAL TASK   PRACTICAL TASK

On your next placement note the professionals and outside agencies who work with pupils in school. If possible investigate their roles and how their input impacts on pupils.

The teacher's emotional state

It should never be overlooked that teachers are human and as such can be affected by the same problems as some of our pupils. In fact for some teachers, the problems being encountered by a pupil can be significantly disturbing if they themselves have also had personal experience of these.

Although often very difficult to do, it is in your own best interest to alert someone within the school if you are having difficulties, who can either guide and support you, or refer you to someone who can. This is not a weakness on your part, it is in fact a strength as you need to be emotionally fit if you are to be able to help and support your pupils.

Professional relationships

A multi-disciplinary approach, involving a range of professionals, is often necessary for supporting pupils with SEND. For children with social, emotional and behavioural difficulties the notion of 'joined-up working' is even more imperative, and it is very often the teacher who will identify and instigate this. The Code of Practice (DfE, 2014) states that pupils with SEND, including those with social, emotional and behavioural problems, should have well co-ordinated and coherent support across education, health and social care.

Working with parents and carers

It has been suggested that inconsistent and harsh parental discipline as well as poor parental supervision and monitoring can result in behaviour and conduct problems in early childhood (DfES, 2003). In an 'ideal' world teachers, along with other professionals, would have the full co-operation and support from parents and carers in all aspects of the child's life. However, we know that this is not always the case, and it is unfortunate that due to many factors, the parents and carers of pupils with social, emotional and behavioural difficulties cannot always offer this support.

Some parents/carers may be affected in a similar way to their children, by for example, experiencing emotional difficulties. Some may not appreciate or may not want to appreciate these problems and this makes effective partnerships more difficult to establish.

Teachers, along with other professionals, often find the support of parents/carers invaluable in all aspects of a child's development and they should be included at every level; a behaviour modification plan which is carried out consistently at home as it is in school is usually far more effective than one which is school based only.

However, we must be realistic and concede that for whatever reason we may not have parental involvement or co-operation, and that while this may cause even further difficulties, it must not impede the support that we and other professionals can give to the child. Parents may feel that they are being blamed by the school for their child's misdemeanours (Gray, 2002) and teachers need to guard against this. Teachers, along with other professionals, often find the support of parents/carers invaluable in all aspects of a child's development and they should be included at every level; a behaviour modification plan which is carried out consistently at home as it is in school is usually far more effective than one which is school based only. However, we must be realistic and concede that for whatever reason we may not have parental involvement or co-operation, and that while this may cause even further difficulties, it must not impede the support that we and other professionals can give to the child.

Planning for pupils with social, emotional and behavioural difficulties

Trainees must develop a fast-growing awareness of the need for effective differentiation of lessons in order to meet the needs of all learners. However, planning for pupils with social, emotional and behavioural difficulties can often add a new dimension to both the planning and the delivery of a lesson. In some circumstances it is not *what* a child learns but *how*, and this is especially true of this group of pupils. With this in mind it may not be the content of the lesson which needs differentiating, but the method of delivery coupled with the pupil's preferred learning style.

As mentioned previously pupils often lack boundaries and structure in their lives, and sometimes all that is needed are these elements in order to enhance teaching and learning. Some examples of how this can be put into practice are as follows:

- Clear outcomes for all lessons in a form understandable to the pupil.
- Clear timetables, once again in an understandable form that is adhered to.
- Now and next: clearly signposting what they are learning now and what they will learn next.
- Resources clearly labelled and accessible.
- A secure working environment.
- Rewards and sanctions.
- Rules and routines.

Clear outcomes

Ensure that the pupil actually knows what they are going to learn and what is expected of them. This can be presented in words, pictures or symbols. The pupil may also require continual reassurance throughout the lesson that they are following the correct 'learning path'.

Clear timetables

A clear overview of the day – again, in a variety of formats – provides learners with a sense of security. Visual timetables can be very useful in creating a sense of routine and order. For some pupils a specific curriculum subject or area of school can be challenging. The use of a timetable provides time for the pupil to adapt and prepare for transitions throughout the day.

Now and next

For some pupils the overview of the day is too complex or challenging, although they still require the security of knowing what is to come. Now and next gives them exactly what it says: what is expected of them immediately and what will happen next. Ensure that all aspects of the day are recorded on this e.g. playtimes, snack time etc. as well as lesson times. Once again this can be presented in a variety of formats. In some cases pupils may require a three-part 'plan': what they have just achieved, what they are working on, and the next step. You will draw on your professional judgement to ascertain the degree of 'security' you need to build into a pupil's visual timetable.

Resources

Ensure that pupils understand where resources are stored and how to access them. For some pupils, opening a drawer marked 'pencils' and finding nothing but rulers could in itself be the trigger for negative behaviour. Clear labels using words, pictures, symbols or even the 'real thing' are vital, and a pupil's self-esteem can be given a positive 'boost' if they are able to be responsible for the retrieval and collection of resources.

Secure working environment

It goes without saying that we all hope to create a classroom or working area that is secure. However, for some pupils this security may not be enough and they will require a modified area in which to work. Some pupils actually need to create their own area in which to work – a personalised desk or an enclosed space – and giving them this will hopefully lead them, in time, to becoming fully included within the classroom space. Security can also often be achieved through a well organised and tidy environment, an aspect which is not always a part of their life out of school.

REFLECTIVE TASK

Think about the classrooms and working areas in your placement schools. Have they been conducive to safe and secure working? What small measures could have been put in place to enhance these aspects?

Rewards and sanctions

O'Regan (2006) has questioned the value of sanctions in response to poor behaviour, arguing that the effects of sanctions can be short term. Rewards affect long-term change in behaviour (O'Regan, 2006) so it is important to praise and reward children when good behaviour is demonstrated. The majority of pupils we teach respond positively to rewards, and while we do not want to get into a culture of 'bribery', they can be a very effective motivator. In contrast sanctions need not be negative and can even be designed to complement rewards.

Pupils often respond more positively if they have the opportunity to choose their own rewards and this can often include other learning opportunities such as time on the computer. When building rewards into the curriculum it is important that you consider the time element i.e. how long will the reward last until the pupil is expected to move to another activity. Timers are ideal for pupils who find telling the time problematic, especially if you want to aim to extend the time on task and reduce the reward time. Now and next cards can include rewards, and for some pupils the 'next' activity will often always need to be a reward. A reward or star chart is often all that is needed in order to motivate, and while a class chart is beneficial for those who achieve, a personalised chart will be more acceptable for those who find competition challenging.

Sanctions need to be understood by the pupil if they are to be effective, and an off the cuff 'sit there for five minutes' will do little good if the pupil does not understand why. As with rewards, sanctions need to have a time implication which the pupil understands, and they can also have positive implications e.g. 'you can still have your chosen reward but due to your behaviour you now need to have five minutes out before that can happen'.

Pupils with behavioural difficulties often require almost 'instant' rewards and sanctions and working towards a reward to be given on Friday when it is only Monday will have little or no effect!

As with all aspects of teaching and learning a reward or sanction system can be differentiated to be effective for all class members and doing so will create a greater feeling of inclusion for all pupils.

Rules and routines

Classroom rules should be positive rather than negative. They should indicate what to do rather than what not to do, and should reflect desired behaviours and positive ways of working. Rules and daily routines often work more effectively when pupils contribute to them.

Teaching and learning styles

Effective teachers use a range of teaching strategies and know how to personalise learning. This of course refers to all pupils you will teach, but this aspect may have greater relevance for those with social, emotional and behavioural problems.

- Visual learners – these learners need to see the teacher's body language and facial expression (difficult for pupils on the Autistic spectrum). They may think in pictures and learn best from visual displays.
- Auditory learners – learn by talking things through and listening to what others have to say. Written information may have little meaning until it is heard.
- Kinaesthetic learners – learn through moving, doing and touching. They need to actively explore the world around them. They find it hard to sit for long periods and can become distracted by their need to explore.

CASE STUDY

Neil was a 14-year-old boy with behavioural difficulties. He attended a mainstream school and had the support of a teaching assistant for two hours each day. His achievement levels were below those of his peers.

I observed him during a geography lesson and was seated in the classroom when he arrived in the room. His teaching assistant was also in the room but had been asked by the teacher to prepare resources and was busy doing so when he arrived. He arrived calmly and took his seat. There was quite a high noise level with other pupils coming in from play and it seemed that the teacher expected them to go to their places and complete the various worksheets that had been handed out without any introduction or input. He sat for at least ten minutes and remained calm, he was not on task and his teaching assistant was still otherwise engaged. Neil seemed interested in his peers who were eventually settling and beginning to work. After ten minutes it became apparent from his body language that he was becoming agitated and he suddenly leapt from his chair, ran to the fire exit, kicked it open, and ran across the school grounds. I was informed later that he was found up a tree!

The teacher informed me that he often displayed this type of behaviour and that someone would eventually find him and return him to class. You have probably come to the conclusion, as I did, that he found the whole situation very stressful and that the only course of action was to escape. He had been denied his allocated support, he found the noise level difficult, and he was aware that his peers were able to access and complete the allotted work while he was not.

When I was able to speak to him, however, his major concern was the format of the work he was expected to complete and the lack of structured instructions. He said he needed someone to tell or show him what to do even though he was capable of reading instructions, and that he needed pictures or diagrams in order to understand the task. Needless to say the worksheets consisted solely of text. He also said that he was happier completing practical tasks, but that he never got the opportunity.

A change in teaching style for this pupil would have been extremely beneficial, and while it was not the only barrier to his learning it was certainly significant. The pupil has now transferred to a special school and is responding extremely well to a curriculum and learning styles better suited to his needs.

A SUMMARY OF **KEY POINTS**

➢ It could be argued that even the 'experts' do not fully understand the complexities of all social, emotional and behavioural problems and their causes. However, during your career take each case as it is presented, and remember you can only do your best!

➢ Use the opportunities presented by these pupils to enhance your teaching, for the benefit of all pupils you will encounter over the years.

➢ Understand that there is a wealth of expertise to be gained from colleagues, literature and research. Use this wisely – you won't have time to reinvent the wheel when working with pupils with difficulties!

➢ Be aware of, and develop relationships with other professionals. Asking for help is not a weakness – it is a strength that will ultimately benefit the pupils you teach.

➢ Use your time in your extended special needs placement to gain a greater insight into pupils with social, emotional and behavioural problems (see Chapter 12 'School-based training').

MOVING *ON* > > > > > > MOVING *ON* > > > > > > MOVING *ON*

Many trainees preparing for their placements often view pupils with social, emotional and behavioural difficulties with trepidation. However, it can be these very pupils who enhance your placement by challenging your teaching and giving you valuable experiences which will enhance your professional development for many years to come. It must also be remembered that you will not be the first teacher to have to deal with a specific problem, and that there is a wealth of expertise, support and resources available in order to help you successfully teach these young people, usually with very rewarding outcomes.

REFERENCES REFERENCES **REFERENCES** REFERENCES REFERENCES REFERENCES

Department for Education (DfE) (2014) *Special Educational Needs and Disability Code of Practice: 0 to 25 Years: Statutory Guidance for Organisations Who Work With and Support Children and Young People with Special Educational Needs and Disabilities*, London: DfE.

Department for Education and Skills (DfES) (2005) *Data Collection by Type of Special Educational Need*, Annesley: DfES Publications.

Gray, P. (ed.) (2002) *Working with Emotions: Responding to the Challenge of Difficult Pupil Behaviour in Schools*, London: Routledge.

Howarth, R. and Fisher, P. (2005) *Emotional and Behavioural Difficulties*, London: Continuum.

Maslow, A. (1954) *Motivation and Personality*, London: Harper and Row.

O'Regan, F. (2002) *How to Teach and Manage Children with ADHD*, Wisbech: LDA.

O'Regan, F. (2006) *Can't Learn, Won't learn, Don't Care: Troubleshooting Challenging Behaviour*, London: Continuum.

Shelton, F. and Brownhill, S. (2008) *Effective Behaviour Management in the Primary Classroom*, Maidenhead: Open University Press.

FURTHER READING FURTHER READING   FURTHER READING   FURTHER READING

Adams, K. (2009) *Behaviour for Learning in the Primary School*, Exeter: Learning Matters.

Cohen, L., Manion, L. and Morrison, K. (2006) *A Guide to Teaching Practice*. Abingdon: Routledge.

Farrell, M. (2008) *Educating Special Children: An introduction to Provision for Pupils with Disabilities and Disorders*, London: David Fulton.

Roffey, S. (2006) *Helping with Behaviour*, London: Routledge.

USEFUL WEBSITES USEFUL WEBSITES   USEFUL WEBSITES   USEFUL WEBSITES

http://www.nasen.org.uk/

http://www.goodschoolsguide.co.uk/help-and-advice/special-needs-advice/types-of-sen/behavioural-difficulties/182/behavioural-disorders

4
Attention deficit hyperactivity disorder

Chapter objectives

By the end of this chapter you should be aware of:

- the signs of attention deficit hyperactivity disorder (ADHD);
- strategies to facilitate the inclusion of a child with ADHD;
- the aspects of a learner-friendly environment for pupils with ADHD.

Teachers' Standards

This chapter addresses the following Teachers' Standards:

TS5: Adapt teaching to respond to the strengths and needs of all pupils

- know when and how to differentiate appropriately, using approaches which enable pupils to be taught effectively
- have a secure understanding of how a range of factors can inhibit pupils' ability to learn, and how best to overcome these
- demonstrate an awareness of the physical, social and intellectual development of children, and how to adapt teaching to support pupils' education at different stages of development
- have a clear understanding of the needs of all pupils, including those with special educational needs; those of high ability; those with English as an additional language; those with disabilities; and be able to use and evaluate distinctive teaching approaches to engage and support them

Introduction

The new Code of Practice (DfE, 2014) places an emphasis on early identification of SEND. ADHD is not a new condition. It has always been around. However, it is only in more recent times that we have become better at identifying it. Pupils with ADHD are not lazy or naughty and ADHD is not caused by bad parenting. It is a neurodevelopmental disorder which reduces the capacity of those affected by it to engage with education. The implications for teachers are significant and there is no single solution or quick fix which will address the multiple manifestations of ADHD across a range of pupils. Teachers need to be reflective and be willing to try out different approaches with different pupils. They need to evaluate systematically these approaches and be willing to adopt different approaches when one approach fails to work. In adopting a social model perspective, teachers need to consider the extent to which their own attitudes towards learners with ADHD, their teaching strategies and styles and the content of the curriculum are partially responsible for creating learner disengagement. Teachers need to be prepared to experiment with creative approaches to teaching and learning in order to maximise levels of engagement for all pupils.

What is ADHD?

- ADHD is a neurodevelopmental disorder – it has a biological origin.
- It affects 5.29% of children and adolescents.
- It is estimated that between 15 and 65% of those affected will carry the condition on into adulthood.
- It is pervasive and enduring – it does not stop when pupils leave a classroom or the school and can be present at home, in school or at work.
- Approximately one third of those affected will experience significant problems with inattention without being impulsive or hyperactive.
- It is more common in boys than girls (ratio 4:1).

Indicators of ADHD

Inattention

	√
Does not listen	
Finds it difficult to follow instructions	
Poor at sustaining attention	
Can be selective – avoids tasks that require attention	
Finds attention to detail difficult and often does not finish tasks	
Organisational problems	
Easily distracted	
Loses things	
Forgetful	

Impulsivity

	√
Shouts out answers	
Poor at turn taking – frequently interrupts	
Easily frustrated/impatient	
Takes risks	
Needs instant rewards	

Focuses on the here and now rather than the future	
Evidence of conduct disorder – stealing/fighting/being unkind to others (starts before age seven)	
Insatiable	
Lacks response inhibition	

Hyperactivity

	√
Fidgets, wanders around	
Cannot sit still – restless	
Moves quickly from one activity to another	
Finds it difficult to work or play quietly and is frequently noisy	
Talks excessively	
Does not listen well	
'Driven by a motor'	
Has an over developed sense of justice	
Has difficulty forming social relationships and friendships	

Physical symptoms

	√
Restless	
Headaches	
Enuresis	
Insomnia	
Hyperactivity	
Perceptual motor problems	
Poor co-ordination	

Mental symptoms

	√
Learning difficulties	
Impulsive	

Stubborn	
Inattention	
Low self-concept and self-esteem	
Insatiable	
Poor short-term memory	
Mood swings	
Obsessive thinking	
Difficulty following instructions	

Strengths within children with attention deficit disorder (ADD)/ADHD

	√
Sense of humour	
High energy levels	
Creative	
Enthusiastic	
Passionate	
Loyal and forgiving	
Willing to take risks	
Inventive thinkers	
Selective high levels of motivation	

The ADHD-friendly classroom

	√
Provide a welcoming classroom	
Provide stimulating areas such as investigation areas/areas for exploration	
Provide working walls to give learners 'tools for learning'	
Reduce teacher talk	
Provide learners with positive, descriptive praise and praise attitude and effort above achievement	
Build in opportunities for collaborative paired and group work, for example using Kagan Structures	

Support teaching with visual cues	
Display class rules and allow pupils to define what the rules are to give them ownership	
Provide an area of low stimulation	
Pair learners with ADHD with a study buddy	
Adults to respond to learners in a consistent, calm, fair manner	
Empower learners with the confidence to speak out	
Establish clear routines	
Divide tasks into small chunks	
Avoid singling out	

Whole class teaching

During whole class sessions teachers can help to maintain attention by physically engaging pupils in the lesson. Whole class sessions should be broken up into shorter chunks in order to maintain pupils' interest. Teachers should aim to use a variety of visual strategies in their teaching including pictures, digital clips and mind maps. Pupils with ADD/ADHD may be able to maintain attention more effectively if they have something to manipulate in their hands such as a soft ball. Building short 'brain breaks' (short periods of physical activity) into sessions can help to maintain good levels of engagement.

Developing new understanding in lessons

When you introduce pupils to new learning it is important to show them what to do as well as explaining to them what they have to do. It is often useful to provide learners with opportunities to talk through new learning in pairs before they are expected to complete tasks. Tasks can be broken down into smaller chunks and the use of clear success criteria ('what you need to do to be successful'/'what am I looking for in your work') can help pupils to monitor their own progress through the task.

Classroom organisation and staying on task

Learners with ADD/ADHD will usually work more effectively if they are provided with clear step-by-step instructions to enable them to complete tasks. They will be more focused if their workplace is organised and if it is positioned away from things which might distract them. Often they will respond better to consistency so it might be better to ensure that they work on the same table and in the same seat, although this is not always possible. Learners with ADD/ADHD need regular and tangible feedback and the use of a timer might help them to stay focused on a task. The use of a visual arrow which moves from left to right can help learners to see how much longer a task is going to last and this can help them to maintain attention.

If you provide a separate workstation for a child with ADD/ADHD then it is important that pupils do not see this space as a punishment. Sometimes classrooms can be too busy and learners may benefit from working in a low stimulus area. To help them stay on task you might consider using 'private' signals with the child, which uses an agreed signal for a first and second warning. This is a private code between you and the child so that other pupils are not aware that a warning is being issued. Avoid public humiliation. Try to issue regular, positive praise – catch them being good. Provide them with opportunities to have a short break as a reward before resuming the task. Allow opportunities for movement as and when they feel this is necessary.

REFLECTIVE TASK

Discuss the following with a colleague:

- What are the pros and cons of treating ADHD with medication?
- What are the consequences of medication?

PRACTICAL TASK   PRACTICAL TASK   PRACTICAL TASK   PRACTICAL TASK   PRACTICAL TASK

In your placement school ask to meet the SENCO. Find out about whether there are any pupils with a diagnosis of ADD/ADHD and if so, what provision has been made available for these pupils.

CASE STUDY

Never giving up on a child: voice of a SENCO

It was whilst in my first teaching post in the 1970s that I first encountered the challenges of working with children with additional needs. The most memorable was David. I was now teaching a Year 4 class and David had transferred from a special school in Sheffield. He had already been educated in three other schools which had all expelled him. There was no Code of Practice and no additional support to meet his needs. He was simply to be integrated into my class. However, the head teacher was adamant that we were never to 'give up' on anyone.

David proved to be without doubt a huge challenge. He introduced himself as 'the bad lad', beaming from ear to ear. The fact that a child of eight years old already accepted this label was, in my view, a disgrace to the teaching profession. I knew very little about how to support him but quickly seemed to develop an understanding with him. He tried to impress and intimidate me and I refused to be openly shocked by his antics. He would lock himself in the class stock room and shout down at me from the top shelf 'Oi I'm up here!' I ignored him and carried on teaching the class. I still do not know if my responses were appropriate but slowly his outbursts became less frequent and we began to focus on his strengths both as a person and academically. His parents and I worked very closely together. At this time there was no expectation or requirement to do so. They would often drop into school at the end of the day. Again it was the positive aspects of his development that I was drawn towards discussing, totally ignoring the fact that he was unable to settle to complete any tasks I set him unless he was 'in the mood'. From his parents I learned about both his likes and dislikes and began to use these as an effective bargaining tool. He adored making models and so a deal was made: when he had completed something for me, he was rewarded with time for himself. I really felt that we were making progress and I was so thrilled by his achievements and my own.

I taught David for the next three years. This was apparently the result of the strong and trusting relationship I had built with him. In reality it was because none of the other teachers were prepared to teach him. At that time I did not feel the pressures of also ensuring that David worked towards national targets in maths and English. Essentially I supported him in joining a mainstream setting as well as coping with and being accepted and happy in that setting. I remember that an educational psychologist did observe David on a couple of occasions during his time in my class. The same psychologist had observed him on previous occasions throughout his short time in education. He was always so positive about the 'difference' in David. Our discussions, in retrospect were so simplistic. No targets were set; there were no suggestions to enable me to further support David, just a pat on the back for me for a job well done. Additionally there was no pressure for me to consider the negative impacts that David's behaviour had on other learners. When he became difficult he would seek isolation in the stock room or leave the classroom, to be greeted by the head teacher who was so supportive in providing David with refuge in his office. He was not punished there, but rather allowed to cool down until he was ready to return to my classroom. This also offered me the opportunity to continue to educate the other children in the knowledge that David was 'in safe hands'. What became of David I have no idea except that I heard that he wanted to pursue teaching as his chosen career in life. I sincerely hope he was successful.

On reflection I am already able to see a clear pattern in the children who, it was deemed, I was particularly successful in supporting. Those that exhibited challenges in their behaviour or did not conform to socially accepted norms, resulted in my determination to support them. I did not want to change them totally. I simply wished to show a degree of empathy, to show patience and set boundaries until they were able to find their own way of coping with the challenges they faced in life. Many of these children did in reality exhibit challenging behaviour and it is without doubt teaching these children in particular that is firmly engraved on my memory to this day.

My next major challenge unveiled itself as I joined another school in 1991 in the form of a five-year-old called Stevie. Stevie and his older brother had come into foster care with a local family who were anxious to eventually adopt the two boys. Stevie and his brother, I recall, had been found by social services in the south of England living in an attic. Their young mother had twins, only twelve months younger than Stevie. The history of Stevie and his brother was that some food was placed in the attic most days although with no regularity. His older brother had ensured that this was shared between them. Stevie had very poor language skills, demonstrated behaviour which was challenging and did not understand or adhere to most expectations.

From the very first day Stevie proved to be a major challenge. He ran around the classroom, knocking things as well as other children over. He frequently left the classroom and ran amok in the school. This time there was no supportive head teacher. He did not challenge Stevie; he did not remonstrate with him. He simply ignored him. He would put his head round my classroom door to ask me: 'Do you know that Stevie is running round out here?' Then he simply left. With 30 young children in my class and no additional support I would leave my classroom door ajar, enabling me to hear but certainly not see my class and go in pursuit of Stevie. With sole responsibility for my class and for Stevie I had no choice but to ensure that I quickly re-captured Stevie and took him back to the classroom where I could at least keep a watchful eye on him and the other children. This often meant that I had to keep a firm hold on

Stevie's hand. As I again attempted to teach the other children Stevie would begin to pull against me. I would 'hold firm' but was often gradually dragged around the classroom as I taught. I was, however, determined that his negative behaviours would be ignored.

The weeks went by and Stevie continued to be a challenge. I recall one Friday when I simply found the whole ordeal too much. I spoke to my head teacher, explaining that I needed him to support me rather than ignore me. His response was to ring Stevie's foster parents and ask them to remove Stevie from the school for the remainder of the day. Stevie's mother was very obliging, very apologetic and acknowledged that she didn't really know how I coped with Stevie. However, his father was nowhere near as understanding. This view was conveyed to me by Stevie's mother who explained that her husband did not understand. He felt that I was a poor excuse for a teacher if I was unable to control a five-year-old. Without really thinking this through I immediately suggested that we should invite Stevie's father to come and work with him in the classroom. Her response was amazing:

> 'Now I think that's a bloody good idea,' she responded. 'He's coming. Don't worry I'll make sure of that.'

To my utter amazement Stevie's father was in my classroom with Stevie at 9 o'clock on the following Monday morning. He spent the day working alongside Stevie and all credit was due to him in that he admitted that he had not realised how challenging Stevie's behaviour was and additionally he acknowledged the need for me to educate Stevie's peers too. Stevie's father was unemployed and Stevie and I enjoyed his support on several occasions during the coming weeks. This was the beginning of a strong school/parent partnership which greatly benefited Stevie. Not once in that first term did it ever occur to me that I did not wish to support Stevie. I often thought about his early childhood and knew that his difficulties were not of his own making. Again I had no desire to completely change Stevie. I simply wanted to find ways of ensuring that he could be educated with his peers, that we understood him and moreover that his 'differences' were accepted by staff and other children alike.

After the first term his mother approached me with a complaint. She had received information that Stevie had a learning assistant to support him in his previous setting. Why was this not the case in our school? This was complete news to the school in which I was working. The school pursued this information and within two weeks I too began to enjoy the benefits of working with support for Stevie in my classroom. The difference was incredible but by no means surprising. In collaboration with his support assistant I set and conveyed boundaries and expectations to Stevie. Unsurprisingly he spent much of the first month challenging those boundaries. With additional support I was now able to ensure that Stevie adhered to my expectations. There were tantrums and he often needed to be withdrawn from the classroom for periods of time. However, I was able to meet the needs of his peers while his support assistant was able to focus on ensuring that he did not return to the classroom until he had met our expectations. Slowly the situation improved. Within three months we enjoyed, initially, a full day when Stevie was not withdrawn from class, followed by several days without the need to withdraw him. Eventually the days turned into weeks. The need to never withdraw Stevie was never realised but he did love school. He made friends, there were disputes and challenges and from time to time his occasional outbursts continued. Stevie stayed with me throughout Key Stage 1 – again, because of the bond I had apparently developed with him. Maybe this was in reality not the reason. He left my class at the age of seven and I knew that I had made a difference. His next teacher was determined to continue the work I had started. Stevie went on to successfully complete his primary education in our school. Many years later I encountered Stevie and his mother one afternoon in Barnsley. His mother flung her arms round me in the middle of a pedestrian crossing. 'You know who this is, don't you?' she said to Stevie. Stevie looked me up and down before replying 'Not a clue.' He shrugged his shoulders and walked on. He did not remember me, but of course I did remember Stevie. I made huge mistakes with him but above all else I learned so much.

Almost 20 years later I now work in another school. The last 15 years of my career have been spent in this school. It is here that I have again supported many children with many diverse needs. It is also in this school that I have learned so much more about supporting children to accept the differences and needs of others. In this respect this school is so successful. I was initially appointed as Early Years Foundation Stage/Key Stage 1 manager before becoming the Assistant Head Teacher. Currently I am the SENCO. It is in this school that I have encountered many more children with a range of diverse needs. Amongst these there have been several other children who have challenged us with behavioural issues, many far more challenging than those of either David or Stevie. Additionally I have supported an elective mute and a child with no speech and language. On a daily basis I work with children with autistic spectrum disorder. The school hosts resourced provision for these children and some of them are included in and access mainstream provision on a daily basis. Most of our children readily accept the needs of others and support one another. We deal firmly with those who torment the children in the Resourced Provision. Sometimes we have caught children standing outside the Resourced Provision upsetting the children inside. However, the vast majority accept their differences and take care of them. This is frequently evident to me when I visit children in other schools and compare their responses to children with additional needs. Such visits highlight the successes of our school and I return with an enormous sense of pride in our achievements. In so many respects I should now be a round peg in a round hole. However, in reality, although I thoroughly enjoy and believe in supporting and educating these children in a mainstream setting, wherever possible, there is a new challenge. It is the challenge of the standards agenda.

I am now charged with the responsibility of identifying, supporting and tracking those children who, for a range of different reasons or for no apparent reasons whatsoever, are not meeting national expectations in terms of their progress and/or attainment. As a teacher of children in the Early Years and Year 1, I am acutely aware of child development. Children are not machines, they develop at varying rates and this is, to me, very evident and supported by specialists in the Early Years. So why do I face the insatiable pressure of justifying what are deemed to be poor results each time I discuss progress with the powers that be? Individual education plans and intervention programmes support children's learning but further reinforce a sense of failure. The school in which I now work has hosted Resourced Provision for approximately 15 years and in that time has been considered very successful in doing so. Our reputation for supporting children with SEN, amongst other local schools, is celebrated and acknowledged. So much so that many of them now recommend us to parents of children with special needs. In discussions with these parents, it has become evident that they have not been made welcome in our neighbouring schools. These schools claim inexperience and parents have been assured that a move to our school is in the best interests of the child. We apparently have the expertise needed. This celebration and acknowledgement of our skills and understanding is that indeed parents frequently decide to place their children in our school.

Today almost 50% of children on roll have SEN status. The result is that the data of neighbouring schools' results is little cause for concern whilst our own data fluctuates from year to year and rarely meets national expectations. Some parents have not welcomed the heavy weighting of children with SEN and many children have been withdrawn from the school, resulting in small cohorts. In small cohorts each child obviously carries a high percentage in terms of data. One child can literally make a huge difference. This year there were only 13 children in Year 6. Of those children nine had SEN and four of those children have a statement of SEN. On paper our data is currently deemed as a huge cause for concern. A school inspection is imminent and under the new inspection criteria the school improvement partner has recently moved the school into a category of high risk of failure. I recently presented my own Early Years Foundation Stage Profile data to this same person having been told at the beginning of the academic year that I must quite simply 'get more children to national expectations'.

Only three of these children began full-time education in September last year. The remaining children joined the class in January. The entry baseline for the majority of children was low and well below national expectations in all areas of learning. One of these children has a statement of SEN (Query ASD), has no language and becomes very distressed by adult intervention. The speech and language of another child is a huge cause for concern and support for the child and the school is still awaited. The remaining two children entered full-time education in January 2011, operating at the approximate level of 36 months in all aspects of their learning. In reality I had only six months in which to support these children to reach national expectations. Many of the children face challenges at home, their parents show little interest in school and it is a huge challenge to engage them in supporting their children. I recount these details only as a means of broadly illustrating that I know why the children in my class have not achieved national expectations in their learning. Data for my class indeed does effectively demonstrate that the children have made extremely good progress. However, armed with this information I recently spoke to the School Improvement Partner. Her attitude was totally dismissive. I provided her with the contextual information related to these children. She merely focused on measuring them against national norms and my data was simply deemed as very disappointing. This response does anger me but above all else I am so upset for the children I have had the responsibility of teaching.

As a new academic year approaches I am already aware that four children with statements of SEN will be included in my class next year. I have visited them in their current settings in local schools. One child in particular has already been labelled as 'naughty'. He has a diagnosis of ADD. During a recent visit to meet him I was approached by another child as I observed my new pupil:

'What are you doing?' he asked.

'I've come to see your lovely new classroom. I am a friend of Mrs T's [head teacher],' I replied.

The child was excited and quickly began to show me round his newly built classroom and to name some of the other children. At this point my new pupil went by on a bike.

'That's Robert,' explained my young companion, 'He's a naughty boy.'

I was standing with the head teacher at this moment in time and waited for her response. Her comment horrified me:

'Yes but you're a good boy aren't you?' was all she replied.

This was the head teacher who, according to Robert's parents, had made them feel so unwelcome in her school and who had said that if he had to stay in her school she would do her best. Instead our school was recommended. Apparently her staff had little experience of dealing with 'children like Robert'. It seemed to me that her children may also have little experience or support in accepting the needs of others.

I make no apologies for my cynical view of aspects of the current system of judging schools and teachers. I continue to believe in a world in which success is celebrated and a need to identify and support children in any aspect of their learning or life skills. It is the narrow measure of success and school effectiveness that I vehemently question. Success for all we hear again and again. No! Success in maths and English is the reality. Little else seems to be of any consequence. My belief is that such a measure of success is narrow and damages many children and their confidence is shattered in its wake. Despite this I have the confidence to challenge such measures, with the knowledge and understanding I hold about the children I teach to support my views. I will continue to value the development and achievements of the whole child and I will continue to celebrate these. Already the battle to do so is becoming harder to fight. I will, however, continue that fight until maybe the unfortunate day arrives when there is no one who is prepared to listen. Sadly I feel that such a day is fast approaching.

REFLECTIVE TASK

Research demonstrates that pupils with ADHD are more likely to underachieve in school (Merrell and Tymms, 2005). What factors do you think influence this underachievement?

PRACTICAL TASK PRACTICAL TASK PRACTICAL TASK PRACTICAL TASK PRACTICAL TASK

When you are next in school ask if it would be possible for you to study a child over a period of time with a diagnosis of ADHD. Observe the child over a period of one week, noting down the triggers which result in incidents of inattention, impulsivity and hyperactivity. Talk to the child about what factors affect their behaviour. Find out:

- what they like about school;
- what they dislike about school;
- what affects their behaviour;
- what would help to control their behaviour.

If possible also speak to the child's parents to collect a parental perspective on their child's behaviour. Speak to the class teacher to ascertain his/her perspective.

A SUMMARY OF **KEY POINTS**

➢ **ADHD is a neurodevelopmental disorder.**

➢ **The symptoms of ADHD can be influenced by the attitudes of teachers and other adults and the provision of an ADHD learner-friendly environment.**

➢ **Be prepared to experiment in your practice and find out what works well and what is less effective.**

➢ **Talk to the child to collect his/her perspectives of the factors that influence their behaviour.**

➢ **Talk to the parents of pupils with ADHD to collect a parental perspective on the child's behaviour.**

➢ **Find out the child's interests and strengths and build on these.**

➢ **Never give up on a child.**

RESEARCH SUMMARY RESEARCH SUMMARY RESEARCH SUMMARY RESEARCH SUMMARY

Research has demonstrated that men and women who had ADHD in childhood were significantly more likely than those without ADHD to experience social exclusion in adulthood (Brassett-Grundy and Butler, 2004).

MOVING *ON* > > > > > > MOVING *ON* > > > > > > MOVING *ON*

Now that you have a basic understanding of ADD/ADHD you now need to consider how you might approach planning to include a child with ADD/ADHD into lessons. During your next block-teaching placement consider carefully how you might break tasks down into smaller more manageable chunks to cater for learners with ADD/ADHD.

REFERENCES REFERENCES **REFERENCES** REFERENCES REFERENCES REFERENCES

Brassett-Grundy, A. and Butler, N. (2004) 'Attention-deficit/hyperactivity disorder: an overview and review of the literature relating to the correlates and lifecourse outcomes for males and females', Bedford Group for Lifecourse and Statistical Studies Occasional Paper 1, London: Institute of Education, University of London.

Department for Education (DfE) (2014) *Special Educational Needs and Disability Code of Practice: 0 to 25 Years: Statutory Guidance for Organisations Who Work With and Support Children and Young People with Special Educational Needs and Disabilities*, London: DfE.

Merrell, C. and Tymms, P. (2005) 'A longitudinal study of the achievements, progress and attitudes of severely inattentive, hyperactive and impulsive young children', Paper presented at the annual conference of the British Educational Research Association, University of Glamorgan, September. Cited in Peer, L. and G. Reid (2012) *Special Educational Needs: A Guide for Inclusive Practice*, London: Sage.

FURTHER READING FURTHER READING **FURTHER READING** FURTHER READING

Peer, L. and Reid, G. (2012) *Special Educational Needs: A Guide for Inclusive Practice*, London: Sage. Read Chapter 14.

USEFUL WEBSITES USEFUL WEBSITES **USEFUL WEBSITES** USEFUL WEBSITES

http://www.edhelper.com

http://www.addiss.co.uk

http://www.adhdtraining.co.uk

http://www.adders.org

5
Dyslexia, dyspraxia and dyscalculia

Chapter objectives

By the end of this chapter you should be aware of:

- theories that help to explain the causes of dyslexia;
- the impact of dyslexia on pupils' self-esteem;
- strategies to support children with dyslexia;
- strategies to support children with dyspraxia and dyscalculia.

Teachers' Standards

This chapter addresses the following Teachers' Standards:

TS5: Adapt teaching to respond to the strengths and needs of all pupils

- know when and how to differentiate appropriately, using approaches which enable pupils to be taught effectively
- have a secure understanding of how a range of factors can inhibit pupils' ability to learn, and how best to overcome these
- demonstrate an awareness of the physical, social and intellectual development of children, and how to adapt teaching to support pupils' education at different stages of development
- have a clear understanding of the needs of all pupils, including those with special educational needs; those of high ability; those with English as an additional language; those with disabilities; and be able to use and evaluate distinctive teaching approaches to engage and support them

Introduction

Most of this chapter focuses on dyslexia and provides examples of strategies for supporting children who fall within this group. However, we wish to emphasise that in focusing on learners with dyslexia, we do not wish to exclude those children who may have reading difficulties but have not been diagnosed with dyslexia. Many pupils with general reading difficulties will have similar problems to those who are dyslexic. The distinction between those who are dyslexic and those with reading difficulties will be explored further in this chapter. Within the chapter we draw upon the social model of disability and we emphasise that with appropriate teaching interventions and positive attitudes, teachers can and do make a difference to children who find reading difficult. We examine the impact of dyslexia on children's self-esteem and we discuss strategies for developing a dyslexia-friendly learning environment. Additionally this chapter also addresses dyspraxia and dyscalculia and provides practical strategies for supporting pupils with these impairments.

What is dyslexia?

Dyslexia is by no means a new word. In 1878 Kussmaul wrote about 'text blindness', stating that 'A complete text-blindness may exist even though the power of sight, the intellect, and the power of speech are intact' (cited in Miles and Miles, 1990: 3).

Shortly after the writings of Kussmaul, the concept of 'word-blindness' was used to explain difficulties in learning to read in apparently intelligent children. Word blindness was given prominence in medical literature for the next two decades. The writings of a Glasgow eye surgeon, James Hinshelwood, in 1917 made links between congenital word blindness and reading failure. Hinshelwood (cited in Miles and Miles, 1990: 5) also noted that the condition might be hereditary and was more common in boys than in girls. However, the American neurologist Samuel Orton, writing in 1937, was critical of the term 'congenital word blindness', arguing that it was misleading: 'There is no true blindness in the ordinary sense of the term nor, indeed, is there even blindness for words' (cited in Miles and Miles, 1990: 5).

Orton noticed a tendency for these types of children to distort the order of the letters in words in spoken and written language. Orton introduced the term 'strephosymbolia', which literally means 'twisting of symbols' to describe this syndrome. Orton, along with Anna Gillingham, pioneered a systematic teaching programme, aimed specifically at pupils who had these problems.

Both Hinshelwood and Orton are respected as great pioneers in this field. Causation for reading difficulties was linked to visual problems and diagnosis of dyslexia centred on looking for an overuse of 'reversals' of letters or 'mirror writing'. Later research cast doubt on the value of this visual model and towards the end of the twentieth century, the emphasis shifted to a phonological model, as an explanation for dyslexia. However, the work of Hinshelwood and Orton in the early twentieth century and their observations are, according to Miles and Miles, 'of lasting importance' (1990: 8).

The actual word 'dyslexia' is made from a combination of two Greek words: *'dys'*, which literally means 'difficult', 'painful' or 'abnormal', and *'lexicos'* which means words of a language. Hence, a literal translation is 'difficulty with words'. According to Riddick 'at a common-sense everyday level, dyslexia is often defined as an unexpected difficulty in learning to read, write or spell' (1996: 1). The media perpetuates the image of the tragedy of the intelligent child who has failed to learn to read. In this sense, dyslexia is commonly defined as a discrepancy between a child's level of intelligence and their reading skills. The difficulty is therefore unexpected and specific and prevents the child from achieving their great potential. Some working definitions have highlighted this discrepancy, for example:

> Dyslexia is a disorder manifested by a difficulty in learning to read despite conventional instruction, adequate intelligence and sociocultural opportunity. It is dependent upon fundamental cognitive disabilities, which are frequently of constitutional origin.
> (World Federation of Neurology, 1968, cited in Riddick, 1996: 2)

Lowenstein (1989, cited in Hall, 2009) favours a definition of dyslexia, which highlights the discrepancy between verbal intelligence and reading ability. Such definitions fail to include children who have difficulties learning to read but also have below average levels of IQ. The term 'garden variety poor readers' (Stanovich, 1988: 96) has been used to categorise children with low levels of IQ and poor reading skills. Poor readers are therefore differentiated as either 'discrepant' or 'non-discrepant' readers. Within these definitions

IQ is taken as an accepted measure of intelligence. However, the use of IQ as a reliable measure of intelligence has been contested. In addition IQ fails to take into account the work on multiple intelligences (Gardner, 1999). There are many famous people with dyslexia who have become skilled artists, sports people or musicians. Therefore it seems unethical to exclude such talented individuals from a diagnosis of dyslexia simply on the grounds that they may have below average levels of IQ.

Arguments against such definitions are further strengthened by research which has investigated the reading profiles of dyslexic and non-dyslexic learners, classified as such under the discrepancy model (Stanovich and Stanovich, 1997). This research has found that the reading profiles of both groups do not differ. It could be argued that IQ is irrelevant and should not be taken into account when defining or diagnosing dyslexia. Some definitions are more inclusive and do not refer to intelligence. For example:

> *Dyslexia is evident when accurate and fluent word reading and/or spelling develops very incompletely or with great difficulty ... it provides the basis for a staged process of assessment through teaching.*
> (British Psychological Society, 1999: 11, cited in Hall, 2009)

> *Dyslexia is a specific learning difficulty that hinders the learning of literacy skills ... and tends to run in families. Other symbolic systems, such as mathematics and musical notation, can also be affected. Dyslexia can occur at any level of intellectual ability. It can accompany, but is not a result of, lack of motivation, emotional disturbance, sensory impairment or meagre opportunities...*
> (The Dyslexia Institute, 1996, cited in Turner, 1997: 11)

These definitions do not make a distinction between dyslexic readers and poor readers with low intelligence. However, the second definition is broader than the first. The British Psychological Society definition focuses on literacy difficulties at word level but the second definition by the Dyslexia Institute focuses on difficulties with symbolic systems in general. In 1989 the International Dyslexia Association adopted a broad definition to include aspects of literacy, numeracy, difficulties with information processing, motor skills and behaviour. In view of these debates it is not difficult to see why dyslexia has become a 'professional battlefield' (Swan, 1985, cited in Riddick, 1996: 21).

Types of dyslexia

The key sub-types of dyslexia are identified below.

Phonological dyslexia

Phonological dyslexics have specific difficulties remembering letter names and sounds and they find it difficult to make sound–symbol relationships. They find it difficult to blend sounds together to read words, they struggle to read non-words and they may find it difficult to detect rhyme.

Surface or morphemic dyslexia

These pupils appear to master the alphabetic code but over rely on a phonological strategy for reading and spelling. Irregular words are often pronounced as though they are regular, for example, the word *island* may be pronounced as *izland* (Snowling, 1998).

These learners generally have no difficulty reading non-words but they may struggle to read sight words, due to an over reliance on the use of phonology.

Hyperlexia

Hyperlexics have good visual memories and are able to learn sight words. They are able to learn sound–symbol relationships and can therefore blend sounds together to read words. The main problem lies in understanding or remembering what they have read. They often struggle to create meaning in their written work, although spelling may be accurate (Hall, 2009).

Causes of dyslexia

Visual deficit theories

Research by Stein and Walsh (1997, cited in Hall, 2009) indicated evidence of a magnocellular deficit. The magnocells are the nerve cells in the eyes and they are linked to the visual area of the brain. Defects in the magnocells disrupt the transfer of visual information between the eyes and the brain. An impaired visual system can result in reduced focus, blurred vision, headaches and the formation of unstable images (Hall, 2009). Acknowledgement of dyslexia as a visual deficit often results in a variety of intervention strategies that aim to reduce the glare from white paper. Such strategies include the use of coloured overlays, coloured paper or tinted lenses.

Phonological deficit hypothesis

Since the 1980s several studies have highlighted phonological processing difficulties in dyslexic children (Shankweiler and Crain, 1986; Share, 1995 and Snowling, 1995, all cited in Snowling, 1998). Snowling (1998) argues that children with dyslexia find it difficult to retrieve phonological information from the long-term memory. Dyslexia is now accepted as a developmental language disorder rather than a visual deficit disorder.

You need to understand theoretical perspectives of how children learn to read before you can develop a full understanding of the phonological deficit model. Bradley and Bryant's research in 1983 showed the relationship between early phonological awareness and subsequent reading acquisition. Thus, children with good early phonological awareness (sound discrimination, understanding of rhyme) are more likely to be good readers in primary school. Sound discrimination and an understanding of rhyme are essential pre-reading skills. If children fail to pick up similarities and differences between sounds they hear and words that are spoken to them it is possible that they will find it more difficult to discriminate between sounds in words when they start to learn to read.

Uta Frith (1985) provides a theoretical model of the stages children go through when they learn to read. These stages can be summarised as follows:

- **Logographic stage**: Children remember words as if they are a logo or a picture. Very young children can recognise environmental print but they are not able to draw on strategies to decipher unfamiliar words. At this stage children memorise word shapes and colours. Think about how children learn to 'read' shop signs, for example. At this stage children rely on a visual strategy for reading words.

- **Alphabetic stage**: At this stage children begin to link letters and sounds together (i.e. they make grapheme–phoneme correspondences). Spelling at this stage tends to reflect an increasing awareness of sounds and may be largely phonetic. At this stage children will start to sound out unfamiliar words through blending the sounds together.
- **Orthographic stage**: At this stage the child is able to memorise spelling patterns, as well as being able to recognise common prefixes and suffixes. They are able to identify larger units of sound within words such as rimes. For example, they are able to read the word *fright* because they recognise the word *light* and the rime *–ight*.

Frith (1985) suggests that in the case of dyslexic learners, development becomes arrested at the logographic stage. They fail to make quick and automatic links between letters and their sounds. They may find it difficult to 'sound out' words and they depend on a small sight vocabulary. According to Snowling, 'they continue to rely for longer than normal readers on a visual strategy for reading words and many have persisting difficulties reading novel words that are not part of their sight vocabulary, such as non-words' (1998: 6).

Therefore it is important to understand why phonological dyslexics may struggle to master the alphabetic code or experience difficulties with early phonological awareness. Abnormalities in the language area of the brain may interfere with the learning of symbol–sound relationships (Hall, 2009). In addition slow processing speeds in general and poor short-term memory may impede the ability to make quick and automatic links between letters and sounds. You might find that learners with dyslexia need to be exposed for longer periods of time to letters, colours, shapes, numbers or words in order to memorise them. Therefore the phonological deficit which occurs as a result of abnormalities in the brain is made worse as a result of slow processing speeds and this has been referred to as a double deficit hypothesis. Research has also indicated that morphemic dyslexics do not perform at age-related norms on phonological tasks, despite the fact that eventually they start to over rely heavily on a phonological strategy (Manis *et al.*, 1996, cited in Coltheart *et al.*, 1998; Stanovich *et al.*, 1997, cited in Snowling 1998). According to Snowling, it would appear 'that the severity of a child's phonological difficulty can affect the way in which their reading system becomes set up' and whether they look like 'phonological' or 'surface' dyslexics' (1998: 7). Dyslexia has therefore been defined as a core phonological deficit (Stanovich, 1986) and this implies that the intervention strategies should operate at a phonological level rather than a visual level.

Genetic factors

There is now a clear research base to suggest that genetic factors can increase the likelihood of dyslexia (Taipale *et al.*, 2003, cited in Hall 2009; Schumacher *et al.*, 2007, cited in Hall, 2009). A boy with one dyslexic parent has a 50% chance of being dyslexic and the chances are increased if the parent is the father (Hall, 2009). However, caution needs to be exercised about these arguments. It is not inevitable that the 'genetic gene' will be passed onto the child (Hall, 2009: 12) and the brain 'develops as a result of the interplay between environmental factors, stimulation of the brain as well as genetic factors' (Hall, 2009: 12). The problem with biological arguments is that they perpetuate the idea that dyslexia is a personal tragedy caused by 'within-child' factors and that little can be done about it. The social model of disability, in contrast, acknowledges the impairment but urges practitioners to make modifications to their teaching style so that the impairment does not become a disability. Thus, with changes to teaching style and the use of access strategies, pupils with dyslexia can, and do, learn to read very successfully.

Defining characteristics

As a classroom teacher you will not be responsible for carrying out psychometric tests on children in order to diagnose dyslexia. Qualified psychologists will be responsible for such assessments. However, it is useful to be able to identify any warning signs through regular on-going formative assessment. The following prompts may help you.

- Does the child have persistent difficulties with reading?
- Does the child find it difficult to learn grapheme–phoneme correspondences?
- Is the child reluctant to read or write?
- Does the child have persistent spelling difficulties? Spelling may be bizarre.
- Does the child have problems with personal organisation or display sequencing difficulties (e.g. learning the order of days of the week)?
- Does the child find it difficult to tell the time?
- Does the child have a poor short-term memory (e.g. remembering instructions or forgetting to bring things to school on certain days)?
- Does the child find rote learning difficult (e.g. memorising multiplication tables)?
- Does the child demonstrate inappropriate behaviour to avoid certain situations?
- Does the child have poor concentration or find it difficult to process information?
- Does the child have poor motor skills or difficulties with co-ordination?

Clearly these points cannot be used to diagnose dyslexia. They simply provide a loose framework for identifying whether a referral for more specialised support is necessary. Hall (2009) provides a very comprehensive checklist for warning signs to look out for in the Early Years, at Key Stage 1 and at Key Stage 2. Early Years educators should pay careful attention to young children who find rhyming difficult. In addition children with dyslexia may have speech problems or difficulties with motor skills such as climbing stairs or riding a bike. They may be slow to write their own name and may find it difficult to make grapheme–phoneme correspondences. At Key Stage 1 children may find blending difficult or they may find it difficult to learn sight words and they may struggle with writing. Although dyslexic learners may overcome their reading difficulties, it is possible that they will experience persistent difficulties with spelling and Hall (2009) identifies that spelling may become increasingly random and idiosyncratic at Key Stage 2.

As a teacher it is important that you listen to parental concerns and take them seriously. Riddick (1995: 462) found that there was an average time of four years elapsing between the parents first suspecting that there was a problem and their children receiving an official diagnosis of dyslexia. Some of the parents in this study expressed their concerns:

> *I thought something was up. I was told I was an overprotective mother and Dean was just a slow learner and there was nothing wrong. And I probably being foolish left it and the next year we went to parents evening and there was absolutely no progress and again I voiced my opinion and again I was told I was being silly.*
> (Riddick, 1995: 465)

> *The thing the teacher did say once, that irritates me now, was that she was very slow at school, slow to learn. And basically, she's not slow to learn. It was the reading that she was slow to learn. And I think that was a lack of understanding.*
> (Riddick, 1996: 88)

A reluctance to take seriously parental concerns can slow down the process of diagnosis and result in parents becoming frustrated.

Diagnosing dyslexia

As a general classroom teacher you are not qualified to make a diagnosis of dyslexia. If you have on-going concerns that a child may have dyslexia you must consult with the SENCO and the child's parent(s). Additional targeted intervention and support should be provided to help the child to make further progress in reading. If progress is limited the school may decide, in consultation with parents and the child, to request support from an educational psychologist. The educational psychologist will provide additional advice to both parents and the school to help them address the needs of the child. In addition, s/he will also be able to carry out more detailed assessments which may indicate the likelihood of the child having dyslexia. These additional assessments can then be used to supplement your own teacher assessments and they can be used as evidence to support an application for a formal assessment by the LA.

Some parents may choose to have their child assessed by a dyslexia-trained teacher in a specialist centre. These teachers have carried out additional training and are qualified to make a specific diagnosis. As a classroom teacher you may wish to ask the SENCO to purchase specialist screening software and tests which you will be able to use. These will not produce a diagnosis of dyslexia as such, but may provide an indicator of the likely chance of a child being dyslexic. It is important that teachers do not provide a specific diagnosis when these assessments are shared with parent(s).

Labelling

One of the key dangers associated with the use of labels is that it can result in a 'within-child' view of the problem. The whole process of observation, assessment, diagnosis and intervention seems to resemble the medical model of disability where disability is conceptualised as a personal tragedy. Labels and categories can also impose on individuals a 'fixed' identity. In essence, people within the specific category are all associated as having similar needs and it may be assumed that they will be equally responsive to interventions.

As a teacher you must remember that children with dyslexia are individuals. Although they may share some defining characteristics, they will not respond in the same way to interventions and they will have different needs. You have a responsibility to the child to develop teaching approaches that are specific to that child. Reading Recovery may not work for all dyslexic learners in the same way that a visual timetable may not work for all learners with autistic spectrum disorder. Rather than adopting a medical model approach, you should aim to adopt a social model approach. This focuses on placing less emphasis on intervening at the level of the individual and placing more emphasis on ways in which you can develop more effective teaching strategies that will benefit not just dyslexic learners, but all learners. Think carefully about wider aspects of your practice, which may result in barriers to achievement. For example, do you use too much text in lessons? Do you ask children to read aloud? Do you over-emphasise auditory rather than visual and kinaesthetic teaching approaches? Do you ask children to record their work in a range of ways, or do you ask them to record through writing? Your practice can erect barriers to achievement for many learners and this should be your starting point. Focus on how you can make adaptations to your practice before you place too much emphasis on 'within-child' factors.

Riddick (1995) found that the official diagnosis of dyslexia was an important milestone for children: the use of the terminology helped them to understand their problems and helped to raise their self-esteem. The term helped them to understand why they had difficulties and they found it empowering. Riddick also found that the parents were pleased with the official diagnosis and they were able to use it to prove to the teachers that there was a genuine problem. One parent in Riddick's study commented: 'Well I was thrilled. I've got the assessment he had here … I took it to school, you know. Vindicated! Rubbish, they said. There's no such thing as dyslexia' (1995: 462).

One key problem with the use of the term 'dyslexia' is that it distinguishes between learners with dyslexia and those who have general reading difficulties. It could therefore be argued that the term excludes a group of poor readers who need support and intervention. The strategies suggested in this chapter will help all children with reading difficulties and as a teacher you will need to implement interventions with all learners working below age-related expectations in reading.

However, although we have highlighted the exclusive nature of the term, we assert that dismissive attitudes towards 'dyslexia' are extremely unhelpful. Thus, teachers need to reflect carefully on their own attitudes towards children with SEN since they are unlikely to undertake further professional development and training if they do not believe that a condition exists in the first place.

CASE STUDY

Issues with labelling

Jasmine was ten years old. She had recently been given a diagnosis of dyslexia after struggling for many years with reading and writing. She was able to sound out simple CVC words but she could not remember the phonemes for more complex graphemes, such as digraphs. Jasmine's mother was thrilled with the diagnosis and had tried to use this to pressurise the school to provide Jasmine with additional support. Jasmine did not respond positively to reading or writing tasks. On several occasions she was overheard to say 'I can't read or write because I am dyslexic'. The teacher had worked hard to develop Jasmine's self-esteem. She had provided Jasmine with one-to-one support and Jasmine had had access to a rich multi-sensory phonics programme. Despite this, progress in reading and writing was minimal.

REFLECTIVE TASK

- What was the impact of the diagnosis on Jasmine?
- What was the impact of the diagnosis on Jasmine's mother?
- What might the teacher do next to support Jasmine?

Impact of dyslexia on self-esteem

According to Lawrence, 'one of the most exciting discoveries in educational psychology in recent times has been the finding that people's levels of achievement are influenced by how they feel about themselves (and vice-versa)' (1996: xi). Although this seems obvious, it is a point worth making. As a teacher, a major part of your role is to nurture within children a positive sense of self. If pupils feel good about themselves this will create optimum conditions for effective learning.

Research has indicated that children with learning difficulties make negative and unrealistic comparisons between themselves and others and, as a result of this, develop low levels of self-esteem (Gurney, 1988; Humphrey, 2001; Humphrey, 2003). Consequently they may feel inferior to their peers and this can have far-reaching consequences. Although there is a lack of research on the links between dyslexia and self-esteem (Humphrey, 2002), some studies have highlighted feelings of disappointment, frustration, anger and embarrassment (Edwards, 1994; Riddick, 1996). Studies have also revealed how some dyslexics feel that they were treated unfairly by teachers (Riddick, 1996; Humphrey, 2001; Humphrey and Mullins, 2002) and also their peers (Humphrey, 2001).

Glazzard's (2010) findings were consistent with the findings in the published studies cited above. This research captured the voices of pupils with dyslexia and highlighted the negative attitudes demonstrated by some teachers and peers towards children with reading difficulties.

Attitude of teachers

The study highlighted both negative and positive attitudes from teachers:

> I had one teacher who I had for a year [Mrs X]. My friend had her as well. She was really against kids who had learning difficulties. She didn't like Asian kids either and she didn't like boys. She was really, really mean to us. Like me and J were really good friends and she was really nasty to us … She used to call us stupid and that we'd fail at this and that. Anything she could to be nasty she'd say it for no reason at all.

> The headmaster was absolutely brilliant … Mr F I'd go and read to him and when he was teaching us I'd say can you just say that again and he'd repeat it … Mrs. D [special needs support assistant] helped me a lot.

> I can't remember any by name but there were some in … the infants that weren't supportive … They were getting onto me about why I wasn't doing as much and they moaned when I always came bottom in the spelling test.

> Well, none of them really understood it. They just left it to this one teacher. She was the special needs teacher … She was basically the only teacher that helped. The others just let me get on with it.

(Glazzard, 2010)

REFLECTIVE TASK

Think carefully about the attitudes above. Discuss the following questions with one of your colleagues:

- How might you adapt a spelling test for a child with dyslexia?
- How might you present reading material to children with dyslexia to make it more inclusive?

- How do you think Mrs X might change her practice to make it more inclusive?
- Why might 'reading aloud' be an unsuitable strategy for children with dyslexia?

Feeling stupid

My reading was worse than the other kids. I couldn't read anything. I had to sound everything out. So 'dog' was 'd-o-g'. It really slowed me down and made me feel stupid. I also struggled with maths. (Tom)

(Glazzard, 2010)

REFLECTIVE TASK

What strategies might help Tom to develop a more positive sense of self? Think carefully about how you might build in frequent opportunities for Tom to experience success. Share your ideas with a colleague.

Attitude of peers

My friends have always supported me. They've always been good friends. As for other people, I keep it to myself. I don't let them know. It's my life, not theirs. Some of them know and they're always grinning and laughing because I work more slowly in class and find spelling difficult. They have made nasty comments to me. But they don't know what it's like 'cos they're not dyslexic. (Paul)

(Glazzard, 2010)

REFLECTIVE TASK

What strategies might you use to address the issues that Paul highlights?

Comparisons with peers

I knew I wasn't as good at spelling as the other pupils were because I never got many correct.

I knew that I was struggling for definite more than the other pupils were because there were sort of a lot of things I did wrong.

In primary school they used to make us read aloud and I always dreaded it 'cos I knew the others would laugh at me. I knew that they were better readers than I was. I can't really blame them for laughing 'cos they didn't know I had dyslexia at that point and neither did I. (Stuart)

(Glazzard, 2010)

REFLECTIVE TASK

Do you think it is more important to work on developing Stuart's self-esteem or on developing his reading skills? Where would you place the emphasis? How can you develop more inclusive practices so that children are less likely to make comparisons between themselves and their peers?

Riddick (1996) has highlighted the reluctance of some teachers to accept the fact that a child may have dyslexia. This can result in feelings of frustration from parents who may be desperately trying to obtain educational support for their child. *Removing Barriers to Achievement* (DfES, 2004) stressed the need for early intervention to enable children to make further progress and this is reinforced in the new Code of Practice (DfE, 2014). If teachers fail to take parental concerns seriously and adopt a dismissive attitude towards dyslexia then intervention will be delayed.

REFLECTIVE TASK

Nosheen is six years old. She finds reading difficult and she is making very slow progress. Her mother approaches you and expresses a concern that she may be dyslexic because of the lack of interest she shows in books. Nosheen's mother is also concerned that other children have made greater progress and are reading more difficult reading books. Discuss the following questions with a colleague.

- What do you think you might say to Nosheen's mother? What advice might you offer her?
- What subsequent action might you take to show the mother that you have taken seriously her concerns?

Glazzard (2010) illustrates the impact of a diagnosis of dyslexia on pupils' sense of self:

> *At last I realised I wasn't stupid. I had a problem but it wasn't related to my intelligence.*

Diagnosis therefore came as a relief to pupils and this is consistent with findings in published research (Riddick, 1996). Parents may also value an official diagnosis of dyslexia, believing that it will inevitably lead to additional funding and support. Therefore there may be value in obtaining a diagnosis. However, the extent of the child's needs ultimately determines whether additional provision will be made available. You should not assume that a diagnosis of dyslexia will automatically result in additional funding and support.

PRACTICAL TASK   PRACTICAL TASK   PRACTICAL TASK   PRACTICAL TASK   PRACTICAL TASK

Think about ways in which labelling children in this way may be detrimental to them. Discuss this with a colleague and then look for literature which explores arguments for and against labelling. Share these ideas with your group in the form of a 10 minute presentation.

Strategies to support children with reading difficulties

The following strategies should help you to meet the needs of learners with dyslexia. However, it is important to stress that you need to respond to the specific needs of individual learners.

Multi-sensory teaching

Multi-sensory approaches are generally inclusive and work for all children. When you are introducing children to graphemes and phonemes all the senses need to be stimulated. They need to see the letter, feel the shape of the letter and they should be encouraged to say the phoneme at the same time. Children should be encouraged to 'air write' the letter or to write it on someone else's back or the palm of the hand. They should be encouraged to make the letter shapes out of dough and draw them in the sand or trace it in the water. Sandpaper letters are useful for dyslexic learners to feel the shape of letters. In PE children can be encouraged to make letter shapes with their bodies. These are practical suggestions for ways in which you can build visual, auditory and kinaesthetic approaches into your teaching.

A structured programme

Dyslexic learners will need a highly structured phonics programme. Reading Recovery is one example of such a programme and is described below. Lessons may have a similar structure but the content of each will vary to ensure progression and continuity.

Over-learning

Children with dyslexia often have problems with short-term memory. They may quickly forget graphemes, phonemes and words that they have been taught. You will need to build in opportunities for revisiting learning that has taken place. We recommend that a multi-sensory approach is adopted to enable children to revisit phonic knowledge that they have already been taught.

Reading Recovery

Reading Recovery is a multi-sensory reading intervention which is taught on a one-to-one basis. The sessions are individualised to the needs of each pupil and learning to read is reinforced using a range of strategies.

Teaching spelling and handwriting

Broomfield and Combley (2003) recommend a cursive script where all letters start with a stroke from the base line and end with a leaving stroke. This approach means that the learner does not have to think about where the letter begins as all letters start in the same place. Learners with dyslexia need to practise writing the letter at the same time as being introduced to the phoneme. This is because the action of actually forming the letter and saying the phoneme at the same time will deepen the learning experience. The sound should always be linked to a hand movement. You will need to make decisions about whether to introduce your learners to a joined script. Broomfield and Combley stress the importance of movement when introducing children to letters. They emphasise that 'the learner needs to be aware of the air moving from the lungs, and being shaped by tongue, lips and throat' (2003: 106).

Waves of intervention

The National Strategies promoted a three-staged model to raise outcomes for all children. This is summarised below.

- **Wave 1**: Inclusive quality first teaching for all children.
- **Wave 2**: Additional interventions (usually group interventions) to enable children to meet age-related expectations.
- **Wave 3**: Highly personalised interventions to meet the specific needs of individual learners. (TDA, 2008)

Although the National Strategies has been disbanded the model still provides a useful framework for levels of intervention. Before a child is diagnosed with dyslexia it is important to establish whether that child has been exposed to inclusive quality first teaching. Quality first teaching of reading was described in the *Independent Review of the Teaching of Early Reading* (Rose, 2006) as teaching which uses a multi-sensory approach and is informed by assessment to meet the needs of individual learners. The report recommended that phonic skills should be taught discretely and within the context of a broad and rich language curriculum. Therefore it is important to question whether struggling readers have had access to rich multi-sensory teaching programmes which meet their specific needs before it is assumed that they may have a reading difficulty. It is also important to examine whether they have had access to a rich language and text-rich environment both at home and in school. This includes ensuring that children can access texts that interest them.

Parents and teachers act as role models for reading and writing. If pupils see parents and teachers enjoying reading and writing there is a greater chance that they too will be motivated. If children with reading difficulties have not had exposure to good role models then this could, partly, explain an apparent lack of motivation to read or write. Some schools enlist the support of famous football players or fathers by asking them to work alongside children in the classroom as readers or writers. This could be a particularly powerful way of raising boys' achievements in literacy, given that dyslexia is more common amongst boys.

As a teacher you also need to think carefully about the inter-relationship between the different strands of literacy and the powerful role of spoken language and listening in laying the fundamental foundations for reading and writing. Your rich language environment should provide opportunities for frequent use of talk, drama or role-play. Children may develop reading difficulties as a result of poor quality teaching and exposure to poor quality learning environments. Although biological factors may also be significant, teachers should not under-estimate the importance of quality first teaching.

If, despite exposure to quality first teaching, children develop reading difficulties, teachers should provide small group (wave 2) or individual (wave 3) interventions to meet the specific needs of individual learners. Reading Recovery has been described above and constitutes a wave 3 intervention programme. *Removing Barriers to Achievement* (DfES, 2004) and the new SEND Code of Practice (DfE, 2014) stress the importance of early intervention and support and teachers should take early action to give children every opportunity to catch up with their peers.

Dyslexia-friendly environments

Pupils with dyslexia typically find reading and writing difficult. Therefore you need to provide them with alternative ways of recording information. Pupils can document their learning visually, orally and practically, as well as using ICT. You might find that a pupil with dyslexia really enjoys science. However, if you ask them to write up an investigation this might demotivate them. Try to be creative in your approaches to recording. Teachers typically like to collect recorded work for assessment evidence. However, you can broaden your range of evidence through documenting the learning that has taken place through the use of teacher observations, photographs and video recordings of pupils at work, as well as audio-recordings of children's conversations. This is common practice in the Early Years and should be built on in Key Stages 1 and 2.

Try not to ask children with dyslexia to copy from the board or to read out in class. You need to be both sympathetic and empathetic. Pupils with dyslexia need to know that you understand their difficulties. Some pupils will find it easier if material is presented on cream or buff paper as white paper can make words difficult to read. Pupils with dyslexia need constructive feedback on their work. An over-emphasis on spelling errors is unhelpful and you should focus on the content of the work instead. Pupils with dyslexia will need lots of positive reinforcement when they read to you.

Pupils with dyslexia may have good ideas but may struggle to write these ideas down on paper. They may benefit from a scribe or a study buddy, who can help them record their ideas. Short-term memory may be a problem so teach pupils strategies to help them remember things. They will need to be taught spelling and reading strategies explicitly and a structured programme to support reading and spelling is essential. You could try pairing a child with dyslexia with an older reader who can read to them or is able to support them with reading. Pupils with dyslexia need to read books which are interesting and you should avoid giving them books which are suitable for younger readers as this could damage self-esteem.

Mathematical learning may be difficult for some pupils with dyslexia as they may quickly forget things. Ensure that there is access to number lines, number squares and practical apparatus to support learning. Try to ensure that your learners understand the learning rather than focusing excessively on how many calculations or problems they have solved within a lesson. They may need access to a calculator to help with problem solving, even if other learners are required to complete a task mentally. In particular, learners with dyslexia may struggle with multiplication tables so you will need to find creative, innovative ways of teaching these.

The classroom should have key words on display for learners to refer to. You could also give these learners additional resources such as word mats, alphabet strips or special dictionaries to support them with spelling. Portable writing aids such as word processors, tablet computers, handheld spell checkers or palmtop devices can be useful. Mind-mapping tools on the computer can be useful for enabling learners with dyslexia to plan and organise information.

PRACTICAL TASK ~~PRACTICAL TASK~~ **PRACTICAL TASK** ~~PRACTICAL TASK~~ **PRACTICAL TASK**

In your placement school identify a pupil with dyslexia. Discuss the specific needs of the child with your teacher-mentor. Find out about prior learning and plan for the child's 'next steps'. Over the period of a week, plan a series of multi-sensory activities to enable the child to make further progress. Evaluate each taught session and make regular assessments of the child's learning. Evaluate the overall progress of the child and write a synoptic critical reflection summarising your own learning from this experience.

CASE STUDY

Multi-sensory intervention

Joshua was six years old. After more than a year in school it was evident that he had some difficulties with the acquisition of phonic knowledge. He could not remember many phonemes and he could not blend sounds together to read words. His teacher decided to provide some additional intervention to enable him to make further progress. A multi-sensory programme was developed to help Joshua to learn the simple alphabetic code. Further progress in reading would be hampered unless he could master this. Each lesson was clearly structured, starting with a recap on phonemes which had previously been taught. Any misconceptions at this point became the focus of the lesson. Phonemes were taught in a multi-sensory way. The letter was shown to Joshua and he was told the phoneme represented by it. He was shown how to form the sound correctly. Joshua was required to repeat the sound made by the letter and he was then provided with opportunities to write the sound in the air, sand, water, soil and on the palm of his hand. Joshua was required to say the sound at the same time as writing the letter. A range of resources were used to reinforce the learning that was taking place. In one memorable lesson he enjoyed making letters out of melted chocolate. After five months on the intervention, Joshua was able to identify all phonemes for all the letters of the alphabet and he also knew the phonemes for some digraphs.

REFLECTIVE TASK

- Why do you think Joshua found it difficult to master the simple alphabetic code?
- Why do you think the strategies worked?
- What are the next steps for Joshua?
- How might the practitioner work with Joshua to achieve these?

Dyspraxia

There are no formal diagnostic criteria for dyspraxia. The term is made up of *'dys'* which means 'difficulty' and *'praxis'* which means the ability to organise and carry out a sequence of movements. Difficulties include:

- reduced muscle strength;
- impaired co-ordination and movement;
- poor balance;
- difficulty in combining movements into a sequence;
- poor fine motor skills;
- poor spatial awareness;

- poor visual–spatial memory;
- problems with hand–eye co-ordination;
- problems with sense of direction (left/right);
- difficulties with organizing and sequencing tasks;
- poor attention and concentration;
- social and behavioural difficulties. (Abdullah, 2012)

Visual timetables may help pupils with dyspraxia to understand the sequence of tasks which need to be completed. They might benefit from completing a series of shorter tasks in a lesson rather than trying to concentrate on one task for an extended period of time. You should plan lessons which provide pupils with opportunities for active, multi-sensory learning with clear steps to success so that pupils are clear about what they need to do in a task. A range of activities to develop finger strength, hand–eye co-ordination and sequencing may need to be planned into the daily timetable.

Dyscalculia

Dyscalculia affects the ability to acquire mathematical skills. Difficulties include:

- counting errors;
- difficulties understanding simple mathematical concepts;
- problems with the recall of number facts;
- difficulties solving mathematical word problems.

Teaching needs to be focused on developing pupils' mathematical understanding rather than relying on rote learning. Teaching for success is also important (Chinn, 2012) and therefore mathematical problems and tasks may need to be broken down into clear steps to success so that pupils know what to do first, second and third. Marking and feedback needs to be diagnostic and provide pupils with clear worked examples and teachers should use very clear modelling in lessons (including using visual images) to model the mathematical skills and processes. Access to concrete resources such as counters, number lines, hundred squares and numeral cards may also be helpful.

A SUMMARY OF **KEY POINTS**

➢ **Dyslexia is now seen to arise as a result of a core phonological deficit rather than a visual deficit.**

➢ **Learners with dyslexia may have low levels of self-esteem. This can increase after the initial diagnosis. Teachers need to preserve the child's self-esteem by being understanding and sympathetic. Above all, children with dyslexia need an empathetic teacher.**

➢ **All learners will benefit from multi-sensory approaches when being introduced to sound–symbol relationships. In addition, dyslexic learners will benefit from a highly structured, multi-sensory phonics programme, which builds in frequent opportunities for assessment.**

➢ **Learners with dyspraxia may benefit from active approaches to teaching and learning, tightly focused tasks and visual timetables.**

➢ **Learners with dyscalculia may benefit from teaching for mathematical understanding rather than rote learning.**

RESEARCH SUMMARY RESEARCH SUMMARY **RESEARCH SUMMARY** RESEARCH SUMMARY

Snowling, M.J. and Hulme, C. (2006) 'Language skills, learning to read and reading intervention', *London Review of Education*, 4(1), 63–76.

This paper argues that speech-processing impairments or broader language-processing impairments can result in reading difficulties. Therefore the paper suggests that speech and language skills determine outcomes in reading.

MOVING *ON* > > > > > > MOVING *ON* > > > > > > MOVING *ON*

Now that you understand the importance of multi-sensory approaches for supporting learners with dyslexia, produce a set of multi-sensory graphemes that you will be able to use during your teaching career to support learners with dyslexia.

REFERENCES REFERENCES **REFERENCES** REFERENCES REFERENCES REFERENCES

Abdullah, J. (2012) 'Developmental coordination disorder and dyspraxia from an occupational therapist's perspective', in L. Peer and G. Reid (eds) *Special Educational Needs: A Guide for Inclusive Practice*, London: Sage, pp. 98–111.

Bradley, L. and Bryant, P. (1983) 'Categorizing sounds and learning to read: a causal connection nature', *Nature*, 301, 419–21.

British Psychological Society (1999) *Dyslexia, Literacy and Psychological Assessment*, report by a Working Party of the Division of Educational and Child Psychology, Leicester: British Psychological Society.

Broomfield, H. and Combley, M. (2003) *Overcoming Dyslexia: A Practical Handbook for the Classroom*, (2nd edn), London: Whurr.

Chinn, S. (2012) 'Mathematics learning difficulties and dyscalculia', in L. Peer and G. Reid (eds) *Special Educational Needs: A Guide for Inclusive Practice*, London: Sage, pp. 169–80.

Coltheart, M. and Jackson, N.E. (1998) 'Defining dyslexia', *Child Psychology and Psychiatry Review*, 3(1), 12–16.

Department for Education (DfE) (2014) *Special Educational Needs and Disability Code of Practice: 0 to 25 Years: Statutory Guidance for Organisations Who Work With and Support Children and Young People with Special Educational Needs and Disabilities*, London: DfE.

Department for Education and Skills (DfES) (2004) *Removing Barriers to Achievement: The Government Strategy for SEN*, Nottingham: DfES.

Edwards, J. (1994) *The Scars of Dyslexia: Eight Case Studies in Emotional Reactions*, London: Cassell.

Frith, U. (1985) 'Beneath the surface of developmental dyslexia', in K.E. Patterson, J.C. Marshall and M. Coltheart (eds) *Surface Dyslexia*, London: Erlbaum, pp. 301–30.

Gardner, H. (1999) *Intelligence Reframed*, New York: Basic Books.

Glazzard, J. (2010) 'The impact of dyslexia on pupils' self-esteem', *Support for Learning*, 25(2), 63–9.

Gurney P.W. (1988) *Self-Esteem in Children with Special Educational Needs*, London: Routledge.

Hall, W. (2009) *Dyslexia in the Primary Classroom*, Exeter: Learning Matters.

Humphrey, N. (2001) 'Self-concept and self-esteem in developmental dyslexia: implications for teaching and learning', PhD thesis, Liverpool John Moores University.

Humphrey, N. (2002) 'Teacher and pupil ratings of self-esteem in developmental dyslexia', *British Journal of Special Education*, 29(1), 29–36.

Humphrey, N. (2003) 'Facilitating a positive sense of self in pupils with dyslexia: the role of teachers and peers', *Support for Learning*, 18(3), 130–6.

Humphrey, N. and Mullins, P.M. (2002) 'Self concept and self-esteem in developmental dyslexia', *Journal of Research in Special Educational Needs*, 2(2), http://onlinelibrary.wiley.com/doi/10.1111/j.1471-3802.2002.00163.x/full (accessed 5 December 2014).

Lawrence, D. (1996) *Enhancing Self-Esteem in the Classroom*, London: Paul Chapman.

Lowenstein, L. (1989) 'Recent investigations and directions in the study of dyslexia', *Education*, 109(4), 424–31.

Manis, F.R., Seidenberg, M.S., Doi, L.M., McBride-Chang, C. and Peterson, A. (1996) 'On the basis of two sub-types of developmental dyslexia', *Cognition*, 58, 157–95.

Miles, T.R. and Miles, E. (1990) *Dyslexia: A Hundred Years On*, Milton Keynes: Open University Press.

Riddick, B. (1995) 'Dyslexia: dispelling the myths', *Disability and Society*, 10(4), 457–73.

Riddick, B. (1996) *Living with Dyslexia*, London: Routledge.

Rose, J. (2006) *Independent Review of the Teaching of Early Reading: Final Report*, Nottingham: DfES.

Schumacher, J., Hoffmann, P., Schmal, C., Schulte-Korne, G. and Nothen, M. (2007) 'Genetics of dyslexia: the evolving landscape', *Journal of Medical Genetics*, 44, 289–97.

Shankweiler, D. and Crain, S. (1986) 'Language mechanisms and reading disorder: a modular approach', *Cognition*, 24, 139–64.

Share, D.L. (1995) 'Phonological recoding and self–teaching: sine qua non of reading acquisition', *Cognition*, 55, 151–218.

Snowling, M. (1995) 'Phonological processing and developmental dyslexia', *Journal of Research in Reading*, 18, 132–8.

Snowling, M. (1998) 'Dyslexia as a phonological deficit: evidence and implications', *Child Psychology and Psychiatry Review*, 3(1), 4–11.

Stanovich, K.E. (1986) 'Cognitive processes and the reading problems of learning disabled children: evaluating the assumption of specificity', in J. Torgesen and B. Wong (eds) *Psychological and Educational Perspectives on Learning Disabilities*, New York: Academic Press, pp. 87–131.

Stanovich, K.E. (1988) 'Explaining the differences between the dyslexic and the garden-variety poor reader: the phonological-core-variable-difference model', *Journal of Learning Disabilities*, 21, 590–612.

Stanovich, K.E., Siegel, L.S. and Gottardo, A. (1997) 'Converging evidence for phonological and surface subtypes of reading disability', *Journal of Educational Psychology*, 89(1), 114–27.

Stanovich K.E and Stanovich P.J. (1997) 'Further thoughts on aptitude/achievement discrepancy', *Educational Psychology in Practice*, 13(1), 3–8.

Stein, J. and Walsh, V. (1997) 'To see but not to read; the magnocellular theory of dyslexia', *Trends in Neuroscience*, 20, 147–52.

Swan, W. (1985) *Dyslexia Unit 25 Block 4 (E206): Personality, Development and Learning*, Milton Keynes: Open University Press.

Taipale, M., Kaminen, N., Nopola-Hemmi, J., Haltia, T., Myllyluoma, B., Lyytinien, H., Muller, K., Kaaranen, M., Lindsberg, P., Hannula-Jouppi, K. and Kere, J. (2003) 'A candidate gene for developmental dyslexia encodes a nuclear tetratricopeptide repeat domain protein dynamically regulated in brain', *Proceedings of National Academy of Sciences of United States of America*, 30 September 2003, 100(20), 11553–8.

Turner, M. (1997) *Psychological Assessment of Dyslexia*, London: Whurr.

Training and Development Agency for Schools (TDA) (2008) *Special Educational Needs and/or Disabilities: A Training Resource for Initial Teacher Training Providers: Primary Undergraduate Courses*, TDA.

FURTHER READING FURTHER READING **FURTHER READING** FURTHER READING

Pollock, J. and Waller, E. (2001) *Day to Day Dyslexia in the Classroom*, Abingdon: RoutledgeFalmer.

USEFUL WEBSITES USEFUL WEBSITES **USEFUL WEBSITES** USEFUL WEBSITES

http://www.dyslexiaaction.org.uk/

6
Supporting children with autistic spectrum disorders

Chapter objectives

By the end of this chapter you should be aware of:

- **the similarities and differences between autism and Asperger syndrome;**
- **the nature of autistic spectrum disorders (ASD) and the barriers to learning and participation for this group of learners, including knowledge of the triad of impairments;**
- **strategies that you can use in the classroom to support the learning of this group of children.**

Teachers' Standards

This chapter addresses the following Teachers' Standards:

TS5: Adapt teaching to respond to the strengths and needs of all pupils

- **know when and how to differentiate appropriately, using approaches which enable pupils to be taught effectively**
- **have a secure understanding of how a range of factors can inhibit pupils' ability to learn, and how best to overcome these**
- **demonstrate an awareness of the physical, social and intellectual development of children, and how to adapt teaching to support pupils' education at different stages of development**
- **have a clear understanding of the needs of all pupils, including those with special educational needs; those of high ability; those with English as an additional language; those with disabilities; and be able to use and evaluate distinctive teaching approaches to engage and support them**

Introduction

Children with autism are often discussed as though they represent a homogenous group of learners. Strategies to support the learning and development of these children will need to be as diverse as the needs of each learner. Warnock (2005) has highlighted key issues associated with the inclusion of autistic children into mainstream learning environments. These concerns will be discussed in this chapter. However, it is likely that at some point during your career you will be responsible for the education of a child with autism and therefore it is crucial that you have a good understanding of how their needs can be met (Amaladoss, 2006). This chapter provides an overview of the evolution of the concept of autism and highlights the challenges faced by this diverse group. Practical strategies for supporting children with autism are discussed.

Autism and Asperger syndrome

The first references to 'early infantile autism' were made by the child psychiatrist Leo Kanner in 1943. Kanner noted the aloofness of people in this group and derived the term 'autism' from *'auto'* which is Greek for 'self'. Kanner and his colleague Leon Eisenberg identified specific criteria for diagnosing this condition. They identified that these children are typically aloof and indifferent to others and tended to develop repetitive routines (Kanner and Eisenberg, 1956, cited in Wing, 2007). Kanner noted the lack of social interaction as a defining characteristic of infantile autism and the existence of echolalia in some children, where words that had been heard were repeated. These children rarely had speech but in cases where speech did exist, none of the children used it as a tool for reciprocal conversation. Kanner believed that this pattern of behaviour was uncommon and quite distinct from all other childhood conditions (Wing, 2007). Kanner initially assumed that all children with this condition were fundamentally intelligent but developmentally delayed. However, this assumption was incorrect and it is now known that the majority of individuals with autism also appear to have additional, and often severe, learning difficulties (Jordan and Powell, 1995). Kanner initially thought that social impairment was present at birth and therefore part of an individual's biological make-up. He later rejected this idea and blamed parenting styles for this pattern of behaviour, although he subsequently dismissed this idea (Wing, 2007).

The following year, Hans Asperger, a Viennese paediatrician, studied a small group of four boys at the University Paediatric Clinic in Vienna. Asperger described the characteristic features that these children had in common and how they differed from children with typical development. These children appeared to have average or above average levels of intelligence and good expressive language but their language skills were not utilised for two-way conversations. Asperger, like Kanner, also used the term 'autism' and it was only in 1981 that Lorna Wing introduced the term 'Asperger syndrome' to describe this group of individuals (TDA, 2008).

The triad of impairments

Lorna Wing used the term 'autistic spectrum disorder' (ASD) as a broad term for children who displayed common characteristics. Wing and Gould (1979) investigated the characteristics of children with autism. Their research identified the existence of a group of children who were socially impaired. This was consistent with the earlier findings of Kanner and his colleague. However, they also found that when social impairment was present, social communication and inflexibility of thought and behaviour were also present (Wing, 2007). They used the term 'triad of impairments' (Wing, 1988) to describe the difficulties experienced by these children.

Social impairment

Social impairment is characteristic of all children with ASD. Children with social impairment may have no interest in social interaction and they may display little interest in other people. They may be socially aloof and indifferent to strangers, although they may be more responsive to people who are familiar to them (Wing, 2007). They may reject approaches from others and may attempt to isolate themselves (Wing, 2007).

As a trainee teacher you need to understand that there are degrees of social impairment. Social impairment lies on a continuum from those who are solitary and withdrawn (classic autism) to those who will respond passively when approached by others but will not initiate interaction themselves. At another end of the continuum may be those children who seek attention from others but often do not know how to deal with it (Jordan and Powell, 1995).

Children with social impairment may fail to grasp social rules. For example, they may not understand the need for one's own personal space. Socialising with others does not come naturally to children with ASD. The company of others is not something they seek or desire. Social situations can be very stressful and they may have difficulty understanding the emotions and feelings of others. They may upset others as a result of failing to understand social codes of behaviour. They may avoid eye contact and find it distressing to make eye contact with others. This has implications for you as a trainee teacher. Never force a child with ASD to make eye contact with you. You will need to teach them explicitly about the effects of their actions on other peoples' feelings and you should therefore not label the child as 'naughty' or 'difficult'.

What are the implications of these difficulties for you as a trainee teacher? The first thing to remember is that autistic children may find social situations distressing or frightening. Do not force social contact and be sensitive to their needs. Social interactions need to be taught. You cannot assume that children with ASD will know how to behave in a group situation. Start slowly and gently to encourage the child to tolerate simple social contact with others (Wing, 2007). Limit the time for social contact initially and limit the number of children in a group. This can be gradually increased as the child gains confidence. Develop positive relationships with parents or carers and plan strategies and interventions carefully in collaboration with them. It is possible that they may have chosen a mainstream placement as a way of helping their child to develop social interaction skills. You will need to develop a 'deep empathy' (Wing, 2007: 27) for these children. After periods of focused social interaction, these children may need to go into their own quiet place for focused one-to-one teaching. They should be 'prepared' for periods of social interaction, rather than interactions being forced on them. A highly ordered routine will be necessary so that children know what is going to happen at specific times during the day. Be aware that noisy environments may distress children with ASD and they may be particularly sensitive to bright lights. They may try to block out noise by putting their hands over their ears. Finally, you need to be calm when a child makes an accurate observation that offends. Children with autism need to be gradually taught the codes of appropriate social behaviour and they will need to be taught very explicitly about the way in which their actions can affect the feelings and emotions of others.

Language and communication

Children with ASD often have limited expressive language. Commonly, they do not understand the function of language as a tool for reciprocal conversation and speech may only be used to satisfy a personal need or to talk about things of immediate interest to themselves (Wing, 2007). They may take the meaning of language literally and they may find it difficult to understand colloquial phrases. In addition, they may take sarcasm literally. Some children may have good vocabulary (particularly children with Asperger syndrome), although they may not use this vocabulary to engage in two-way conversations.

They may echo words that they have heard and their comprehension of language may be weak. Some children may talk 'at' other people or even speak in different languages, thus demonstrating a failure to grasp the fundamental function of language as a tool for communication. Therefore, although speech may be developed, an understanding of speech as a tool for communication may be lacking. The extent of a child's difficulties with communication will lie on a continuum from those with no speech to those who have quite well developed speech. Some children have excellent grammar and pronunciation and a talent for a foreign language (Jordan and Powell, 1995). However, poor communication remains a fundamental problem in all children with ASD. Many children with ASD do not understand facial expressions, expressive gestures and body postures (Jordan and Powell, 1995).

What are the implications of this for your classroom practice? Instructions may need to be accompanied by visual prompts or modelling. You will need to teach conversational skills such as listening, turn taking and the value of sharing knowledge with others. You cannot assume that these skills will be secure. Think carefully about the way in which you phrase instructions. A simple request such as 'can you draw a triangle?' is intended to elicit more than a reply of 'yes' (Jordan, 2005). Tasks may need to be explained pictorially rather than through verbal instructions.

Rigidity of thought and behaviour

Children with ASD often develop rigid patterns of behaviour. They may repeat certain behaviours, such as dropping an object on a table repeatedly or spinning a coin. They may develop obsessions with a favourite object or they may become obsessed on cars, trains or motorbikes. Changes to familiar routines may cause distress and they may resist change. They may find imaginative play very difficult. Pretend play is often delayed or absent altogether (Jordan and Powell, 1995) and they may find it difficult to differentiate between reality and imagination. Creativity is often lacking.

As a trainee teacher you will need to ensure that the teaching day is very well structured. The use of a visual timetable (discussed below) will help the child to see what activities are scheduled during the day. Creative teachers can integrate the child's 'obsessions' into the daily schedule. If a child has a particular obsession with castles, you might wish to build in some time during the day when the child can build castles out of construction kits or read about castles in the book area. You might want to provide the child with opportunities to play a simulation game on the computer where the simulation is based inside a castle. The activities you provide will depend on the skills and interests of the child. If this time is scheduled on the daily timetable and the timetable is followed in order, you can then use this as a bargaining tool. For example, if number work comes before 'castles' on the daily schedule, you can teach the child that they must complete the first task before they can move onto their obsession. This becomes a 'rule' which the child learns to follow and helps to ensure that the child receives access to a broad and balanced curriculum. The best teachers will use children's obsessions and draw on these for curriculum-planning purposes. However, children need to know that they cannot spend all their time engaging in their obsessions. Try to keep changes to the classroom layout to a minimum and warn children about any changes to the curriculum or the classroom systems, routines and organisation. Slowly you should aim to introduce learners to new experiences and interests in order to give them access to a broad and rich curriculum.

Causes of autism

During the 1940s and 1950s it was thought that parental style was responsible for autism (Wing, 2007). However, later research in the 1960s confirmed that autism is caused by irregularities in brain development, often before birth (Wing, 1997). Strong evidence now confirms that genetic factors play a part in brain dysfunction (Bailey *et al.*, 1995; Jordan and Powell, 1995; Rutter, 1999). There is no one single cause of autism but the evidence supports biological explanations. Autism is therefore explained as a product of nature rather than a product of nurture, although this does not exclude the possibility of environmental factors at the pre-natal stage (Wing, 2007).

Barriers to learning and participation

The key barriers to learning and participation have been discussed above. These can be summarised as follows.

- Impairment in the ability to understand social behaviour.
- Impairment in the ability to understand and use non-verbal and verbal communication.
- Impairment in the ability to think and behave flexibly. (TDA, 2008)

The Code of Practice for Special Educational Needs and Disabilities (DfE, 2014) identifies some key principles. Local authorities and schools must have regard to:

- the views, wishes and feelings of the child or young person, and the child's parents;
- the importance of the child or young person, and the child's parents, participating as fully as possible in decisions, and being provided with the information and support necessary to enable participation in those decisions;
- the need to support the child or young person, and the child's parents, in order to facilitate the development of the child or young person and to help them achieve the best possible educational and other outcomes, preparing them effectively for adulthood. (DfE, 2014: 8)

These principles are designed to support:

- the participation of children, their parents and young people in decision making;
- the early identification of children and young people's needs and early intervention to support them;
- greater choice and control for young people and parents over support;
- collaboration between education, health and social care services to provide support;
- high quality provision to meet the needs of children and young people with SEN;
- a focus on inclusive practice and removing barriers to learning;
- successful preparation for adulthood, including independent living and employment. (DfE, 2014: 8–9)

The principles of early intervention, removing barriers to learning, partnership working and raising expectations and achievement were also emphasised in Labour's SEN strategy (DfES, 2004). As a trainee teacher or even as a qualified teacher you are not expected, nor would it be appropriate for you, to make a diagnosis of autism. However, you may have observed specific characteristics in a child which may cause you to question whether the child may have ASD. The diagnosis must 'be made on the pattern of development of skills and behaviour from infancy onwards' (Wing, 2007: 25) and should, where possible, be made by a multi-disciplinary team made up of health professionals. Medical professionals may consult with teachers during the process of making a diagnosis.

As a trainee teacher you will want to implement strategies to remove potential barriers to learning and to increase participation and achievement. Some strategies are suggested below. It is vital that you develop positive and respectful relationships with parents and other professionals who may be involved with the child. You should aim to implement any recommendations made by outside agencies and you should discuss the child's progress regularly with your teacher-mentor, parents or carers.

It was mentioned above that children with ASD might be sensitive to certain stimuli. Some may be sensitive to light or temperature. Others might be sensitive to specific textures such as sand, soil or certain foods. It is possible that children may display sensitivities to specific smells, such as the smell of perfume or after-shave. Teachers need to be aware of these sensitivities so that children are not placed in stressful situations. Of course, these sensitivities may become barriers to learning. How can you engage children in sand play or water play in the Early Years Foundation Stage if they have a specific sensitivity with sand or water? How can you teach a lesson relating to light if a child becomes distressed with bright lights? How can you create a colourful and stimulating classroom environment if a child is sensitive to colour or becomes distracted with displays? These are all critical questions, which you may need to ask yourself, and there are no magic answers. Sometimes you may avoid putting the child in a specific situation. At other times it might be appropriate for you to gradually give the child experience of specific stimuli.

Strategies to support learning

If you have a child with autism in your class on placement the first thing you need to do is to research into this area thoroughly. You need to talk to your teacher-mentor to find out which strategies work and identify any strategies that do not work. All children are individuals and will respond differently to interventions. Amaladoss (2006) stresses the importance of a whole school approach. All staff, including teaching and support staff, need to have knowledge of the particular child and the strategies which are being employed to manage the child's behaviour and learning. Teachers need to meet with parents and carers to discuss their approach and to agree on systems for managing the child's behaviour. A daily home–school diary is a very useful way of communicating with parents and allows successes and challenges to be shared.

Creating safe learning environments

As a trainee teacher you need to ensure that the tasks that you are providing do not include elements of social learning which are beyond the capabilities of the child. Identify the intended learning outcomes and focus on how these are best achieved for individual pupils. Review your classroom provision and pedagogical approaches. Could they be responsible for creating undesirable behaviours? Remember the social model of disability and how it conceptualises disability as a social construct caused by factors that are external to the child. A classroom, which lacks structure and routine, could generate undesirable behaviours. Many children with ASD are visual learners. Capitalise on this and take account of this when you plan learning opportunities. Resources should be clearly labelled using both words and pictures. Think carefully about providing calm areas and areas that provide quiet spaces for work. Individual workstations may be appropriate for some learners with ASD but some children may be able to work happily alongside their peers. The needs of the child should determine your classroom organisation. Consider whether you need to use lighting. The flicker of fluorescent lighting may be distracting and patterns can be a source of fixation. Excessive use of colour or over-crowded displays may also be distressing.

You will need to ensure that the rest of the class are understanding and knowledgeable about children with ASD. Talk to them about the child's specific difficulties and ways in which they might be able to offer support. However, it is important not to conceptualise any form of disability as a personal tragedy. The aim is not to seek tolerance and sympathy from others, but to create an ethos where diversity is viewed positively and celebrated. The social model has helped to emancipate and empower disabled people and teachers need to ensure that children with ASD are not viewed as inferior.

Unstructured social times such as playtimes and lunchtimes may be difficult for children with ASD. Some children with ASD may choose to walk the perimeter of the playground or follow lines on the floor to avoid social contact. Some children may run around flapping their arms because they feel distressed. All staff need to be aware of how to communicate with children with ASD. This includes lunchtime staff. Some children with ASD can gently be encouraged to join in with playground games. Initially the game will need to be modelled by an adult and you may decide that a game with one partner is sufficient. You can then judge whether it is appropriate to increase the size of the group, depending on the specific needs of each child. Some children may be happy to be left alone and should not be forced to socially interact.

Visual approaches

Adults with autism have described how pictures enable them to think (Grandin, 1996). Visual timetables provide children with a clear structure to the day and help to reduce anxiety (TDA, 2008). The daily schedule can be presented horizontally or vertically and laminated picture cards can be attached to denote the daily activities. Symbols or photographs are used to represent the tasks, activities or lessons that are to be completed during a day. The child can then access the visual timetable at the start of the day and know the sequence through which s/he will work through the tasks. Whole class visual timetables support a more inclusive ethos and ensure that no child is singled out from the rest. A visual timer (TDA, 2008) with an arrow will help children to see how much time is left in a lesson. Choice cards can be offered at the end of an activity and symbol cards can be used to give specific commands.

A whole class approach to inclusion

CASE STUDY

Sally was a reception teacher and was preparing for a child with autism to join her class. Luke was four years old. He displayed all the traits of classic autism. He had no speech and was unable to socially interact. His parents had adopted the use of a visual timetable at home and this was working well. Sally was keen to build on the strategies that Luke was already familiar with. She decided to talk to the class about autism. She explained that Luke often got very upset if he did not know what was going to happen during the day and she showed the children an example of a visual timetable. She discussed how important it was for Luke to know the order of his daily activities. Sally was surprised when several other children also expressed a desire to know what was going to happen during the day. She asked for their suggestions and the children were given some 'thinking time' to come up with suggestions.

The children decided to create a planning board. The children's names were printed on cards and displayed on the board. Cards were then created representing different classroom activities (sand, water, mathematics, literacy, construction, mark making, computers, etc.). Each child was given a set of 12 cards representing the different activities in the classroom. These were stored in each child's tray. On a daily basis, the children were given 'planning time' where they were required to select the activities they wanted to do that particular day. Activities relating to literacy and mathematics were placed on the board daily by the teacher next to a specific time slot. However, there was flexibility about which of the remaining activities the children selected and the order in which these were undertaken. After selecting the relevant cards, these were then displayed by the child on the board next to their name in the order of their choice. At the end of the day the cards which had been displayed on the board were removed and were not available for future selection until the child had used up all their remaining cards.

REFLECTIVE TASK

- Why was this approach more inclusive?
- How did the teacher involve the pupils in the decision making?
- Do you think it was a good move to talk to the whole class about autism?

Picture exchange communication system (PECS)

PECS is a communication system for children with no speech. In this system if a child wants an object, they must firstly search through their personal book of picture symbols to find the relevant picture that represents the sought object. The child can then offer the picture in exchange for the desired object. This strategy prevents lack of speech becoming a potential barrier to participation. After this initial stage children can then be introduced to a simple phrase such as 'I want', which they may learn to use before offering the symbol. Phrases or words can then be attached to Velcro strips in the PECS book and the adult can model the phrase by verbalising it and the child may repeat this. Initially PECS will be used in situations where the child will be motivated to communicate, such as when they require food. Its use can then gradually be extended to cover other purposes.

Structure and routine

The visual timetable described above will help to outline the daily structure. However, simple routines must be consistent and this is beneficial to all children. Try to implement consistent early morning routines. For example, what do the children do when they first enter the classroom in the morning? Where do they put their lunch boxes? Where do you ask them to sit? What are the early morning activities? Then think carefully about the routines during the day. How do you stop the class and gain their attention? Do you play a particular piece of music at the end of a session when the children are tidying away? Where do the children line up? Where are the resources kept? There are so many things for you to think about but try to keep changes to a minimum and if changes are necessary, these should be communicated in advance.

Social stories and comic strips

Social stories are a strategy developed by Carol Gray (1994) in America. Some children with ASD may find particular situations or experiences difficult. A social story is built around this experience and aims to describe the events that happen and the feelings of the 'characters' in the story. They can help children learn to cope with specific social situations, such as going to the dentist, having their hair cut, lunchtime or going into assembly. Children can read these stories prior to an event (or have them read out) to help them rehearse the experience.

Comic strip conversations can be used as a way of representing social situations, similar to social stories. They are made up of stick people, and speech and thought bubbles so that children can think about the sequence of events, what was said during a particular situation, and the thoughts and feelings of the people involved in the experience (Amaladoss, 2006).

Individual teaching

The decision for a child to receive individual teaching is a professional decision informed by the needs of each child. You will need to discuss the teaching style with parents and carers. They may be keen to avoid too much individualised teaching and this may be the reason why they have chosen to send their child to a mainstream school in the first place. Some children with ASD may have specific needs that mean that social learning is not possible. Some children with ASD may be able to cope with some peer-to-peer interaction combined with some individual teaching. Some learners with ASD may not need individual input and it may be possible to support these learners in a group situation. You will need to exercise your professional judgement in the decision-making process.

Adequate staffing ratios are essential if you are supporting a child with ASD. If individual teaching is appropriate, you should make use of bookcases, cupboards and screens to create a working space for the child with ASD. However, you should be aware that such approaches could perpetuate segregation. In developing your systems for classroom organisation you should consult with specialist staff from other agencies who are involved in supporting the child. For younger children with ASD, individual workstations may be appropriate whereas older children may be able to work at an open table (TDA, 2008). You will also need to make decisions about whether they work alone at an open table or whether they can work in parallel, opposite another child or working alongside a group of children.

Classroom environment

The flicker and hum of fluorescent lighting may cause a distraction for learners with ASD. Think carefully about possible sensitivity to light. Classroom blinds can be used to good effect to minimise light. Think about the visual appeal of your classroom. Try to avoid brightly coloured backing paper. Use calming colours instead. You could divide the classroom into low stimulus areas and high stimulus areas. In the low stimulus area there could be minimal display and calming colours. This might be the most appropriate place for the child with ASD to work. However, other children could also work in this area. In the high stimulus area there could be colourful displays of pupils' work. This solution is a compromise to balancing the needs of one child against the needs of all children (TDA, 2008).

PRACTICAL TASK   PRACTICAL TASK   PRACTICAL TASK   PRACTICAL TASK   PRACTICAL TASK

Arrange to meet a specialist teacher from the communication and interaction team in the LA. You may get the chance to shadow one of these teachers during your placement or you may have to meet at the headquarters. Find out about their role and responsibilities. Find out how the service supports practitioners and parents or carers. Find out about how teachers are able to undertake further professional training within this field in order to become specialist teachers of autism.

ICT

Many children with ASD have visual learning styles, although some children will demonstrate other learning styles (TDA, 2008). For this reason, the computer can be a very powerful learning resource for children with ASD. Try to make the learning visual. Teachers should maximise use of the interactive whiteboard during lessons and children with ASD should have frequent opportunities to explore a range of software. Sometimes, they may develop a preference for a specific piece of software and this can, in itself, become a barrier to learning. You should gradually aim to increase their experience of a range of software in order to give each child access to a broad and balanced curriculum. The use of a personal laptop computer with a range of software specifically targeted at learners with ASD may increase motivation in some sessions. It may be appropriate to section off the computer area with screens so that the child with ASD is not distracted when they are working in other areas of the classroom. The use of headphones for children working on computers may minimise levels of distraction.

PRACTICAL TASK   PRACTICAL TASK   PRACTICAL TASK   PRACTICAL TASK   PRACTICAL TASK

Arrange to spend some time in a LA resource base for children with autism or a school which includes autistic learners. Your initial teaching trainer (ITT) provider may arrange this for you but if not you could pursue your own professional development during your periods of 'flexible training'. This will need advance planning as the children may need to be 'prepared' for your visit. Spend some time observing in the setting.

- What visual strategies are used to support teaching and learning?
- How is the teaching space organised?
- How are the children taught?

- What behaviour management strategies are adopted?
- How are the staff deployed to support teaching and learning?

Talk to the lead teacher and discuss the following points.

- What are the specific needs of learners with ASD?
- What strategies are used to support teaching and learning and why are these strategies used?
- How do staff in the setting work in partnership with external agencies and parents or carers?

Managing anger

If you have a child in your class with ASD you are advised to keep a mood diary. The purpose of a mood diary is to look for triggers that may cause a child to become angry or distressed. If you are able to identify the trigger you may be able to reduce the expressions of anger. Some children may benefit from being taught to sit in a calm place until the feelings of anger have subsided. Remember to reward the child when s/he stays calm. Ensure that you consistently model positive values in your teaching – an angry teacher could produce angry children!

CASE STUDY

Attitudes to inclusion

Read the following episode, written by a parent of a child with autism.

His teacher had very low tolerance levels. He would shout at Sam all the time and Sam used to cry constantly. He used to send him out of class with his TA when he couldn't cope with him. Sam became a very distressed little boy. I am sure that he just knew that Mr X didn't like him. Mr X just doesn't recognise that children are not all the same and cannot be programmed to behave in the same ways. Children are not robots. I saw all my hard work going down the drain and it made me so angry. I found out one day Sam was wailing and screaming because Mr X had shouted at him. I couldn't believe what Mr X did. He tape recorded him and took it round the staff and played it to them. He wanted to humiliate Sam. I was furious and so was the SENCO (Bev) because she told me what had happened. Bev was deeply disturbed by the tape and she told Mr X that it said more about him and his classroom ethos than it did about Sam. Mr X clearly thought the tape was funny and was laughing about it in the staffroom. I was appalled.

REFLECTIVE TASK
REFLECTIVE TASK

- What do you think the parent means when she says that 'children are not all the same and cannot be programmed to behave in the same ways'?
- What do you think the parent means when she says 'I saw all my hard work going down the drain'?
- How important are teachers' attitudes in fostering an inclusive ethos?
- Why do you think Mr X demonstrated such unprofessional behaviour?

CASE STUDY

Managing individual needs

Michael was placed in a Year 2 class within a mainstream school. Initially there were occasions when Michael demonstrated signs of distress. He cried and screamed and the other children quickly became frightened of Michael and were reluctant to go near him. The teacher decided to keep a behaviour diary. She recorded the events leading up to an incident and she later analysed the episodes with Michael's support worker. Upon analysis it was evident that Michael's 'outbursts' occurred when there were sudden changes to his routine. He had a visual timetable but changes to routines were frequent and are not uncommon in primary schools.

Working in partnership with Michael's parents a policy was established to help Michael cope with sudden changes to his routine. A staff meeting was called and in the meeting it was agreed that any changes to routines had to be communicated to Michael's support worker first. This enabled the support worker to discuss the change with Michael before it actually happened, pre-warning him using either a social story or a visual comic strip. This approach was very successful and Michael soon learnt to cope with changes to his routine. On one occasion Michael even took part in a fire drill without getting upset.

REFLECTIVE TASK

- How useful was the behaviour diary?
- Do you think a behaviour diary would be useful for parents?
- Why did Michael get upset?
- How was the issue addressed?

CASE STUDY

One size fits all?

Read the following extract from a teacher who had a child with ASD in her class:

The advisory teacher from the LA seemed to have 'textbook' strategies for dealing with autistic children. She insisted that David had a daily schedule, even though I thought that we should try him without one in the first instance. I was anxious not to make him feel different. She said that he had to be escorted to the toilet. She wanted him to go out to play before the others so that he was not distressed by being in a busy cloakroom. She said that David would need one-to-one support in the playground. She wasn't very happy because I said 'no' to all of her recommendations. These strategies would have isolated David and were not practical in a mainstream classroom and a mainstream school. There was simply no way that we could escort him everywhere and the bottom line was that his parents had chosen to send him to a mainstream school for a reason. They did not want us to operate a mini special school. She also wanted David to have one-to-one teaching which I am totally opposed to. I was glad when she left us alone. After a couple of days he settled brilliantly. He didn't need a schedule. He didn't need one-to-one supervision and he didn't need to be taught in a one-to-one situation. He coped with getting ready to play with the other children. He coped with our normal classroom routines. I remember that sometimes he used to throw himself on the floor. This was often when he needed his own space. We used to withdraw him to give him the space he needed but not as a punishment. It allowed him to calm down.

REFLECTIVE TASK

Think carefully about the following questions:

- Why was the teacher reluctant to implement the suggested strategies?
- Do you think the teacher was right to avoid implementing the suggested strategies?
- How might the adoption of special school practices in mainstream environments perpetuate exclusion rather than inclusion?
- What do you think are the dangers associated with labelling?

CASE STUDY

Tom was diagnosed as having Asperger syndrome in Year 2. He was given a statement of SEN which gave him access to a teaching assistant for 15 hours a week. Tom was very vocal in class but often appeared not to be listening. He would make loud squawking noises whilst the teacher was talking to the class which was very distracting. Tom was very good at maths and would always shout out the answers to oral questions, not allowing others to have their turn. He took all state-ments very literally, for example, when the class was told to 'pull up your socks' he would follow the instruction to the letter! As Tom got older he began to be fascinated by writing. He would write very literal stories which were peppered with his own comments on his writing always enclosed in square brackets. He used unusual vocabulary which was often far in advance of his years and was sometimes inappropriate to the context. Children found him difficult to play with in the playground as he would want to join in on his terms and 'wind-milled' his limbs in a very forceful manner. He would often complain that children hurt him, but could not recognize when he had hurt them. Tom also had a strong fascination for computers which at times became an issue when he redesigned access codes for the school network.

The school used a variety of strategies including one-to-one sessions, small group sessions and lunch-time support. At times Tom was able to go home for lunch on days when his mother was not at work. Parents of other children were aware that Tom had difficulties socializing and in the main were sup-portive and understanding. When Tom transferred to high school he was allowed to move classes five minutes before the end of lessons to give him the chance to relocate away from the crowd.

A SUMMARY OF **KEY POINTS**

➤ **Children with Asperger syndrome may have average or above average IQ levels and well-developed speech, but essentially children in both groups typically share commonalties.**

➤ **Children with ASD typically display impairments in the three areas of social interaction, social communication and rigidity of thought and behaviour.**

➤ **Visual systems, such as visual timetables and PECS can be used to support the specific needs of children with ASD.**

RESEARCH SUMMARY RESEARCH SUMMARY **RESEARCH SUMMARY** RESEARCH SUMMARY

Bass, J.D. and Mulick, J.A. (2007) 'Social play skill enhancement of children with autism using peers and siblings as therapists', *Psychology in the Schools*, 44 (7), 727–35.

This article discusses the role of peer initiation strategies and peer buddy systems as interventions to improve the social play skills of children with autism.

MOVING ON > > > > > > MOVING ON > > > > > > MOVING ON

Now that you have developed a basic understanding of the specific needs of learners with ASD, try to arrange a short placement in either a school for autistic learners or in resourced-based provision attached to a mainstream school. Find out about the systems that are used to organise the teaching and find out about strategies which staff use to manage challenging behaviour.

REFERENCES REFERENCES **REFERENCES** REFERENCES **REFERENCES** REFERENCES

Amaladoss, K. (2006) 'Supporting children with autistic spectrum disorders in a mainstream class-room', in G. Knowles (ed.) *Supporting Inclusive Practice*, London: David Fulton, pp. 111–25.

Bailey, A., LeCouteur, A., Gottesman, I., Bolton, P., Simonoff, E., Yusda, E. and Rutter, M. (1995) 'Autism/Asperger syndrome: a strongly genetic disorder: evidence from a twin study', *Psychological Medicine*, 25: 63–77.

Department for Education (DfE) (2014) *Special Educational Needs and Disability Code of Practice: 0 to 25 Years: Statutory Guidance for Organisations Who Work With and Support Children and Young People with Special Educational Needs and Disabilities*, London: DfE.

Department for Education and Skills (DfES) (2004) *Removing Barriers to Achievement: The Government Strategy for SEN*, Nottingham: DfES.

Grandin, T. (1996) *Thinking in Pictures: And Other Reports from My Life with Autism*, London: Vintage.

Gray, C. (1994) *The Social Storybook*, Arlington, TX: Future Horizons.

Jordan, R. (2005) 'Autistic spectrum disorders', in A. Lewis and B. Norwich (eds) *Special Teaching for Special Children*, Berkshire: Open University Press, pp. 110–22.

Jordan, R. and Powell, S. (1995) *Understanding and Teaching Children with Autism*, Chichester: John Wiley and Sons.

Kanner, L. (1943), 'Autistic disturbances of affective contact', *Nervous Child*, 2, 217–50.

Kanner, L. and Eisenberg, L. (1956) 'Early infantile autism, 1943–1955', *American Journal of Orthopsychiatry*, 26, 55–65.

Rutter, M. (1999) 'Autism: Two-way interplay between research and clinical work', *Journal of Child Psychology and Psychiatry*, 40, 169–88.

Training and Development Agency for Schools (TDA) (2008) *Special Educational Needs and/or Disabilities: A Training Resource for Initial Teacher Training Providers: Primary Undergraduate Courses*, TDA.

Warnock, M. (2005) 'Special educational needs: a new look', *Impact*, 11, Salisbury: Philosophy of Education Society of Great Britain.

Wing, L. (1988) 'The continuum of autistic characteristics', in E. Schopler and G. Mesibov (eds) *Diagnosis and Assessment in Autism*, New York: Plenum Press.

Wing, L. (1997) 'The history of ideas on autism', *Autism*, 1, 13–23.

Wing, L. (2007) 'Children with autistic spectrum disorders', in R. Cigman (ed.) *Included or Excluded: The Challenge of the Mainstream for Some SEN Children*, Oxon: Routledge.

Wing, L. and Gould, J. (1979) 'Severe impairments of social interaction and associated abnormalities in children: epidemiology and classification', *Journal of Autism and Developmental Disorders*, 9(1), 11–29.

FURTHER READING   FURTHER READING   **FURTHER READING**   FURTHER READING

The following texts provide excellent reading material to help you understand autism:

Haddon, M. (2003) *The Curious Incident of the Dog in the Night-time*, London: Doubleday.

Sainsbury, C. (2000) *Martian in the Playground*, London: Sage.

USEFUL WEBSITES   USEFUL WEBSITES   **USEFUL WEBSITES**   USEFUL WEBSITES

http://www.autism.org.uk/autism

This website by the National Autistic Society has a wealth of background information about autism.

7
Visual and hearing impairment

Chapter objectives

By the end of this chapter you should be aware of:

- the symptoms of visual and hearing impairment;
- strategies to support pupils with visual and hearing impairment;
- characteristics of an inclusive classroom for pupils with visual and hearing impairment.

Teachers' Standards

This chapter addresses the following Teachers' Standards:

TS5: Adapt teaching to respond to the strengths and needs of all pupils

- know when and how to differentiate appropriately, using approaches which enable pupils to be taught effectively
- have a secure understanding of how a range of factors can inhibit pupils' ability to learn, and how best to overcome these
- demonstrate an awareness of the physical, social and intellectual development of children, and how to adapt teaching to support pupils' education at different stages of development
- have a clear understanding of the needs of all pupils, including those with special educational needs; those of high ability; those with English as an additional language; those with disabilities; and be able to use and evaluate distinctive teaching approaches to engage and support them

Introduction

This chapter will provide you with a basic understanding of how to identify pupils with visual and hearing impairments and the strategies that you could implement to facilitate the inclusion of learners with sensory impairments in mainstream schools. The chapter will not tell you everything that you need to know about this aspect of SEN but it should provide you with a basis upon which to further develop your knowledge.

Hearing impairment

'Hearing loss' is a broad term which includes children who are culturally deaf, those who are hearing impaired and those who use signed or spoken language (Duncan, 2012).

Children who have a permanent hearing loss are likely to have been diagnosed as such before entering school. They may have hearing aids or even cochlear implants. In most cases they will have some support as part of their schooling and you will be able to ask for advice from the SENCO to understand their difficulties.

However, children whose hearing problems are less severe are often not identified at birth and can go undetected for some time. It is estimated that as many as one in four children in a Reception class may have a mild or slight hearing loss (Tassoni, 2003). Children who are prone to heavy colds and coughs can experience a mild conductive hearing loss which fluctuates. The reason for this is that the Eustachian tube which connects the nose and the ear becomes blocked causing sound to be distorted. The case study below illustrates the signs you need to look for.

Signs of hearing impairment

The following signs may be evident in children with hearing impairment:

- The child fails to respond to instructions.
- The child repeatedly asks for clarification about what to do despite being told clearly.
- The child watches others to see what they have to do then follows their lead.
- The child constantly asks others to repeat what they have said.
- The child hears on some occasions but not on others.
- The child misinterprets information or questions.
- The child only responds partially to what has been said.
- The child is unable to locate a speaker or source of sound.
- The child daydreams or has poor concentration, especially during group discussions.
- The child has delayed language development.
- The child sometimes shouts without realising they are being noisy.
- The child makes speech errors (misses out letters or omits sounds from the end of words).
- The child confuses words that sound similar (that/fat/vat).
- The child fixes their eyes on a speaker as though lip reading.
- The child may become disruptive during lessons in which children are required to listen to a teacher.
- The child experiences difficulties with reading, spelling and/or writing.
- The child has coughs or colds frequently. (Adapted from Frederikson and Cline, 2009)

CASE STUDY

Mary, a child in a Reception class, often suffered from colds and a runny nose. When she had such symptoms Mary seemed to spend a great deal of time playing by herself. She had difficulty following instructions and often looked confused. She didn't appear able to settle in whole class situations and didn't engage in group discussions. Her speech could appear muffled or indistinct. The class teacher suspected that Mary might have a fluctuating hearing loss. She talked to Mary's mother and they agreed that a visit to the family doctor would be made the next time Mary's symptoms re-occurred. The school arranged for the school nurse to conduct a hearing test using specialist equipment. These actions did indicate that Mary did have a fluctuating hearing loss and a hospital appointment was made where a full range of tests confirmed the diagnosis. Mary's ears were fitted with grommets to drain the fluid from her ears more effectively. Her class teacher ensured that Mary always sat facing people who were talking to her, and that they spoke clearly.

Impact of hearing impairment

- Children with hearing impairment may be working at a lower cognitive level of development than other pupils because they have gaps in their knowledge, skills and understanding. However, this is not always the case and some children with hearing impairment may be cognitively very able.
- Children with hearing impairment may struggle with reading because they may struggle to develop adequate phonological representations.
- Some children with hearing impairment may have low self-concepts.

Strategies to support pupils with hearing impairment

The strategies that you adopt will largely depend on the severity of the hearing impairment, although the following may be useful:

- Always face the child when you are talking to them.
- Speak slowly and pronounce your words carefully.
- Use short sentences or phrases.
- Sit the child close to you when you are teaching the whole class.
- Use concrete objects and visual images and representations to support your teaching.
- Use all the senses when you are teaching – use a multi-sensory approach.
- Use signing to help communication. Introduce signing to all the class to enable the child's peers to communicate with him/her.
- Use a visual timetable to help structure the day.
- Communicate with the child using the appropriate modality: some children with hearing loss use sign language and others use spoken language. Some children use a combination of signed and spoken language (Duncan, 2012).
- Ensure that the child is using assistive hearing technology (hearing aids/implants) where these have been provided by specialist services.
- Plan for learning in collaboration with specialist practitioners.
- Think about background noise and reduce this where possible.

Visual impairment

The severity of visual impairment will vary. Some children may have no vision whilst others may have some vision which is impaired. Others may have vision but may struggle with focusing on an object or tracking a moving object. It is estimated that between 10 and 15% of the child population has visual inefficiencies (Holland, 2012). These visual inefficiencies can affect learning to a greater or lesser extent. Children with poor visual discrimination skills for example may struggle with learning to read because the task of reading demands both visual and auditory perception. Children need to be able to distinguish between graphemes on the basis of their visual representation as well as through the sounds they make.

There is no longer a national school eye examination service in the UK (Holland, 2012) and therefore it is important that teachers are able to identify pupils who may have visual difficulties. Holland (2012) has produced a useful checklist of symptoms which may warrant further investigation by specialists. These include but are not restricted to those listed in the following table.

Evidence of visual difficulties	√
Misses out words or re-reads the same words	
Loses their place when reading and needs to use their finger to keep their place	
Becomes tired quickly when reading	
During close work they experience blurred or double vision	
They complain that words jump around on the page when reading	
Finds copying from the board difficult	
Frequently complains of headaches during close work	
Loses concentration during close work	
Needs a short working distance	
Continuous reading of text is inaccurate, although is able to read isolated words	
Has poor co-ordination – frequently bumping into things or knocking things over	
Poor spatial awareness	
Reluctance to complete jigsaws	
Untidy handwriting	

Strategies to support children with visual difficulties

Pupils with visual difficulties may benefit from one or more of the following strategies:

- The use of tinted lenses to reduce glare.
- The use of coloured paper to reduce contrast with black text, for example on worksheets.
- The use of a coloured background on the computer or interactive whiteboard to reduce glare and contrast.
- A portable desk slope to increase working distance.
- A space to work in which has no visual distractions, for example plain walls rather than the use of colour.
- Flicker-free lighting or the use of high frequency fluorescent lighting.
- The use of size 12 or 14 font for pupils with tracking difficulties; fonts smaller than this should be avoided.
- Avoid asking pupils to copy from the board.
- Ensure that printed material is clear and sharp. (Holland, 2012)

Other useful strategies to support pupils with visual difficulties include:

- Making resources tactile and textured, for example making letter shapes out of sandpaper.
- Making displays interactive by using textured materials.
- Use of magnifiers to support reading.

- Avoiding glossy finishes to resources such as laminated sheets which are reflective.
- Using real objects and artefacts as much as possible in your teaching.

REFLECTIVE TASK

Consider the advantages and disadvantages of separate provision for pupils with sensory impairment within a mainstream school. Discuss this with a colleague and draw up a list of pros and cons.

PRACTICAL TASK   PRACTICAL TASK   PRACTICAL TASK   PRACTICAL TASK   PRACTICAL TASK

In your next placement school arrange to meet with the SENCO. Discuss whether there are any pupils in the school with visual or hearing impairment. If so, find out what strategies are used to support these pupils in lessons. Ask if you can observe these pupils in lessons to identify the specific adjustments which are embedded into daily practice to provide these learners with equality of opportunity.

REFLECTIVE TASK

Consider how visual and hearing impairment can impact on pupils' abilities in communication, reading and writing. How might these barriers to communication, language and literacy be overcome to give pupils the best chance of success?

PRACTICAL TASK   PRACTICAL TASK   PRACTICAL TASK   PRACTICAL TASK   PRACTICAL TASK

Arrange to visit Resourced Provision for pupils with sensory impairment. You will need to spend at least one day in this provision. Observe pupils in this provision and find out what the barriers to learning are. Research the strategies which are being implemented to remove these barriers to learning.

CASE STUDY

A pupil with no sight was admitted to a mainstream school with the support of a special needs support worker. The pupil was in a nursery class, providing access to a range of resources including sand, water, role-play and malleable play. The child was only allowed to access the play-based provision under the direct supervision of the support worker and the child had separate playtimes.

- Do you think the inclusion of this child was managed effectively?
- How would you manage this differently?

A SUMMARY OF **KEY POINTS**

➢ **A neutral, low sensory learning space may be more effective for learners with visual and hearing impairment.**

➢ **Small changes to your teaching and classroom environment can make a significantly positive impact on pupils with visual and hearing impairment.**

➢ **Capitalise on the senses which are working efficiently and use those as channels for facilitating learning.**

➢ **Children with sensory impairments are full members of the mainstream classroom – they are entitled to be there and should be treated as full members.**

➢ **Vision impairment may be associated with other disabilities, especially in cases of severe vision impairment.**

RESEARCH SUMMARY RESEARCH SUMMARY **RESEARCH SUMMARY** RESEARCH SUMMARY

Stein (2001) demonstrated that the use of blue or yellow tints can increase visual stability and improve reading ages.

MOVING *ON* > > > > > > MOVING *ON* > > > > > > MOVING *ON*

Now that you have a basic understanding of sensory impairment, try contacting the service for supporting learners with sensory impairment within your LA. Ask if they have any literature that could be sent to you to further your knowledge and understanding of this area and if possible arrange a meeting with the services to help you further understand this aspect of SEN.

REFERENCES REFERENCES **REFERENCES** REFERENCES REFERENCES REFERENCES

Duncan, J. (2012) 'Students with hearing loss', in L. Peer and G. Reid (eds) *Special Educational Needs: A Guide for Inclusive Practice*, London: Sage, pp. 211–25.

Frederickson, N. and Cline, T. (2009) *Special Educational Needs, Inclusion and Diversity*, Berkshire: Open University Press.

Holland, K. (2012) 'Vision and learning', in L. Peer and G. Reid (eds) *Special Educational Needs: A Guide for Inclusive Practice*, London: Sage, pp. 112–26.

Stein, J. (2001) 'The magnocellular theory of developmental dyslexia', *Dyslexia*, 7, 12–36.

Tassoni, P. (2003) *Supporting Special Needs: Understanding Inclusion in the Early Years*, Oxon: Heinemann.

FURTHER READING FURTHER READING **FURTHER READING** FURTHER READING

Frederickson, N. and Cline, T. (2009) *Special Educational Needs, Inclusion and Diversity*, Berkshire: Open University Press, chapter 17.

USEFUL WEBSITES USEFUL WEBSITES **USEFUL WEBSITES** USEFUL WEBSITES

http://www.scope.org.uk

http://www.rnib.org.uk/guidanceonteaching

8
Speech, language and communication difficulties

Chapter objectives

This chapter will enable you to:

- develop your knowledge and understanding of the factors which affect the development of speech, language and communication difficulties;
- develop your knowledge and understanding of how to support learners with speech, language and communication needs (SLCN).

Teachers' Standards

TS5: Adapt teaching to respond to the strengths and needs of all pupils

- know when and how to differentiate appropriately, using approaches which enable pupils to be taught effectively
- have a secure understanding of how a range of factors can inhibit pupils' ability to learn, and how best to overcome these
- demonstrate an awareness of the physical, social and intellectual development of children, and how to adapt teaching to support pupils' education at different stages of development
- have a clear understanding of the needs of all pupils, including those with special educational needs; those of high ability; those with English as an additional language; those with disabilities; and be able to use and evaluate distinctive teaching approaches to engage and support them

Introduction

This chapter focuses on speech, language and communication needs (SLCN) and briefly touches on other conditions where speech, language and communication difficulties may also be evident. Increasingly teachers in mainstream schools are encountering children with a range of SLCN and need further guidance on how to support these learners. Speech refers to the pronunciation of sounds within words. Language refers to the ability to combine words together within sentences to produce meaning. Communication refers to the interaction between people engaged in conversations. It includes rules such as listening, turn taking, looking at the speaker, building on what others have said as well as non-verbal communication. This chapter will provide you with a basis upon which to develop your practice and knowledge further.

Language and communication

Language is what differentiates mankind from all other species. It is an extraordinary system of communication, making use of symbols, words and a complex range of sounds. Societies have evolved many different languages. Each language uses a different set of symbols, stringing them together in different ways (grammar), and using different sound ranges (speech) and, for languages that are not oral, different signs on paper.

(Penn, 2008: 58)

Language is essential to the human species, and understanding how it is acquired and how it develops is very significant for teachers, especially when considering how to support children with SEN where the difficulty relates to SLCN.

The role of language

Jean Piaget's studies of child development concluded that a child acquired language as if by magic once s/he reached a certain stage in their development. However, the work of Vygotsky on cognitive development suggests that language development is an interaction between the environment and the pupil's cognitive skills. It does not occur in a vacuum, but:

- develops in a socio-cultural context;
- is influenced by the cognitive skills pupils bring with them;
- develops gradually and at varying rates.

Vygotsky describes a process where communication develops through social interaction with others and suggests that thought evolves separately and at a later stage of cognitive development (Jarvis, 2005). This suggests that it is only later that language becomes internalised, allowing the child to mentally manipulate ideas and follow instructions. The implication of this has major significance for children whose special needs involve any kind of speech and language difficulties as their ability to internalise and comprehend information may be severely compromised.

Making sense of language

When children first begin to speak they react to the environment around them. Initially this means using single words which are followed by two or more words which may appear to the listener to be unconnected. Many researchers such as Chomsky (1953; 1957), Skinner (1957) and Crystal (1976) have attempted to find a pattern for early language acquisition but there is still further work to be done to fully understand how children's language develops. Language development is affected by a combination of biological and environmental influences and the social environment in which a child is raised can have a significant impact on language development. Communication with young children tends to take place at a slower pace than adult conversations, vocabulary is often repetitive and simple, the intonation is exaggerated and the grammatical structure is simpler.

The impact of social environments

The home environment significantly impacts on the development of children's speech, language and communication. Children learn to communicate by listening to and imitating the world around them. If the child does not have access to a language-rich home environment it is possible that they will experience speech and language difficulties.

The influence of virtual technologies on children's development of language is also a matter of concern. Children entering school do seem to be less advanced in speech, language and communication than in the past. At this time much of the evidence for this is anecdotal and based upon reports from head teachers.

Gross (2011) recommended the need for Early Years practitioners working in disadvantaged communities to undertake a programme of professional training in language development. Additionally she emphasised the need for schools to view improvements to children's language and communication as central to whole school improvement. This has significant implications for improving programmes of initial teacher training so that language and communication development is given an increased priority. Programmes of professional development also need to be provided to serving teachers so that they have the knowledge and skills to support children's development in this area.

Non-verbal communication

What is clear is that children do manage to make themselves understood to their parents or those closest to them. This may be made easier by contextual clues such as where the child is looking, facial expression and tone of voice or body movements (Wood, 1998). For children with specific educational needs, such as those with autistic spectrum disorder, there may be problems 'reading' such non-verbal signals as they may not be recognised as interpretive clues to meaning. Similarly some children with a visual impairment may have limited experience of using and seeing non-verbal communication.

REFLECTIVE TASK

- Consider the link between social deprivation and the development of speech, language and communication.
- Why do more children from areas of social deprivation have SLCN?
- How can schools support the parents in these cases to develop language-rich environments in the home?

Strategies to facilitate communication

The following strategies may help you to support pupils with SLCN:

- reduce background noise;
- face the child when speaking to him/her;
- provide them with thinking time so they can process what you have said;
- simplify your language – use short, clear statements;
- slow down your speech;
- show them what you want them to do as well as explaining what they have to do;
- be patient;
- build on what they have said;
- do not finish their sentences;
- model the correct language;

- rephrase what they say using the correct language;
- teach new vocabulary explicitly;
- provide opportunities for paired talk;
- provide opportunities for collaborative group work and discussion.

All teaching spaces should be language-rich environments and this is no different for children with SLCN. They enjoy taking part in songs, rhymes and action games and should be encouraged to join in whenever possible, including using signing if appropriate to their needs. For example, many schools now include signing when singing in assembly whether or not they have children who rely upon this means of communication. This not only acknowledges diversity, but also is a way of helping all the children to think more carefully about the words they are singing.

You will need to consider the complexity of the language you use with children who have SLCN. They will become disinterested in talking to you if they find it difficult to interpret your conversation. Generally adults naturally repeat and emphasise key words in a sentence with young children and this continues to be a useful strategy for older children with SLCN.

Children with SLCN need a relaxed atmosphere in which to learn. One of the best ways to achieve this is through adopting a play-based approach to learning. The Early Years Foundation Stage is based around play and it may well be appropriate to continue to use some of this methodology for older children in some of their learning. It allows the adult to scaffold the development of new vocabulary during child-initiated interactions.

Some physical aspects of the classroom environment can make it difficult for children with SLCN to communicate. This is especially true if a child has a hearing or visual impairment. Try to avoid standing with your back towards a bright light such as a window or display screen. Your face is then in shadow and a child who relies on your face for visual clues to grasp the full meaning of your conversation will struggle to fully comprehend you. Similarly make sure the room is light enough for your face to be clearly visible, and do not engage children in conversation when you have your back to them. Whenever possible ensure that the classroom environment is free from echoes. This can be achieved by having curtained windows and carpeted floors. It is an interesting fact that children with hearing impairments are generally at least twice as good at lip reading as their hearing peers. You can also employ visual aids to support the development of communication such as puppets and pictures or objects that relate to the teaching objective of the lesson.

Much of the above reflects good educational practice for all children, but it is especially important for children with SLCN.

Support and differentiation for pupils with SLCN

Throughout this chapter we have emphasised that children with SLCN require the same if not more access to language as other children. The difference lies in the way this access is provided. Children with SLCN need more one-to-one and small group teaching than their peers, which may be enhanced by the presence of some support within the classroom. This may take the form of a specialist teacher or a suitably trained education teaching assistant. Nevertheless it is you, as the class teacher, who must plan and prepare lessons that are differentiated according to the needs of all the children in your class. The first action you need to take is to become familiar with the specific needs of the child in your class who has SLCN difficulties. This is not simply knowing what the problems are, but identifying the next steps of learning for the child. They will need more time to understand and practice new vocabulary and concepts. It may be useful to introduce this to them in advance of your lesson through pre-teaching. This will allow them to concentrate upon the content and your delivery rather than simultaneously having to make sense of the vocabulary. Your daily planning needs to detail how you will ensure this takes place.

Some children are born with facial disorders such as cleft palate or what is commonly referred to as being 'tongue tied' where the skin under the tongue prevents the child from being able to communicate effectively. These problems rarely stop the child from communicating, but their ability to produce certain sounds may be affected. These issues are usually identified by health visitors before a child starts nursery or school and a referral is often made to a speech therapist.

Down's syndrome

Down's syndrome is a learning disability. Children are born with the condition and it can be mild or very severe. Many children with Down's syndrome can cope very well in mainstream schools but some may experience difficulties when using speech and language. Their speech may appear slurred, especially if they are tired, and some may experience difficulties with their vision and/or their cognitive development.

Neurological problems

Some children are born with central nervous system disorders such as cerebral palsy. This affects the muscles and can result in involuntary muscle contractions which may affect their speech. Again it is likely that they will already have been referred to a speech therapist before starting school.

Selective mutism

Some children acquire early language skills but are unable to apply them because of emotional or social difficulties. One form of this is known as selective mutism. Children with this difficulty tend to communicate well in certain situations and environments but choose not to communicate in others. This occurs most commonly when a child leaves the family home for the first time and enters school and refuses to communicate with the teacher and/or their peers. The most effective strategies to deal with this issue have focused on the parents or peers working with the child on school tasks in the classroom during the school day and the gradual withdrawal of their input over a long period of time. Additionally, the use of pictorial communication systems can also be effective.

Look at the Development Matters statements and Early Learning Goals in the Early Years Foundation Stage framework (DfE, 2014). Identify those statements which require a child to demonstrate their development through talking. What impact could this have on a child with selective mutism?

Stammering

Children who stammer might struggle to pronounce specific words and may struggle to articulate their sentences. Focused and regular intervention with a speech and language therapist can have a positive impact over a sustained period of time. However, teachers can support stammering pupils by:

- not asking them to read aloud in class;
- not targeting a question at them without warning;
- giving them time to process their thinking;
- giving them time to orally rehearse an answer;
- praising them for their attempts at communication;
- not finishing their sentences for them;
- not rushing them when they are trying to speak;
- giving them opportunities to respond to questions in other ways, for example, by writing an answer on a whiteboard;
- not asking them to speak in front of the class without warning.

Case Study

Alex was a six-year-old child with a stammer. He was about to join a new school. Before Alex arrived at the school the head teacher was keen that he had a positive experience of the school right from the start. She decided to talk to the whole school community about stammering in an assembly. She showed the short DVD 'Wait, wait, I'm not finished yet' produced by the Michael Palin Centre for Stammering Children (available on You Tube: http://www.youtube.com/watch?v=hwjO-vWo4Oc) to help all pupils and adults to understand more about stammering and she then talked about Alex who would be joining them the following week. As a community they drew up a contract to demonstrate how they would support Alex.

How do the actions of the head teacher demonstrate a proactive approach to inclusion?

A SUMMARY OF **KEY POINTS**

➤ **Provide children with a language-rich environment.**

➤ **Do not assume that pupils with SLCN are automatically less able.**

➤ **Praise their attempts at communication, use short, clear commands and provide learners with SLCN access to correct models of language.**

PRACTICAL TASK   PRACTICAL TASK   **PRACTICAL TASK**   PRACTICAL TASK   **PRACTICAL TASK**

On your next placement investigate the support given to a child with SLCN. What is the nature of their difficulty? When was it discovered? What support has the child and his or her family received from the primary care practitioners and the school?

MOVING *ON* > > > > > > MOVING *ON* > > > > > > MOVING *ON*

If you are not familiar with signing watch some children's television which provides signing alongside the programme (e.g. 'Mr Tumble'). Try turning off the sound and following the programme without oral clues. This may provide you with useful insight into the difficulties that may be encountered by a child with a hearing loss.

REFERENCES REFERENCES **REFERENCES** REFERENCES REFERENCES REFERENCES

Chomsky, N. (1953) 'Systems of syntactic analysis', *Journal of Symbolic Logic*, 18, 242–56.

Chomsky, N. (1957) *Syntactic Structures*, The Hague: Mouton Publishers.

Crystal, D. (1976) *Child Language, Learning and Linguistics: An Overview for the Teaching and Therapeutic Professions*, London: Edward Arnold.

Department for Education (DfE) (2014) *Statutory Framework for the Early Years Foundation Stage*, London: DfE.

Gross, J. (2011) *Two Years On: Final Report of the Communication Champion for Children*, London: The Communication Trust. https://www.thecommunicationtrust.org.uk/media/9683/nwm_final_jean_gross_two_years_on_report.pdf (accessed 6 December 2014).

Jarvis, M. (2005) *The Psychology of Effective Teaching and Learning*, Cheltenham: Nelson Thornes.

Penn, H. (2008) *Understanding Early Childhood Issues and Controversies*, (2nd edn), Maidenhead: Open University Press.

Skinner, B.F. (1957) *Verbal Behavior*. New York: Appleton-Century-Crofts.

Wood, D. (1998) *How Children Think and Learn*, (2nd edn), Oxford: Blackwell.

FURTHER READING FURTHER READING **FURTHER READING** FURTHER READING

Garner, P. (2009) *Special Educational Needs: The Key Concepts*, Abingdon: Routledge.

Pugh, G. and Duffy, B. (eds) (2008) *Contemporary Issues in the Early Years*, (4th edn), London: Sage.

USEFUL WEBSITES USEFUL WEBSITES **USEFUL WEBSITES** USEFUL WEBSITES

https://www.thecommunicationtrust.org.uk/media/12285/let_s_talk_about_it_-_final.pdf

https://www.thecommunicationtrust.org.uk/resources/resources/resources-for-practitioners/lets-talk-about-it/

http://www.stammeringcentre.org/michael-palin-centre

http://www.youtube.com/watch?v=hwjO-vWo4Oc

9
Identification and assessment

Introduction

The Code of Practice (DfE, 2014) explicitly emphasises the importance of identifying SEN early. However, it is important that the formal identification of SEND does not result in a lowering of expectations or excuses for lower rates of progress (NASEN, 2014). Before needs can be formally identified it is necessary to ask critical questions about whether pupils have received their entitlement to high quality, differentiated teaching. If a child is making less than expected progress this does not automatically mean that the child has special needs. This chapter will introduce you to the process of identifying needs and the graduated response which follows on from the identification process.

Identifying needs

The Code of Practice (DfE, 2014) emphasises the importance of:

- the early identification of needs;
- the importance of maintaining high expectations of all pupils;
- the importance of establishing high aspirations for children and young people;
- integrated assessment processes;
- integrated planning and intervention with a focus on outcomes;
- high quality, differentiated and individual provision to meet the specific needs of pupils.

All teachers have a responsibility to adapt their teaching to meet the specific needs of individual pupils. This accountability is embedded within the Teachers' Standards (specifically TS5). Additionally the Teachers' Standards make all teachers accountable for the progress and outcomes of their learners (see TS2). Thus, the accountability for identifying SEND and meeting the individual needs of pupils does not solely rest on the SENCO.

It is important that the SENCO establishes a whole-school agreed approach to the identification of SEND. It is not sufficient to assume that just because a pupil has received tailored interventions then their needs have been met and that lack of progress must mean that the pupil has SEND. The SENCO will need to check that:

- pupils' progress during an intervention has been carefully monitored;
- class teachers have been informed of pupils' progress during interventions and these assessments of pupils' learning have been used to inform planning for the child when the child is not undertaking the intervention;
- the knowledge and skills that the intervention addresses are further addressed during times when the child is not undertaking the intervention.

SENCOs will need to ensure that a record-keeping system is established so that teachers can record any concerns in relation to those pupils who appear to make little or no progress despite high quality teaching and targeted intervention. The use of an initial concern form may be a useful starting point. This form can be used to collate evidence of formative and summative assessments undertaken with the child and observational assessments undertaken by TAs and teachers.

Sources of evidence

Evidence to support the identification of a pupil's needs may be drawn from:

- teachers' assessment and experience of the pupil;
- pupil progress, attainment and behaviour;
- the individual's development in comparison with their peers;
- the views and experience of parents;
- the pupil's own views;
- advice from external support services. (NASEN, 2014)

The most effective identification processes result in a 360 degree evaluation of need. Sources of evidence should be collated from key stakeholders and the child's own views should be captured to inform the assessment process.

Range of assessment tools

The SENCO will need to make decisions about which assessment tools to use to identify whether or not a pupil has SEND. There are a range of commercial resources available on the market including:

- standardised tests;
- criterion-referenced assessments and checklists;
- profiling tools, for example for behaviour and speech, language and communication needs;
- observation schedules and prompt sheets;
- questionnaires for parents;
- questionnaires for pupils;
- screening assessments, for example for dyslexia. (NASEN, 2014)

However, it is important that schools do not over-identify SEND as a justification for a pupil falling behind in a specific area of the curriculum. SEND should only be identified if a child is consistently making little or no progress within a specific area despite high quality teaching and targeted support to address the need.

The graduated approach

Once a pupil has been identified as requiring SEN Support a graduated approach should be followed. This is summarised below:

Plan

Schools should ensure:

- that expectations of the child remain high;
- that they have high aspirations for the child and the child shares these;
- access to high quality differentiated teaching for individual pupils;
- that the SENCO supports class or subject teachers in planning to meet the needs of the pupil;
- that all colleagues who work with the child are aware of their specific needs;
- that parents are consulted and included in the planning process;
- that pupils are consulted and included in the planning process;
- that class and subject teachers remain accountable for planning to meet the needs of the child;
- that skills and knowledge developed during intervention sessions are subsequently applied in the classroom when the intervention is not taking place;
- that class and subject teachers are fully aware of the progress a child is making during an intervention and take account of this in their daily planning;
- those interventions are fully evaluated on the basis of the extent to which they address the needs of the child and accelerate achievement.

There is no expectation that schools will plan in a particular way to meet the needs of individual pupils. Some schools will continue to use individual education plans but there is no legal requirement for schools to do so and schools should adopt innovative approaches that best meet the needs of specific pupils.

Do

It is important that the planned actions to address the specific need are implemented and the SENCO will play an important role in ensuring that planned interventions take place and that the impact of these interventions is evaluated. All pupils deserve to be taught by a qualified teacher and it is important that class and subject teachers continue to teach pupils with SEND. It is common for pupils with SEND to be supported by TAs during lessons. However, class and subject teachers must never use this as an opportunity to abdicate their responsibilities. They are the ones who remain accountable for pupils' progress and their involvement in teaching pupils with SEND is critical to successful outcomes.

In cases where TAs are responsible for delivering interventions for addressing specific areas of need the following points need to be taken into consideration:

- the TA must have the knowledge, skills and training to deliver the intervention;
- the TA should have received up-to-date training in the intervention;
- the TA should know how to use an intervention flexibly to meet the specific needs of pupils.

It is important that parents of pupils with SEND are kept fully informed about the progress their child makes during an intervention. Collaboration between TA, teachers, parents and external agencies is essential so that everyone is clear on the effectiveness of the provision. Schools should discuss with parents how the knowledge and skills which the intervention addresses can be further developed by the parent at home.

Review

It is important that schools do not wait for formal reviews to evaluate the impact of the provision offered for pupils with SEND. The provision should be reviewed regularly and adaptations should be made to the teaching to ensure that pupils get the opportunity to catch up. When reviewing the quality of provision, SENCOs, class and subject teachers need to consider the following:

- Are the pupils on track to achieve their targets?
- Is the gap narrowing between pupils with and without SEN?
- Is the provision enabling learners with SEND to make progress?
- What are the views of support staff?
- What are the views of the child?
- What are the views of the parent?

Interventions which are not successful and are not having the desired impact on pupil progress should be discontinued and replaced with more effective interventions. Additionally, interventions need to be time-limited rather than permanent. The aim of an intervention is to enable pupils to catch up with their peers as quickly as possible so that they can continue with the differentiated work in the classroom.

Checklists

The checklists below should not be used for the identification of SEND. They have been included merely to illustrate possible characteristics of specific impairments. They are not, however, formal assessment tools and should not be used for the purpose of identifying specific needs. The SENCO will be responsible for developing a whole school approach to the identification of SEND and s/he may purchase specific approved assessment tools which can be used to identify SEND. The checklists below simply provide, in a very condensed form, traits which may be evident within individuals with specific needs. It is important to point out that all assessments of SEND should take place in the context of discussions with external agencies; parents, pupils and teachers should not feel that they need to take sole responsibility for making an assessment of SEND.

Possible indicators of autism

- Difficulties with social relationships and communication may affect functioning as a member of a group
- May have difficulties in understanding that s/he is part of a group
- There may be signs of poor hand–eye co-ordination
- Unusual responses to sensory stimuli e.g. bright lights, loud noises
- May show signs of stress and anxiety particularly at times of transition
- Difficulties understanding whole class instructions and general information

- May only understand spoken language which is literal, and speech may be delayed or unusual
- Finds abstract concepts difficult
- Prefers own agenda and may be reluctant to follow directions or accept a change in routine
- May/may not have a diagnosis of autism by an appropriately qualified professional
- May have difficulties with fine and gross motor skills
- May have difficulties with reciprocal social interaction with peers
- Poor concept of time and sequencing of events

Possible indicators of behavioural, social and emotional difficulties

- May be withdrawn or isolated
- May show signs of stress and anxiety
- Immature social skills
- Occasional disruptive and disturbing behaviours
- Low-level hyperactivity and lack of concentration
- Follows most but not all routines in the learning environment
- Difficulties with social relationships
- Difficulties complying with the structure of a group
- Difficulties joining in group/whole class work
- Difficulty following whole class instructions

Possible indicators of hearing impairment

- Mild/unilateral, sensori-neural/conductive hearing loss which may be temporary or permanent in nature
- May have hearing aids
- Possible difficulty with listening, attention, concentration, speech, language and class participation
- May have Auditory Processing Disorder/Auditory Neuropathy
- May have additional language/learning difficulties associated with hearing loss

Possible indicators of visual impairment

- May find concentration difficult
- May peer or screw up eyes
- Use a short working distance
- May present a limited or no awareness of visual cues/landmarks in an environment without prior awareness being raised
- May be unable to follow visual cues such as routes around a building and keep left of corridors

Possible indicators of physical difficulties

- Some problems with fine motor skills, pencil/pen control, scissor skills, dressing and undressing/self-care skills
- Exhibits some difficulties with written recording
- Some problems with gross motor skills often seen in PE/outside environment
- Lack of co-ordination e.g. difficulty carrying a tray at meal times
- Movement unsteady in crowded areas and/or on uneven surfaces
- May have continence issues
- Possible low levels of self-esteem

Possible indicators of specific learning difficulties

- Low level difficulties in the acquisition and use of language/literacy/numeracy/motor/memory/organisational skills
- Evidence of unexpected/inconsistent/unusual pattern of strengths and specific weaknesses in skills development
- Only specific curriculum areas may be affected whilst demonstrating high cognitive abilities in other areas

Possible indicators of speech, language and communication difficulties

- May have underdeveloped social skills
- May struggle to listen
- May have a limited vocabulary
- May talk in shorter sentences or not in sentences
- May struggle to understand language
- Some problems with accessing the curriculum e.g. following instructions, answering questions, processing verbal information and following everyday conversations
- Low-level difficulties in the acquisition/use of language
- May have difficulties in expressing themselves
- May stammer
- Language difficulties have an impact on social inclusion
- May struggle with some aspects of phonics work
- Speech sound production may be delayed or muddled

Possible indicators of general learning difficulties

- Some problems with concept development and logical thought
- Below average range of cognitive ability which varies in severity
- Delayed acquisition or use of language/literacy/numeracy skills
- May need support to organise resources for familiar activities
- Difficulties with pace of curriculum delivery
- Low self-concept

REFLECTIVE TASK

Consider the advantages and disadvantages of using labels to understand and communicate a pupil's learning needs. Think about this first then discuss it with a colleague. Draw up a table to show the benefits and limitations of labelling.

PRACTICAL TASK PRACTICAL TASK PRACTICAL TASK PRACTICAL TASK PRACTICAL TASK

In your next school arrange to meet with the SENCO and find out about the school's approach to identifying SEND. In particular find out about specific assessment tools which are used to identify specific needs and find out how teachers record their concerns.

CASE STUDY

James entered his Reception at the age of four. The practitioners in the setting noticed that James had significant difficulties with communication and social interaction. James did not use language for communication and often communicated through pointing or crying. James preferred to play alone and he became distressed when it became too noisy or when other children invaded his space. He quickly became upset if he was asked to complete unfamiliar activities. The practitioners in the class were concerned about James' communication and social development. In consultation with the SENCO and his parents they decided to place James on SEN Support.

James' parents were invited into school for a meeting. Their views, experiences and observations of James in his home setting were discussed to form a holistic assessment of James' development. James' parents confirmed that they also had concerns about his limited verbal communication. At the meeting, some targets were agreed to support James' communication development and his parents agreed to make an appointment with their General Practitioner.

- Why might James' parents have decided not to initially raise any concerns with the school?
- What do the characteristics displayed by James suggest?
- What other action might the school need to take?

REFLECTIVE TASK

Consider whether pupils should be withdrawn from lessons to carry out specific interventions. What are the advantages and disadvantages of this?

PRACTICAL TASK

In your next placement school, research the specific interventions that are used to address pupils' needs. How is the impact of the interventions measured?

A SUMMARY OF **KEY POINTS**

➢ **Do not assume that pupils who are working below age-related expectations automatically have SEN.**

➢ **Teachers should have high expectations of pupils with SEN.**

➢ **Pupils, parents, teachers and external agencies should work collaboratively in identifying specific needs, planning for learning and reviewing progress.**

➢ **The SENCO should develop a whole school approach to support the identification of pupils with SEN.**

RESEARCH SUMMARY RESEARCH SUMMARY **RESEARCH SUMMARY** RESEARCH SUMMARY

Glazzard (2010) found that the diagnosis of dyslexia was empowering for students. They found that the diagnosis helped them to understand the difficulties they were experiencing and the diagnosis had a positive impact on their self-concepts.

PRACTICAL TASK PRACTICAL TASK **PRACTICAL TASK** PRACTICAL TASK **PRACTICAL TASK**

Now that you are familiar with some of the principles of identification of SEN, research:

- interventions to support pupils with dyslexia;
- picture exchange communication system (PECS);
- interventions to support behaviour modification;
- language intervention programmes.

MOVING *ON* > > > > > > MOVING *ON* > > > > > > MOVING *ON*

Now that you are familiar with the process of identification of needs ensure that you maintain high expectations of all learners during your next placement. Do not assume that all pupils with SEND have cognition difficulties and do not assume that learners with SEND will always require tasks which are cognitively less demanding.

REFERENCES REFERENCES **REFERENCES** REFERENCES **REFERENCES** REFERENCES

Glazzard, J. (2010) 'The impact of dyslexia on pupils' self-esteem', *Support for Learning*, 25(2), 63–9.
NASEN (2014) *Everybody Included: The SEND Code of Practice Explained*, Tamworth: NASEN.

FURTHER READING FURTHER READING **FURTHER READING** FURTHER READING

Peer, L. and Reid, G. (2012) *Special Educational Needs: A Guide for Inclusive Practice*, London: Sage.

This text provides guidance on symptoms of categories of SEN.

USEFUL WEBSITES USEFUL WEBSITES **USEFUL WEBSITES** USEFUL WEBSITES

http://www.nasen.org.uk/tresed21/

10
An inclusive classroom

Chapter objectives

By the end of this chapter you will be able to:

- understand how the term 'inclusion' applies to the work of a school;
- know about the importance of modifying planning and teaching styles and the necessity to build access strategies into your teaching;
- understand the importance of collaborative working;
- know how to identify barriers and make learning challenges faced by pupils feasible;
- make reasonable adjustments for a range of learning needs.

Teachers' Standards

This chapter addresses the following professional standards:

TS5: Adapt teaching to respond to the strengths and needs of all pupils

- know when and how to differentiate appropriately, using approaches which enable pupils to be taught effectively

Introduction

This chapter provides guidance on how to create learner-friendly environments to support all learners. It addresses the need to consider the adaptation of teaching styles, developing access strategies to overcome barriers to learning as well as the modification of learning objectives to meet individual needs.

How the term 'inclusion' applies to the work of a school

Creating an atmosphere that motivates children to learn is always a priority. Teachers and TAs within the classroom are responsible for creating a learning environment where all pupils can be included in the learning process in a supportive and purposeful way.

Creating learner-friendly environments within schools will help learners to feel safe, happy and welcome, and will engender a sense of belonging, thus enabling them to make good progress. Essentially learner-friendly environments allow all children to enjoy a high quality education where all aspects of the curriculum are accessible, yet pupil individuality is both welcomed and appreciated. If you want to get the best out of your learners this must be a major focus of your work.

No child should be excluded from participating in learning and every attempt must be made to support those pupils who have barriers to participation, learning and achievement. The Equality Act 2010 places a statutory duty on schools to make reasonable adjustments to cater for the needs of learners with disabilities and the statutory framework for inclusion in the National Curriculum (DfE, 2013) emphasises the need to identify and remove barriers to learning and participation. This process ensures equality of opportunity. All teachers must therefore ensure that any barriers to pupils' learning are identified and eradicated. This might involve some or all of the following processes:

- carefully differentiating the task in a range of ways;
- building in access strategies;
- using a range of teaching strategies.

These elements will be examined in more detail in this chapter.

It is essential that you provide a welcoming inclusive environment for all learners. A commitment to inclusive practice demands a value-led principled approach to education. Values are central to inclusive education and personal experiences, values and principles shape our identities as educators. You should spend some time reflecting on your own values and principles in relation to inclusion. Inclusive teachers believe that all children are important and deserve the best possible education and care. Additionally inclusive teachers believe that with high quality teaching and support all learners can achieve to a high level. They communicate this to their learners by creating a 'can-do' culture in their classrooms. This genuine commitment to both education and care is critical because it enables teachers and other educators to focus on children's holistic needs rather than solely their academic needs.

In order to develop an inclusive classroom you have a responsibility to model inclusive values. You need to demonstrate that you respect all children and adults in the setting. You need to provide a welcoming environment where parents and pupils feel a genuine sense of belonging. Parents should be provided with opportunities to express their own views and they should be empowered to influence policies and practices within the school. The learning environment should be designed to reflect a genuine affirmation and celebration of diversity, for example through displays which reflect positive images of various disabilities, sexualities and cultures. Classroom resources should challenge gender stereotypes and reflect a deep commitment to social and cultural diversity.

Behavioural issues present teachers with considerable challenges. However, resistance can invigorate teachers by energising us to re-think our own practices. Inclusive teachers continuously reflect on their practice and refine it to engage pupils in learning. They make opportunities to give learners a voice and they listen genuinely to their perspectives. They provide learners with opportunities to shape their learning experiences and they continuously seek to establish positive connections with their learners. Their practice is built around their learners and is constantly reviewed and re-shaped to meet the needs of different learners. Inclusive teachers experiment with new approaches. Their practice is never static but always in a state of flux because inclusion is viewed as a process rather than an end point.

All children need to experience a genuine sense of belonging. This is a critical element of inclusive practice. Additionally teachers should celebrate pupils' diversity. Diversity is neither something which should be hidden nor ridiculed. It is a positive, energising force which should be harnessed to improve learning and teaching for all pupils. Additionally all pupils have a right to be taught in a supportive environment where they are able to make mistakes without fear of ridicule from peers or adults. An inclusive ethos will prevail in classrooms where there is evidence of much collaborative learning taking place. Pupils should be taught to understand that they can all play a part in supporting each other to succeed and that at various times everyone will benefit from being supported. A classroom environment, which encourages competition, is not inclusive nor is it healthy. This will serve only to create winners and losers and the losers are often those with SEN (Cole, 2005).

Your learners will develop in different directions. Some learners thrive in academic areas, whilst some excel at sports or others have strengths within creative and performing arts. As an inclusive teacher it is your role to find the strengths within each child and to celebrate these. This will undoubtedly have a positive impact on pupils' self-concepts and their self-esteem. In inclusive classrooms educators and learners are partners in the learning process. There are no hierarchies and learning is facilitated through a process of mutual support and collaboration. Inclusive educators aim to develop within learners a sense of confidence and focus on making pupils feel positive about their efforts. All achievements are recognised and celebrated irrespective of how small they may appear to be.

Inclusive classrooms are warm, friendly and full of fun and laughter. Pupils do not learn if they are intimidated, stressed and anxious, or made to feel that they are worthless. Unfortunately the standards agenda places significant value on pupils' academic development as school effectiveness is dependent on high achievements in relation to a set of narrow performance indicators. This creates an education system which effectively fails those learners who are unable to demonstrate achievement in the dominant sense. The standards agenda erects barriers to learning, participation and achievement (Lloyd, 2008) and the education system marginalises those learners who are neither capable of nor interested in demonstrating academic excellence (Goodley, 2007). In this respect inclusion as a policy agenda has tended to act as a normalising, disciplinary force (Armstrong, 2005) which uncritically assumes that all learners are able to achieve the same academic standards.

Teachers should celebrate achievement across the full breadth of the curriculum. A child with Asperger syndrome may learn slowly to play co-operatively with his/her peers. In terms of achievement this might be outstanding for that particular child. However, achievements of this kind do not register on school performance tables. Despite this, it might well be a significant achievement for a child with autistic spectrum disorder (ASD) and should be celebrated and rewarded.

Inclusive schools do not seek to normalise learners. Children with ASD may have no desire to play co-operatively with their peers or wish to carry out group tasks. They may prefer to work or play alone. These learners should not be forced to conform to the demands of a normalising society. Systems within schools and classrooms therefore need to be sufficiently flexible to cater for the needs of all learners. Some learners with SEND may not be able to sit through a ten-minute whole class session or be able to sustain concentration on one task for the duration of a lesson. Others may need additional support within lessons or extra resources to help them access the learning. You might need to develop different boundaries of acceptable behaviour for individual learners and be willing to experiment with various lesson structures which best support the needs of pupils with very specific needs. It is clear that one uniform set of rules for a whole class, or indeed school, may not be the best way of developing an inclusive ethos.

Highly positive and secure relationships with all learners are evident in inclusive class-rooms. Take time to find out what their interests are and take account of these during the planning process. Consult with pupils about their education and genuinely listen to their views. Challenge all forms of discrimination including bullying and harassment. If children feel upset or rejected then they will not feel included. Teachers have a statutory duty to keep children safe and all forms of bullying should be challenged.

Identifying barriers and making learning challenges feasible

The Equality Act protects pupils with disabilities from direct or indirect discrimination and every attempt must be made to help pupils to overcome barriers to learning, partici-pation and achievement. This should be done by adapting tasks, resources and levels of support to enable learners with SEND to succeed.

REFLECTIVE TASK

Consider the following examples and how a pupil may be excluded from participation if they are unable to:

- see the interactive whiteboard;
- hear the teacher;
- read a text or book;
- access the computer;
- contribute in a talk session.

Add further examples to the list given above and consider how these barriers may be reduced. How could these barriers be addressed to maximise pupils' achievements in lessons?

Developing learner-friendly environments

Ofsted has identified specific criteria to enable schools to evaluate their practice in rela-tion to inclusion. According to Ofsted (2010) effective provision includes the following characteristics:

- a clear focus on outcomes for children and young people rather than simply ensuring that provision is in place;
- rigorous monitoring of pupils' progress;
- early interventions to address gaps in pupils' knowledge and skills;
- careful monitoring of the impact of interventions on the progress of learners;
- high aspirations for all pupils;
- a clear determination to enable children and young people to be as independent as possible;

- a clear focus on ensuring that the quality of teaching is high;
- ensuring that pupils are not identified as having SEND because they are falling behind as a result of weak teaching.

Inclusion in practice can be addressed through:

- choosing appropriate learning objectives;
- modifying teaching styles;
- building in access strategies to remove potential barriers to learning.

Choosing appropriate learning objectives

When planning for learners with special educational needs and/or disabilities your starting point must be what your learners already know and can do. This knowledge will come from accurate assessment information, much of which will be formative. There is sufficient flexibility within the National Curriculum (DfE, 2013) for teachers to select objectives from earlier or later year groups and some children may still need to work on developmental milestones within the Early Years Foundation Stage framework (DfE, 2012).

Sometimes it will be inappropriate for learners with SEND to work on the same learning objectives as their peers. In these circumstances you will take the decision that these learners need to focus on different learning objectives which more sharply address their individual needs. However, in other cases it is possible that learners with SEND may be able to work on the same learning objectives as their peers if appropriate access strategies are built into the task to enable them to access the learning. These might include access to additional support or additional resources. In other situations learners with SEND may be quite capable of working on the same area of learning as their peers but following objectives which are earlier or later in a progression sequence. It is also very important to remember that not all learners with SEND have cognitive difficulties – some may be very able.

PRACTICAL TASK   PRACTICAL TASK   **PRACTICAL TASK**   PRACTICAL TASK   **PRACTICAL TASK**

Identify a learning objective from the National Curriculum in mathematics for pupils in Year 2. Now identify an earlier objective in the National Curriculum which links to the objective you have identified. Share your ideas with a colleague. Now repeat this task for English.

You need to be flexible in your approach and take decisions about which learning objectives are suitable for individual learners and which are inappropriate. However, in all situations you should maintain consistently high expectations of all learners in your class. Learners with special educational needs and/or disabilities may have an individual education plan which identifies clear learning targets which they need to focus on. These should have been negotiated with the parents or carers and the child and other agencies where applicable. You should aim to take these learning goals into account when you plan for learners with additional needs. These should be additional and different from targets which you identify as part of your normal classroom differentiation.

Learners with SEND may work on:

- the same objectives as the rest of the class, providing adaptations are made;
- linked learning objectives which follow the same theme which the rest of the class are following but a stage (or several stages) earlier or later in a sequence of progression;
- distinct and different learning where pupils work on their individual targets alongside others in the classroom;
- alternative work.

Modifying teaching styles and approaches

Some learners with SEND will need different resources to enable them to access the learning, thus removing barriers to participation and achievement. The nature of the adaptation will clearly depend on the individual needs of each child. As a general rule you should aim to make the learning experience as multi-sensory as possible by providing learners with as many opportunities to learn using their senses. Inclusive teachers use visual, auditory and kinaesthetic teaching strategies in their lessons to meet the needs of all learners.

CASE STUDY

A multi-sensory approach

Jabina struggles to identify phonemes from their corresponding graphemes. This is impeding her progress in blending phonemes for word recognition because she often cannot say specific phonemes in words. Her teacher made a set of graphemes from sandpaper, enabling Jabina to trace over the graphemes at the same time as being introduced to the phonemes. This was reinforced in a range of ways including tracing graphemes on the floor, in the air and in glitter in response to a given phoneme.

REFLECTIVE TASK

Can you think of other teaching strategies that would support Jabina to make correct correspondences between phonemes and graphemes?

PRACTICAL TASK   PRACTICAL TASK   PRACTICAL TASK   PRACTICAL TASK   PRACTICAL TASK

In English you are focusing on teaching sentence structure and sentence punctuation in a Year 1 class. You have a child with learning and cognition difficulties and he finds it difficult to understand the concept of a sentence. Discuss with a colleague how you might adapt your teaching for this child to enable him to understand sentence structure and sentence punctuation.

Developing access strategies

Simple access strategies can enable learners with SEND to access the same learning that the rest of the class are doing. Some suggestions that you might try are listed below:

- pre-teach pupils before the lesson so that they can make good progress in the lesson;
- make good use of ICT, for example a child may struggle with writing but may be able to use a word processor to record their ideas. They might be able to record their ideas digitally on a sound file or you might be able to purchase specialist software which can convert speech to text;
- allow learners to work with a TA;
- allow learners to work with a study buddy;
- find alternative ways of recording ideas. If writing is a barrier to learning, the pupils might be able to present evidence of their learning through making a film, taking photographs of their learning or using pictorial images;
- ensure that pupils have access to resources that will support them in their learning, e.g. working walls, spellings, number squares, number lines, word mats, grapheme cards and dictionaries.

This is not an exhaustive list and you will be able to add to it to cater for the specific needs of the learners in your class. The National Curriculum statutory framework for inclusion (DfE, 2013) states that schools have a statutory duty to set suitable learning challenges, respond to pupils' diverse learning needs and overcome potential barriers to learning and assessment. The strategies suggested above will help you to achieve these duties. Some barriers to learning can be attitudinal. Staff and other pupils may have negative attitudes towards learners with SEND. This will certainly not contribute to an inclusive culture. Some barriers may be physical, such as a child needing a specially designed chair or special pair of scissors to enable them to complete a task. Some barriers may be organisational and it is the responsibility of the school to ensure that SEN provision (staffing) is appropriately deployed throughout the school to enable learners with SEND to have equality of opportunity.

CASE STUDY

Adaptive technologies

Sadie has limited verbal communication. Other children experience difficulties communicating with Sadie and are unwilling to play with her. The school has contacted the speech and language therapist who now comes into the school on a regular basis. One of the devices recommended was a USB keyboard overlay. The TA was asked to attend a training course so that she could learn how to use the equipment. The equipment was programmed using overlays of pictures that when pressed omitted simple vocabulary. Sadie was able to use the equipment to communicate and express simple choices. In addition the equipment generated interest from the other pupils in the class who also wanted to work with it.

REFLECTIVE TASK

Think of ways in which technological modifications could be used to aid other pupils with additional needs.

PRACTICAL TASK   PRACTICAL TASK   PRACTICAL TASK   PRACTICAL TASK   PRACTICAL TASK

When you are next on placement discuss with the ICT co-ordinator or the ICT technician the range of adaptive technologies available to support learners with SEN.

Creating an inclusive environment is not always easy and requires careful detailed planning. There is no single approach because all pupils are different. However, the responsibility does not lie with the classroom teacher alone and in inclusive schools all colleagues, parents, pupils and external professionals work collaboratively to find ways of addressing barriers to learning, participation and achievement.

PRACTICAL TASK   PRACTICAL TASK   PRACTICAL TASK   PRACTICAL TASK   PRACTICAL TASK

In your placement school speak to the SENCO about the range of people who support learners with SEN and try to find opportunities to shadow at least one of these professionals.

REFLECTIVE TASK

Consider which aspects would contribute to your ideal learner-friendly environment for a target group of pupils or an individual pupil with specific needs.

Do all schools have inclusive learner-friendly environments?

People assume that schools are purpose built for the number, age and type of pupils they educate. However, in practice you will find that this is not the case and environments have to be adapted to make them as learner-friendly as possible.

Inclusive environments should include the elements of good classroom practice. For example, they should be:

- comfortable;
- welcoming;
- well-lit;
- friendly – not stifling;
- spacious;
- calm;
- well-organised.

Developing an inclusive, learning-friendly environment

An inclusive, learning-friendly environment should benefit the *whole* school community.

Children

In inclusive environments children gain confidence and have high self-esteem. They are able to work independently and develop creativity which benefits learning across the curriculum. They feel able to ask for help and their attempts to produce work and answer questions are valued and not ridiculed. In inclusive schools pupils' self-respect grows as children gain confidence to work independently and they learn to communicate better with others both inside and outside the school. Learners develop respect for others and value achievements made.

Teachers

With collaboration, teachers expand their knowledge and understanding of how to meet the needs of learners with special educational needs and/or disabilities. These inclusive teachers seek further professional training to update their knowledge and skills and they value a multi-disciplinary approach. They challenge stereotypical responses and become more creative as they search for ways of addressing pupils' diverse learning needs. Inclusive teachers seek feedback from parents and carers as well as pupils and colleagues. They are prepared to modify their practices to cater for pupils' individuality. Effective teachers can empathise with pupils and they are able to develop new ideas and techniques. In addition they are willing to try new technologies to address pupils' needs. Inclusive teachers make very effective use of classroom support, helpers and outside agencies as they develop their inclusive practice. They value the very small steps that some children take and they celebrate these so that the children begin to feel important and develop a feeling of self-worth.

Parents

Many parents of pupils with SEND start to take an active role in their children's education. These parents welcome the fact that their children are valued and made to feel welcome in a supportive learning environment. Many become involved and contribute willingly to reviews of progress. However, some parents may be reluctant to develop home–school partnerships and schools will need to find ways of reaching out to these parents. Above all a sense of pride in their child's progress must develop.

Parents have told us that good, honest and open communication is one of the important components of building confidence and good relationships. Face-to-face communication with parents, treating them as equal partners with expertise in their children's needs is crucial to establishing and sustaining confidence. Where things go wrong, the root causes can often be traced to poor communication between school, local authority and parent.

(Lamb, 2009: 3)

The community

By fostering a community approach better relationships develop and the pride felt by many children, parents and teachers spreads into the wider community. People from wider social backgrounds are willing to participate and become involved in the activities of a school. They may also work with individual pupils.

CASE STUDY

Access strategies

Michael was made redundant. He had previously worked as a joiner. The teacher approached him to see if he would be interested in working with small groups and individuals, supporting them to use tools for design and technology. Initially Michael was reluctant but after meeting with other helpers in the school he realised that he had a lot to offer. He was able to go into school one afternoon a week and support small groups of children making buggies. Michael was able to introduce the children to new skills and the teacher valued his knowledge and support. Michael further considered the difficulty of holding and cutting wood and was able to make simple modifications to the task to enable a learner with motor neurone problems to access the activity. He devised a cutting sleeve to hold the saw so that the child was able to control it.

REFLECTIVE TASK

- What are the advantages of developing community links to support learners with SEN?
- Think of adjustments that you could make to enable such a learner to access practical activities, such as sewing, cooking and painting.

Barriers to inclusion

This section briefly examines the barriers to inclusion and the facilitators of effective inclusion.

PRACTICAL TASK   PRACTICAL TASK   PRACTICAL TASK   PRACTICAL TASK   PRACTICAL TASK

Read the following quotes from teachers and discuss the key barriers and facilitators to effective inclusion.

We've got a teacher who sees his job as just to teach and get them through the SATs. He expects every child to conform and that is against inclusion. You can't have a child coming in with behaviour problems and the teacher not recognising these problems. It is the difference between – if there is a problem in the classroom ... blaming the child, or thinking ... what can I do to make this easier? Or what is wrong with my environment if I am not meeting this child's needs. That is a massive difference. Teaching styles have a lot to do with it. Inclusion is harder if you just want them all to sit there quietly. (Fran)

It will be interesting to see how his next teacher copes because he won't continue what we have started. I don't think he will last very long. The child will meet fire with fire. He will not tolerate his behaviour – he likes them all to be quiet! (Joan)

It is about everyone knowing the children, not just the support staff being palmed off with the low abilities and that's what it amounts to. We know of support staff in our school who are writing review reports about the children because the teacher does not know them. We are paid for that responsibility. I heard a teacher say she was not paid to 'baby-sit' children who she felt were incapable of learning. She just sends them out of class with a member of support staff. Some teachers are not capable of writing reports on children because they simply do not know them. (Bev)

(Glazzard, 2011)

When you are next in school take some time to notice the attitudes of different members of staff towards pupils with specific needs. You may hear conversations in the staffroom or you will observe interactions between adults and pupils around the school, in the playground and in classrooms.

REFLECTIVE TASK

Discuss the following questions with a colleague.

- How can teacher attitude impact on the creation of inclusive environments?
- Should all pupils work on the same learning objective at the same time?
- How can the learning environment be designed to demonstrate a commitment to inclusion?

A SUMMARY OF **KEY POINTS**

➢ **Learning objectives may need to be modified to meet the needs of all learners.**

➢ **The same learning can be accessible to all children with the implementation of carefully considered and appropriate access strategies.**

➢ **The careful consideration of multi-sensory approaches can effectively address the needs of all learners.**

➢ **Positive attitudes by staff in relation to inclusive education are conducive to positive outcomes for all learners.**

MOVING *ON* > > > > > > MOVING *ON* > > > > > > MOVING *ON*

In your placement school take the opportunity to reflect upon access strategies used by teachers across the curriculum. Consider the following points in relation to one specific pupil.

- What are the barriers to learning?
- What access strategies are in place to support the child?
- Are these access strategies effective?

Consider additional strategies to support and enhance the learning of this child.

REFERENCES REFERENCES **REFERENCES** REFERENCES **REFERENCES** REFERENCES

Armstrong, D. (2005) 'Reinventing "inclusion": New Labour and the cultural politics of special education', *Oxford Review of Education*, 31(1), 135–51.

Cole, B. (2005) 'Good faith and effort? Perspectives on educational inclusion', *Disability and Society*, 20(3), 331–44.

Department for Education (DfE) (2012) *Development Matters in the Early Years Foundation Stage*, London: DfE.

Department for Education (DfE) (2013) *The National Curriculum in England: Key Stages 1 and 2 Framework Document*, London: DfE.

Glazzard, J. (2011) 'Perceptions of the barriers to effective inclusion in one primary school: voices of teachers and teaching assistants', *Support for Learning*, 26(2), 56–63.

Goodley, D. (2007) 'Towards socially just pegagogies: Deluzoguattarian critical disability studies', *International Journal of Inclusive Education*, 11(3), 317–34.

Lamb, B. (2009) *Lamb Inquiry: Special Educational Needs and Parental Confidence*, Annesley: DCSF Publications.

Lloyd, C. (2008) 'Removing barriers to achievement: a strategy for inclusion or exclusion?', *International Journal of Inclusive Education*, 12(2), 221–36.

Ofsted (2010) *The Special Educational Needs and Disability Review: A Statement is Not Enough*, Manchester: Ofsted.

FURTHER READING FURTHER READING **FURTHER READING** FURTHER READING

Ainscow, M., Booth, T. and Dyson, A. (2006) *Improving Schools, Developing Inclusion*, London: Routledge.

Armstrong, F. and Moore, M. (2004) *Action Research for Inclusive Education: Changing Places, Changing Practices, Changing Minds*, London: RoutledgeFalmer.

Knowles, G. (ed.) (2006) *Supporting Inclusive Practice*, London: David Fulton.

This is an excellent text. It is clear, concise and offers support and advice to practitioners. The book considers practical strategies to support a range of learning needs.

Nutbrown, C. and Clough, P. (2005) *Inclusion in the Early Years*, London: Sage.

Ross-Watt, F. (2005) 'Inclusion and the early years: from rhetoric to reality', *Child Care in Practice*, 11(2), 103–18.

Thomas, G. and Loxley, A. (2007) *Deconstructing Special Education and Constructing Inclusion*, Maidenhead: Open University Press.

Thomas, G. and Vaughan, M. (2004) *Inclusive Education: Readings and Reflections*, Maidenhead: Open University Press.

Topping, K. and Maloney S. (eds) (2004) *The RoutledgeFalmer Reader in Inclusive Education*, London: RoutledgeFalmer.

Warnock, M. (1978) *Special Educational Needs, Report of the Committee of Enquiry into the Education of Handicapped Children and Young People*, London: HMSO.

USEFUL WEBSITES USEFUL WEBSITES **USEFUL WEBSITES** USEFUL WEBSITES

http://www.csie.org.uk/resources/free.shtml

11
Practical strategies for supporting and teaching children with special educational needs and disabilities

Chapter objectives

By the end of this chapter you should be aware of:

- specific strategies to support learners with SEND;
- strategies for working with parents;
- strategies for working with other professionals.

Teachers' Standards

TS5: Adapt teaching to respond to the strengths and needs of all pupils

- know when and how to differentiate appropriately, using approaches which enable pupils to be taught effectively
- have a secure understanding of how a range of factors can inhibit pupils' ability to learn, and how best to overcome these
- demonstrate an awareness of the physical, social and intellectual development of children, and how to adapt teaching to support pupils' education at different stages of development
- have a clear understanding of the needs of all pupils, including those with special educational needs; those of high ability; those with English as an additional language; those with disabilities; and be able to use and evaluate distinctive teaching approaches to engage and support them

Introduction

The Code of Practice (DfE, 2014) makes it clear that schools should provide pupils with SEND access to high quality, differentiated teaching to meet their needs. The Code is explicit that the provision of additional interventions cannot compensate for lack of good quality teaching and therefore the suggested strategies offered in this chapter should be available to learners as part of a package of high quality, differentiated teaching. There is a clear focus within the Code on strengthening partnerships with parents and external agencies. Parents are expected to have more strategic influence in relation to the services which are available within communities and there is an expectation that parents and carers will be involved at school level in reviewing progress and setting targets. Parents will also be given more choice and will be able to make decisions about how to spend financial resources (DfE, 2014). Agencies represented from education, health and social care will be expected to work collaboratively in ways which are more effective and local agreements will be established to determine how agencies from different services will work together.

Specific strategies for supporting learners with SEND

The strategies suggested in this section should be offered to pupils as part of a package of entitlement which ensures that all pupils receive access to high quality teaching. It is important to emphasise that learners are individuals and respond differently to various strategies, even though they may share a common impairment. As a reflective teacher you will need to be prepared to use different strategies for different pupils. It is a case of trying out strategies and constantly evaluating their effectiveness with specific pupils. You will need to be prepared to adapt the strategies for different pupils and it is important to recognise the child rather than the label. Some pupils with autistic spectrum disorder (ASD) do not need to rely on visual timetables and therefore 'blanket' strategies should be avoided. Additionally, many of the strategies suggested in this section will be useful for all pupils, not just learners with SEND.

Need	Key characteristics	Useful strategies
Dyslexia	• Poor standard of written work compared to oral ability. • Unusual spellings of words. Unusual sequencing of letters/ words. • Sees blurred word shapes/ words moving around on the page. • Frequently loses their place when reading. • Reverses numbers and letters. • Has difficulty remembering simple sequences e.g. months of the year/ days of the week. • Makes frequent errors when copying. • Has low self-concept and motivation. • Poor organisation/time management. • Poor handwriting/reversals/badly formed letters. • Poor progress in reading. • May struggle with comprehension in reading – getting meaning from print. • Employs work avoidance tactics e.g. sharpening pencils/looking for books. • Easily distracted. • Excessively tired due to the amount of concentration required in tasks. • Lack of automaticity in reading/ writing.	• Raise ideas, content and effort. • Do not expose their weaknesses. • Do not make them read out loud. • Key vocabulary on display e.g. mathematical words/science words. • Use of mind maps to aid planning/ structuring of ideas. • Use of writing frames with prompts to support writing. • Active learning. • Break up text, e.g. leave spaces between paragraphs. • Use bullet points rather than continuous prose. • Keep sentence length to a minimum. • Give clear, concise instructions. • Present information visually using flow charts. • Use coloured paper, e.g. pastel/cream/ blue. • Keep lines left-justified with a ragged edge. • Use a clear font (size 12/14). • Ensure repetition of learning. Use word and language games. • Use coloured overlays where appropriate. • Teach the use of spell checking. • Use different methods of recording, not just writing. • Keep oral instructions short and clear. • Don't ask them to copy from the board – they find it hard to keep their place.

(Continued)

(Continued)

Need	Key characteristics	Useful strategies
		• Use a study buddy/scribe so that they do not always have to do the writing. • Give them a reading buddy in class. • Find other ways of recording learning other than writing – capture learning in photographs/films/ask them to do oral presentations. • Give short, clear visual or written instructions. • In mathematics give them access to a tables square to help them. They often struggle to remember times tables. • Change background colour on the interactive whiteboard. • Give them spell checkers or access to laptops in lessons to take away some of the pressure of writing. • Give them a dictaphone/iPad to record lessons. • Display graphemes, key words, and sequences e.g. days of the week/months. • Use off-white background on whiteboard or any paper used. • Use a rounded script e.g. Arial. • Represent information visually using concrete objects/photographs/pictures. • Provide whiteboards and magnetic letters. • Don't make children with dyslexia read out loud. • Don't expose their weaknesses. • Use other methods of recording such as photocopying work, video and photographs. • Provide prompts and tools, e.g. key words lists, spelling rules, alphabet cards. • Do lots of partner work and shared writing – swap partners around. • Repeat instructions, break them down. Give children time.

Need	Key characteristics	Useful strategies
Autistic spectrum disorder (ASD)	• Finds it difficult to look others in the eye. • Has difficulty dealing with others invading their space. • Has delayed speech. • Has difficulty understanding jokes or sarcasm. Things are taken literally. • May have difficulties with language.	• Ensure there is continuity in routine. Warn if it is to change. • Be consistent with rules and managing behaviour. • Use visual timetables. • Keep instructions simple and clear – repetition is needed. • Use visual symbols to give instructions.

	• Dislikes a change in routine. Needs structure and rules, e.g. might always need to go to bed at exactly 8.30pm. • Sensory sensitivity – light, colour, smell, touch, taste, sound. • Obsessions, e.g. love of trains • May have learning difficulties. • Fascination with signs. • Talking sounds like 'thunder'.	• Use the pupil's name and check their understanding of tasks. • Explain jokes and sarcasm. • Low arousal areas – limit visual disturbance. • Use headphones for sound reduction. • Maintain a predictable physical environment. • Clearly designated work areas. • Resources labelled clearly with words and pictures. • Clear daily/lesson routines. • Show them when an activity has finished. • Use picture exchange communication system (PECS).

Need	Key characteristics	Useful strategies
Attention deficit disorder (ADD) or attention deficit hyperactivity disorder (ADHD)	• May display impulsive behaviour. • Talks or calls out continuously. • Stands up and wanders around. • Lashes out verbally or physically. • May be easily distracted. • Task avoidance strategies. • Has poor social interaction. • Finds following instructions difficult. • Finds writing difficult. • Has limited concentration and listening skills. • Constantly fidgets.	• Use a consistent approach with routine and rules. • Praise even small achievements. • Provide opportunities for movement within the classroom, e.g. brain gym, responsibilities. • Use time out as a benefit rather than a sanction. • Give short, simple instructions. • Teach social skills. • Be realistic in the targets that you set. Make them short and achievable.

Need	Key characteristics	Useful strategies
Dyspraxia	• Appears clumsy and bumps into objects/people. • Has difficulty judging distances. • May find physical activity especially ball games difficult. • Appears unco-ordinated when running, jumping etc. • Has an immature use of equipment, e.g. pen, scissors etc. • Has difficulty pronouncing speech sounds. • Has limited concentration and listening skills. • Gets upset easily. • Becomes frustrated.	• Give clear, simple instructions. • Offer encouragement and praise achievements and effort. • Practise simple exercises to improve co-ordination. • Offer support in practical subjects.

Need	Key characteristics	Useful strategies
Moderate learning difficulties (MLD)	• Immature listening/attention skills. • Immature social skills. • Relies on friends and TAs to direct them in class. • Has a poor memory. • Has difficulty with basic literacy and numeracy. • Needs a high level of support in more independent tasks such as problem solving.	• Use a lot of praise and encouragement. • Provide TA support at the beginning and end of a lesson but encourage pupils to work independently where possible. • Simplify and differentiate tasks. • Provide a multi-sensory approach to learning. • Keep language simple where appropriate. • Make use of songs and rhymes to aid learning sequences. • Keep instructions short and concise. • Ask pupils to repeat instructions to check they have understood tasks. • Allow extra time for tasks when appropriate. • Monitor and record progress so that even the smallest achievements are recognised.

Need	Key characteristics	Useful strategies
Speech, language and communication needs (SLCN)	• Speech that is difficult for staff and other children to understand. • Struggles to say words or sentences and this can be very frustrating for them. • May not understand words that are being used, or the instructions they hear. • Difficulties knowing how to talk and listen to others in a conversation.	• Create a respectful, listening environment where you encourage turn-taking, kind and thoughtful behaviours. • Teach emotional literacy, strategies to recognise feelings. • Manage your language – use names, speak clearly and slowly. Give thinking time. • Use questioning carefully. • Introduce other forms of communication, e.g. photographs, symbols, signing. • Encourage discussion, e.g. teach debating skills.

Need	Key characteristics	Useful strategies
Stammering	• May struggle to pronounce words or may stutter. • May repeat words within a sentence. • Communication may not be fluent.	• Slow down your rate of speech but don't tell the child to slow down. • Allow them to speak at their own pace. • Use lots of pauses in your own speech to give the conversation a relaxed pace. • Ask one simple question at a time and give children time to answer. • Get down to the level of the child so that they can see they have your attention. • Don't interrupt or ask children to stop, slow down or to start again.

Need	Key characteristics	Useful strategies
Mutism	• The child may choose not to communicate with specific people although may communicate with others.	• Try to discover the cause of any anxieties and work on building up self-confidence by being very positive. • Give children opportunities to contribute without needing to talk. • Use objects, symbols and photographs to communicate. Give praise. • Encourage parallel play alongside confident speakers. • Allow children to use a whiteboard to communicate. • Set aside a 'safe area' which is calm and quiet where children can relax when anxiety starts to build up. • Provide children with opportunities to record their voice away from others – removing the anxiety caused by speaking in front of other people. • *Remember*: children with mutism can hear everything that is said so make sure everyone is always respectful around them.

Need	Key characteristics	Useful strategies
Behavioural, emotional and social difficulties (BESD)	• Children may be physically or verbally aggressive. • They may harm themselves or other children. • They may be anxious and suffer from depression. • They can seem very alone and withdraw from other people.	• Use a visual timetable to structure short periods of time. • Clearly display classroom rules. • Use timers. • If possible have a calm area in your classroom with fewer stimuli. • Use a 'praise book' and write in positives which have happened during the day – send it home. • Make an 'I can' book for the child to write down achievements. • If staff are available, develop 1:1 listening time for five minutes a day. • Go through the visual timetable – use it. • Give children an active role, or a 'job' to do. • Use non-verbal signals. • Use 'what should you be doing?' • Give children choice with a clear consequence – (refer to the rules). • Find positives, give specific praise. • Be consistent and clear. • Set realistic time targets, e.g. for sitting and concentrating.

Need	Key characteristics	Useful strategies
Visual impairment (VI)	Pupils with VI have different levels of severity.	• Use a font of at least 14 with a round script such as Arial when producing work for all children. • Make resources tactile and textured, e.g. make letter shapes out of sandpaper. • Make displays interactive by using textured materials. • Avoid glossy finishes to resources, e.g. laminated sheets. They can be very reflective. • Use an off-white background on the whiteboard and a bold clear font. • Make sure background and foreground are contrasting. Don't put words over the top of an illustration. • Use real objects and artefacts as much as possible in your teaching.

Need	Key characteristics	Useful strategies
Hearing impairment (HI)	Pupils with HI have different levels of severity.	• Always face the child when talking. • Speak slowly and pronounce your words carefully. • Sit the child close to you on the carpet. • Use concrete objects to make teaching 'real' where possible. • Use all the senses when teaching – a multi-sensory approach. • Use signing to help communication. Introduce to all the class to help reduce the need for too much noise. • Use a visual timetable to help structure the day. • Think about background noise and reduce where possible.

(Drawn from: Buttriss, J. and Callander, A. (2008) *A–Z of Special Educational Needs for Every Teacher*, (2nd edn), London: Optimus Education.)

Strategies to support pupils on the autistic spectrum

- Be flexible.
- Agree on a signal for the pupil to use if they are becoming anxious or in need of 'quiet time'.
- Develop a visual timetable for the whole class.
- Prepare pupils for changes to their normal routine, e.g. by presenting a timeline of key events during the day and marking the change.
- Provide an area which is calm and low in stimuli.
- Provide opportunities for the pupil to have quiet time during the day.
- Simplify your language – give clear instructions.
- Use the pupil's name at the start of an instruction/question.
- Mark their page so they know precisely where to start writing.
- Break down tasks into smaller 'chunks' using visual step-by-step cues.
- Avoid sarcasm.

- Use pre-teaching.
- Use over-learning.
- Use an individual and immediate reward system.
- Directly teach social skills through modelling.
- Give clear instructions, e.g. how many questions to answer, how many sentences to write, how long to listen.
- Use a timer to support completion of tasks.
- Never insist that a pupil looks at you.
- Structure playtimes and dinner times.
- Use clear success criteria in lessons so that a pupil can tick them off once they have been achieved.
- Use the child's strengths and interests as a starting point for planning.
- Support teaching through visual strategies, e.g. using models and images and a range of visual cues.
- Bring conversations back to the point when the child diverts from it.
- Teach other children about autism and teach them how they can support the child.
- Keep a daily home–school diary.
- Use visual cues on cards to give the child commands.
- Build interests and obsessions into the daily timetable (within reason!).
- Start each new lesson with a clean sheet! Don't dwell on what has happened.

Strategies to support pupils with general reading difficulties

- Pre-teach: read a story to a child before a shared reading experience with the whole class.
- Provide an individualised multi-sensory phonics programme but at a slower pace (using magnetic letters for word building; writing graphemes and words in sand, salt, sugar, glitter, etc.). Focus on grapheme–phoneme correspondences first and reinforce this in a multi-sensory way. Then focus on blending and segmenting.
- Paired reading: pair able/less able readers (taking turns to read).
- Reading together in pairs (reading at the same time).
- Reading Recovery: 1:1 sessions with a specialist-trained teacher.
- Use pause, prompt, praise (PPP) when they reach a word they cannot read straight away.
- Some children need further intervention on rhyme awareness, auditory and visual discrimination and awareness of syllables.
- Develop a love of stories: share 'real' books with them together.

Strategies to support pupils with writing difficulties

- Alphabet mats on tables.
- Key word mats on tables.
- Jumbled sentences: put a separate word on each card and ask the child to read the words and arrange the cards together to make a sentence. Use when the child is attempting to write a sentence by asking them to think of and say the sentence out loud. The teacher writes each word on a separate card and then the child orders the cards to make a sentence, then copies the sentence.
- Dictation: dictate sentences within the child's phonic knowledge (daily).
- Paired writing: less able and more able writers work together to compose a story. More able collects ideas from the other child and notes them down. Then the more able starts the writing process and gradually hands responsibility over to the other child.
- Patterned/repetitive writing: child follows a simple repetitive structure (as in the story of the *Little Red Hen*).
- Writing frames help children to structure their writing: planning frameworks, e.g. story boards, story maps, mind maps, flow charts.

- Give prompts: Where does the story take place? Who are the characters? What happens? (Could be part of a planning framework/writing frame.)
- Use word processors.
- Handouts on coloured paper.
- Access to simple dictionaries and spell checkers.
- Plan writing using mind maps.
- Sensitive marking, e.g. not over-focusing on spelling. Praise content.
- Clear success criteria: 'This is what I am looking for in your work' rather than asking them to think about too much at once.
- Pre-teach.
- Use a multi-sensory approach to writing, e.g. writing in coloured sand or with chalks.
- Visual strategies to support teaching – show them as well as tell them what to do.
- Short focused tasks with breaks.
- Active learning.

Strategies to support pupils with mathematical difficulties

- Access to number lines.
- Access to counting squares on tables/hundred squares.
- Access to concrete apparatus, e.g. counters, multilink cubes, counting rods, beads.
- Pre-teaching mathematical skills/concepts.
- Clear modelling of mathematical skills.
- Use a multi-sensory approach to number recognition/number formation, e.g. writing numbers in sand and tracing over sandpaper numbers.
- Use a developmental approach, e.g. knowing the stages in counting so that you can plan for next steps.
- Active teaching to provide hands-on learning.
- Make maths relevant to everyday life so that children can see its value, e.g. looking at mathematics in the environment.
- Build in outdoor mathematical opportunities – learning maths through the environment.
- Paired support: pair a less able with a more able pupil – children explain things better to each other.
- Present 'word problems' as pictures or let pupils solve word problems using concrete/practical apparatus, e.g. access to real coins to work out totals and change.
- Use visual representation where possible.
- Identify their misconceptions and work on these.

Additional strategies to manage children's behaviour

- Use proximal praise: 'Thank you Charlotte, I like the way you are listening. It shows me that you are learning'.
- Assertive language: 'John, you need to listen so that you can learn'; 'Emma, you need to put your hand up'.
- Gaining attention, e.g. when tidying away: ensure they are all listening to you; do not talk over the children; insist on silence, then give them instructions.
- Don't let low-level disruption build – 'nip it in the bud' immediately as soon as you see it happening. Don't ignore it, especially if it is repeated.
- Use instant rewards when you catch them being good. Instant rewards are better for children with challenging behaviour.
- When one child is talking or when an adult is talking, insist that they all listen.
- Tell them how to modify their behaviour – 'You need to sit still or you will sit on the thinking chair' – then make sure you follow it through.

- Use a thinking mat/chair.
- Provide a learning space which is distraction free.
- Time out: use a sand timer then ask them to explain what they have done wrong and how they intend to modify their behaviour or resolve disputes with their peers.
- Always use clear instructions.
- Clear classroom rules – continually remind them.
- Individual reward systems for pupils with challenging behaviour.
- Do not accept rudeness or direct challenges to your authority – you are in charge and they must accept this. If they are rude to you, explain why the behaviour is not acceptable and give them a warning: 'If you speak to me like that again X will happen' – follow school policy.
- Do not get into confrontations with children: do not debate with them about behaviour – they must accept what you say.
- Sometimes allow children the opportunity to choose their own rewards for good behaviour/work.
- Always ensure children understand why sanctions are being applied.
- Tactically ignore occasional incidents.
- Use non-verbal cueing, i.e. eye contact
- Use tactical diversion: ask them to do a job to re-focus them or ask them about their work to re-focus them.
- Ask direct questions: 'What is our rule for answering questions?'
- Choice/deferred consequence: state the consequence of a continued disruptive behaviour in the context of a 'choice' – 'If you choose to not do your work and waste time, I will need to talk to you at playtime'.
- Commands: 'John, *stop* that now'. Use sparingly because commands carry a danger that the child will not comply. This places you in a confrontational situation.
- Make learning active.
- Use short, focused tasks rather than one long task.
- Use praise.
- Find their strengths and capitalise on these.
- Separate the behaviour from the person.
- Give them achievable and focused clear behaviour targets which you negotiate with them.
- Use a reward system (might be individualised for the child).
- Involve the parents as much as possible and develop consistency between home and school.
- Build the curriculum around their interests.
- Ignore minor behaviour problems.
- Apply sanctions fairly: use time out/thinking spot, but make this reasonable and proportionate to the issue.
- Use an arrow to show how long a task will last.
- Use visual timetables so they can see what is happening in a day.
- Solution-focused approach – 'John, you need to …' – rather than focusing on what they have done wrong.
- Deal with issues in school and don't always tell parents unless it is serious.
- Don't allow the other children to victimise or tell tales – instead focus on how we can all help the child.
- Use circle of friends.
- Don't get into confrontations – think before you speak!
- **Think**: what is wrong with my teaching rather than with the child.

Lesson examples

- In a phonics lesson a child with poor motor control is asked to demonstrate his skills in segmenting words into their constituent graphemes by using magnetic letters on a small whiteboard, whilst his peers are asked to write the target words on whiteboards.
- The teacher introduces a new grapheme–phoneme in a phonics lesson. A child with dyslexia is introduced to the same grapheme–phoneme but is provided with a sandpaper version of the grapheme which he is allowed to trace over with his finger.

- In an English lesson a Year 1 class are learning to write simple sentences. They are asked to think of a sentence they want to write, say it, count the words and then write it down. Jasmin struggles with written sentence structure although she is able to say a sentence. The teacher asks Jasmin to verbalise her sentence and writes the words down for her. Each word is written onto a separate card. The cards are jumbled up and the teacher supports Jasmin to rearrange the cards into the correct order to make the sentence.

Reflection

How have the barriers to learning been removed in the above examples? Consider how the following resources or adaptations to lessons might be used to remove barriers to learning:

- spell checker;
- writing frame;
- key word mats;
- set of grapheme cards;
- number line or counting square;
- counters;
- visual timetable;
- distraction-free space;
- access to a TA;
- set of instructions to remind a pupil how to complete a task;
- altering the lesson structure.

Working with parents

Children never develop at a faster rate, both physically and mentally, than during their formative years. Much of this time will have been spent with parents or carers. Parents and carers hold key information regarding children's strengths, interests and anxieties. This information enables practitioners to build an early and accurate picture of a child. Parents and carers may have ideas and opinions and these must be taken into consideration. Most parents will have their child's best interests at heart and an effective partnership between parents and schools is an essential means through which to best support and develop a child.

Teachers may have a wealth of professional experience to support the child's development. However, it is vital that they do not dominate and over-rule the opinions of the parents and carers. Parents of children with SEN may be anxious about their child's progress. They need to be reassured that teachers are working with them in the best interests of their child. Essentially, it is vital that parents feel that their concerns are taken seriously and that teachers are doing their very best to enable their child to reach his/her full potential.

The value of strong parent–school partnerships will ensure that targets for a child's development are formulated and reviewed collaboratively. However, the strongest partnerships will ensure that this effective practice is embedded and reinforced by daily communication between home and school. This can effectively be addressed through the use of daily home–school diaries. Practitioners and parents or carers should use these diaries to communicate the child's strengths and thus communicate the child's achievements.

Communication which over-emphasises what the child cannot do may damage partnerships between home and school. This is pertinent in the case of a child with behavioural issues. Parents and carers do not need a daily diary entry regarding their child's challenging behaviour. They are already aware of this and are working with you to address relevant targets. As a trainee teacher you should therefore focus on identifying positive aspects of a child's development. There is of course a need to record the child's 'next steps' but these should be small, measurable, achievable, realistic and timed (SMART targets).

Think carefully about the way in which you communicate with parents. You will need to think about the clarity of your diary entries. It is important to avoid jargon, which some parents may not understand. You also need to communicate 'negatives' with extra care and attention. It is important to provide parents and carers with advice on how they can support their child to achieve the targets that have been set. Think about how you will communicate with parents who do not speak English or those who are illiterate. This may present you with considerable challenges and you may need additional support to address these issues. Some parents may be reluctant to work with you in partnership. They may be influenced by their own negative experiences of school and some parents may not value education. Additionally some parents may have problems in their own personal lives, which they may not wish to share with you. This can negatively impact on the school–parent partnership. These are real challenges facing professionals in school. Schools can encourage parent partnership but there is no obligation for parents to comply. Ultimately, whatever resistance you are faced with, you must do your best to meet the needs of all children. Your efforts to develop effective partnerships with parents and carers must be consistent and ongoing, even in the face of adversity. Practitioners must have high expectations for every child and with or without the support of parents they must endeavour to raise outcomes for all pupils.

Teachers/practitioners should ensure that they consult with parents or carers when making decisions about the appropriate level of intervention (graduated response) for their child. Practitioners should ensure that parents fully understand the graduated response and their role within the Code of Practice (DfE, 2014). Parents or carers should be involved at all stages of the graduated response and they should be consulted and advised about specific interventions that will be implemented to support the child. Parents or carers should be fully involved in monitoring and evaluating the success of interventions and the setting of new targets.

Barbara Cole's (2005) research with mother-teachers found that parents' experiences of raising a child with SEN influenced their professional thinking. The study found that these teachers developed greater empathy when working with parents of children with SEN after raising their own child. The mother-teachers became more conscious of the feelings of the parents. This research illustrates that personal experiences can impact on professional practice. These professionals became more acutely aware of the impact of their use of language on the parents. They became aware of how abrupt and 'clinical' they may have previously been when talking to parents.

Cole's research has implications for all teachers who work with children with SEN. Think carefully about what you say to parents and your tone of voice. Many parents of children with SEN may have experienced emotional challenges and will already be aware that their child finds some aspects of life challenging. Others may not be aware that their child is encountering any difficulties. You need to be sensitive in the way you communicate your concerns to the parent. It is crucial that you do not over-emphasise 'within-child' factors and that no blame is apportioned to either the child or the parent. You must keep an open mind. The child's difficulties could have arisen due to inappropriate 'teaching' either at home or school. The child's difficulties could have a biological origin but appropriate teaching can help to alleviate these. It is essential that you listen carefully to the parents' perspectives, concerns and opinions. It must be a two-way conversation and both parties must be fully included in the discussion. Joint problem solving is essential.

The teachers in Cole's study wanted their own children to be treated with dignity and care and this impacted on their professional practice. From this study it is evident that parents value the progress their child makes but they give equal value to the child's holistic needs. Reflect on your own attitudes towards children with SEND. Do you treat them all with care, dignity and respect? Consider the way you communicate with pupils and their parents or carers. Ensure that you are sensitive to their needs and feelings. Aim to develop their self-esteem and confidence.

Cole found that the mother-teachers often valued words of encouragement and 'an arm around the shoulder' (2005: 338). An open-door policy would clearly facilitate regular and meaningful communication between teachers and parents. It is not necessarily the amount of time offered to a parent that proves to be the most productive element of good communication. The key element is the ability to display genuine interest in a child and his or her parents and the ability to demonstrate a willingness to do your very best for a child. The little things really do matter. These may include:

- giving parents time when they need it;
- ensuring that there are opportunities for sharing incidental information;
- providing opportunities for parents to celebrate their child's achievements as well as sharing their concerns;
- sharing mutual successes and challenges;
- developing an honest and open professional relationship;
- developing an atmosphere of mutual respect.

Cole (2005) found that the mother-teachers needed to feel, above all else, that schools and teachers genuinely wanted and welcomed their child. This has vital and far-reaching implications for all teachers. The initial meeting with all parents and their child is the most important point of contact. Parents may be understandably judgemental at this stage. They are ready to embark on trusting you with the education and care of their child. This is a huge responsibility and privilege and you must understand the huge importance of your role. Always ensure that you:

- smile;
- listen;
- interact positively with the child;
- ask questions to create a better picture of the child's needs, interests and strengths;
- answer questions about your systems and routines, ensuring that the parent and child are also able to develop a clear picture of you and the school;
- assure parents that your systems are flexible to accommodate the specific needs of their child;
- invite the parent and child to visit the working classroom;
- introduce the parent and child to other practitioners in both the classroom and the wider school;
- provide opportunities for the child to interact with their peers and adults.

Consider how the visual environment of the school and the classrooms reflects diversity. A child who is a wheelchair user will feel empowered and have a sense of belonging when displays and resources reflect this aspect of daily life. In turn parents or carers will greatly value a school that totally embraces diversity through:

- positive attitudes towards *all* children and an atmosphere of mutual respect between all members of the school community;
- displays that celebrate diversity;
- teaching materials that reflect diversity;
- adaptations to meet the needs of all learners.

REFLECTIVE TASK

Consider the following questions:

- Do you value parental contributions?
- Do you think parents should be able to influence practice in schools?
- Do you believe that parents hold vital information about their child that would be useful for you to access?

PRACTICAL TASK   PRACTICAL TASK   PRACTICAL TASK   PRACTICAL TASK   PRACTICAL TASK

In your next placement research the strategies that your school has adopted to develop effective partnerships with parents and carers.

Working with other professionals

The Code of Practice (DfE, 2014) states that schools should involve specialists in cases where there is evidence to suggest that a child is making little or no progress, despite intervention. External specialists might involve (but are not limited) to the following:

- educational psychologists;
- Child and Adolescent Mental Health Services (CAMHS);
- specialist teachers – e.g. teachers for pupils with visual and hearing impairments;
- specialist support services – e.g. Communication and Interaction teams;
- therapists – e.g. speech and language therapists/physiotherapists;
- other colleagues from the National Health Services e.g. nurses/healthcare professionals/doctors;
- Social Care services.

A multi-agency approach can help to ensure that a child's holistic needs are addressed. In some cases pupils with SEND have multiple needs which extend beyond education and therefore a multi-agency approach is needed to address all of their needs. There are challenges associated with multi-agency collaboration which are worthy of consideration. These include:

- The need for a shared language of communication to ensure that everyone is clear about the messages which are being conveyed.
- The need to find time to allow all agencies to meet.

- The need for a clear understanding of the roles and responsibilities of each service.
- Professional respect: the importance of valuing the opinions of colleagues from different services.
- Sharing information: ensuring that agencies share vital and necessary information while also ensuring that confidentiality is protected at the same time.

REFLECTIVE TASK

Consider the following questions:

- Have you encountered any outside agencies on your placements?
- What was their role within school?
- Was the class teacher able to liaise with the external colleagues?

PRACTICAL TASK PRACTICAL TASK PRACTICAL TASK PRACTICAL TASK PRACTICAL TASK

In your next placement school, research which agencies are involved in supporting pupils with SEND and talk to external colleagues to find out what their roles and responsibilities are.

A SUMMARY OF **KEY POINTS**

➢ **The suggested strategies for supporting pupils with SEND in this chapter might not work for individual pupils in your class. You need to try various approaches with specific pupils to find out what works best for those learners.**

➢ **Building effective partnerships with parents and carers is essential and will give each child the optimum chance of experiencing success.**

➢ **Developing professional, respectful relationships with colleagues from external agencies will enable you to meet the needs of individual learners more effectively.**

RESEARCH SUMMARY RESEARCH SUMMARY RESEARCH SUMMARY RESEARCH SUMMARY

Desforges, C. and Abbouchaar, A. (2003) *The Impact of Parental Involvement, Parental Support and Family Education on Pupil Achievement and Adjustment: A Review of Literature, Brief No: 433*, Nottingham: DfES.

This research identifies a positive correlation between parental involvement and pupil achievement. The research found that levels of parental involvement are influenced by social class and children's attainment. In addition the research found that levels of parental involvement tend to diminish as children get older.

MOVING *ON* > > > > > > MOVING *ON* > > > > > > MOVING *ON*

Now that you have a bank of strategies for supporting learners with SEND, start to keep a log of different strategies you use for pupils with specific needs in your classes during your placements and evaluate their effectiveness.

REFERENCES REFERENCES **REFERENCES** REFERENCES REFERENCES REFERENCES

Cole, B. (2005) 'Good faith and effort? Perspectives on educational inclusion', *Disability and Society*, 20(3), 331–44.

Department for Education (DfE) (2014) *Special Educational Needs and Disability Code of Practice: 0 to 25 Years: Statutory Guidance for Organisations Who Work With and Support Children and Young People with Special Educational Needs and Disabilities*, London: DfE.

FURTHER READING FURTHER READING **FURTHER READING** FURTHER READING

Buttriss, J. and Callander, A. (2008) *A–Z of Special Educational Needs for Every Teacher*, (2nd edn), London: Optimus Education.

USEFUL WEBSITES USEFUL WEBSITES **USEFUL WEBSITES** USEFUL WEBSITES

http://www.autism.org.uk

http://www.nas.org.uk

http://www.bdadyslexia.org.uk

http://www.dyslexiaaction.co.uk

http://www.dyslexia.uk.com

http://www.livingwithadhd.co.uk

http://www.adhd.org.uk/

http://www.addiss.co.uk

http://www.dyspraxiafoundation.org.uk

http://www.rnib.org.uk/guidanceonteaching

http://www.scope.org.uk

http://www.gosh.nhs.uk

https://www.thecommunicationtrust.org.uk/

12
School-based training

Chapter objectives

By the end of this chapter you will

- understand inclusive practice;
- develop skills in SEN teaching;
- have the confidence to try new approaches;
- understand partnership working.

Teachers' Standards

This chapter addresses the following Teachers' Standards:

TS5: Adapt teaching to respond to the strengths and needs of all pupils

- know when and how to differentiate appropriately, using approaches which enable pupils to be taught effectively
- have a secure understanding of how a range of factors can inhibit pupils' ability to learn, and how best to overcome these
- demonstrate an awareness of the physical, social and intellectual development of children, and how to adapt teaching to support pupils' education at different stages of development
- have a clear understanding of the needs of all pupils, including those with special educational needs; those of high ability; those with English as an additional language; those with disabilities; and be able to use and evaluate distinctive teaching approaches to engage and support them

Introduction

Your extended placement in special needs provision can be exciting, enlightening and rewarding. It can challenge many ideas and beliefs you may already hold, and for some it can shape their future career. It can, however, give rise to anxiety and trepidation, often due to an unavoidable lack of experience or knowledge. But with the correct preparation and organisation this could be the highlight of all your placement experiences!

This chapter aims to give a practical, rather than a theoretical overview of your placement, as the theory of this will have been covered by your ITT provider, and it is often the practical experience about which trainees feel they need information and guidance.

Placement overview

The specific length and organisation of the placement will be determined by your ITT provider. It is designed to offer trainees a range of experiences which can help meet the

Teachers' Standards, especially those in relation to SEND. It is envisaged that trainees will be able to:

- learn skills and approaches that are not exclusive to special provision but can enhance all aspects of teaching and learning;
- learn about the wide range of professionals involved in specialist provision and the importance of team working;
- try out new approaches and be able to accept that outcomes are not always predictable, and that behaviour can play a big part in this.

This placement may be designed to take place in the middle or near the end of the ITT course, so that trainees already have substantial mainstream experience, have had taught input in relation to SEND, and are able to make links between theory and practice in order to assess their own learning.

The theory behind the practice

Your ITT provider should provide taught input prior to undertaking the placement on themes such as:

- development and diversity;
- areas of need set out in the SEN Code of Practice (DfE, 2014);
- classroom management and partnerships.

These themes should provide you with the knowledge and theory you require in order to complete a successful SEN practice. Content may include the following.

Development and diversity

- Inclusion – the individual and the environment
- Inclusive planning and assessment of the curriculum
- Overview of the inclusion statement
- Planning
- Removing barriers for disabled pupils
- Understanding key aspects of the Equality Act 2010

Areas of need set out in the SEN Code of Practice

- Overview of cognition and learning needs
- Learning and teaching for pupils with dyslexia
- Speech, language and communication
- The particular needs of pupils with an ASD
- Behavioural, emotional and social difficulties
- Planning for pupils with behavioural, emotional and social difficulties

Classroom management and partnerships

- Creating an inclusive learning environment
- Managing pupil groupings
- Working in partnership with parents/carers
- Working with other adults in the class

- Working in partnership with pupils
- Partnerships with outside agencies

The new Code of Practice covers children and young people from 0 to 25 years, to facilitate successful transitions. There is a greater emphasis on obtaining the views of children and young people, especially in decision-making processes. There is to be joint planning and commissioning of services to ensure close co-operation between education, health services and social care.

Statements will be replaced by an EHC Plan (Education, Health and Care Plan), which includes preparation for adulthood, including employment, independent living and participation in society.

The definition of SEN remains the same.

A focus on practice

The main objective of this chapter is to help you put theory into practice, to help you understand the practicalities of your time in a SEN placement and to help you fulfil the Teachers' Standards.

Understanding inclusive practice

Inclusion in education involves:

- Valuing all students and staff equally.
- Increasing the participation of students in, and reducing their exclusion from, the cultures, curricula and communities of local schools.
- Restructuring the cultures, policies and practices in schools so that they respond to the diversity of students in the locality.
- Reducing barriers to learning and participation for all students, not only those with impairments or those who are categorised as 'having special educational needs'.
- Learning from attempts to overcome barriers to the access and participation of particular students to make changes for the benefit of students more widely.
- Viewing the difference between students as resources to support learning, rather than as problems to be overcome.
- Acknowledging the right of students to an education in their locality.
- Improving schools for staff as well as for students.
- Emphasising the role of schools in building community and developing values, as well as in increasing achievement.
- Fostering mutually sustaining relationships between schools and communities.
- Recognising that inclusion in education is one aspect of inclusion in society. (Booth, 2011)

REFLECTIVE TASK

Looking back at your previous school experiences, what inclusive approaches did the teacher/school offer? Did it work well?

While it is vitally important that all schools are inclusive, and that pupils with SEN and disabilities should be able to access mainstream education through appropriate training, strategies and support, we all need to be realistic and realise that this is not always an option.

Special needs provision is often the most viable option for some pupils, but inclusion must not be taken for granted, as it can be just as difficult to achieve as it is in a mainstream school.

Inclusion can be hard work! Consider a class of eight pupils in a special school. The school caters for all aspects of SEN and disabilities, and there is full inclusion in the sense that all classes have a wide range of abilities and needs. But what about the planning? What about the environment? What about the resources? What about the delivery? All these and much more have to be inclusive, and this may be one of your greatest challenges. This, however, is where pre-placement visits become beneficial, as having first-hand experience of inclusive practice is the best way to learn. Inclusion will therefore be covered again in the section on extended placements below.

Case Study

Whilst involved in pre-placement theory, a trainee undertook a short task with her peers concerning inclusion. The task was for the trainees to discuss and record the feelings they would experience if they were to be included/excluded in an activity.

The trainee was very interested and often surprised at the responses, and how this gave an insight into the perceptions of her peers. Therefore, with this in mind she decided to conduct this task with some of the pupils at her placement school. She had to devise appropriate ways of doing this (e.g. using feelings cards, photos, etc.) but she found it a very beneficial exercise. Not only did it give her an insight into how the pupils felt, but it also helped her during her extended placement when she had to consider an inclusive environment.

Organisation of your placement

Wherever possible it is recommended that trainees should be paired with other trainees for special school placements. This could be within the classroom or the wider school. This offers mutual support, as trainees have the opportunity to observe each other, share experiences and plan and evaluate together.

Schools normally appoint a lead mentor to co-ordinate the placement, who ideally should be a member of the leadership team. They will be responsible for ensuring a coherent and successful placement, including the day-to-day organisation of the placement. A mentor should also be identified, most importantly as a 'critical friend' but also as a point of reference for information about the school.

The class/group teacher along with the placement co-ordinator will have responsibility for planning, monitoring and supporting the trainee's teaching activities. They are also the first point of call for information concerning individual pupils, and will also have a clear overview on many aspects relating to an individual child, e.g. medical concerns and history.

The placement should give you the opportunity to complete study tasks, prepare learning materials and engage in discussions with a range of professionals. The placement may also include a visit to a linked school/mainstream provision and a visit to a setting providing for a different area of need.

Pre-placement visits

You are armed with your theory and knowledge – so this is the start of putting it into practice! The first visit you make to any new school can be daunting, and for many of you this may be your first experience of a special needs provision. Initial reactions often include:

> *'It's so different to a mainstream school.'*
> *'It's not as different as I thought it would be!'*
> *'There seems to be a lot more movement and noise.'*
> *'What a lot of equipment!'*
> *'What a lovely atmosphere!'*

The specific needs of the pupils will inevitably depend on the school or setting but expecting the unexpected is probably a good motto to start the placement with!

Pre-placement visits are the time to gather information and orientate your way around the school. It is very beneficial if your placement co-ordinator is available during these visits – make use of them.

The layout of the school may be quite different to what you are used to in terms of both physical and human resources. The school may have a hydrotherapy pool and all the resources to make it accessible such as hoists. There may be physiotherapy, occupational therapy, speech and language therapy, a medical team, light and sound, soft play and, of course, classrooms! It will often seem that children are coming and going to these areas in a continuous stream – and they often are. But because of detailed planning and extreme timetabling these actions have very little impact on the teaching and learning within the school. Try to acquaint yourself with all these different areas as this will make it easier for when you are shadowing a child or meeting professionals for discussions.

Within your given classroom or area familiarise yourself as far as possible with the 'housekeeping' aspect, as well as with aspects related to teaching and learning. Many SEN classrooms have designated bathrooms/hygiene areas where some pupils will be taken on a timetabled basis and some will have free access. Some may also have their own light and sound, or 'chill out' room which will have very deliberate functions relating to the curriculum – not for hiding in (you or the pupils!). Snack time can play an extremely useful role for the pupils as it encourages independence, turn taking, communication, social skills and food preparation skills, and how it is organised and how long it can take can vary greatly dependent on the pupils' needs.

Areas such as cloakrooms and playgrounds can often be specific to the class, and require a much higher staffing level than those in mainstream. Remember that pupils will probably arrive by school transport and this in itself can be a major operation at the start and finish of the school day. Add to this the logistics of making sure that all pupils reach designated areas at the correct time (e.g. the hydrotherapy pool) and you can begin to see that there is far more to take into account on this placement than perhaps on any other!

You will also notice higher than average staffing levels, both in the classrooms and in the school in general. If your experience is mainly mainstream with a 1:20 (or more) ratio, it can often feel busy. Do not feel intimidated! Support assistants are an excellent asset, and often, due to the nature of their duties, get to know the pupils very well and can be invaluable to you when you are assessing a pupil.

During your pre-visits it is also helpful if you are given timetables, details of the pupils, school documents and prospectuses, and schedules for individual pupils. Try to have discussions with other professionals specifically in relation to school protocols, e.g. relating to absence. Familiarise yourself with names of staff with a significant responsibility and make sure you obtain a map of the school.

It is also beneficial for you to see schemes of work, examples of planning, methods of assessment, resource provision and individual education plans. As some pupils can find it difficult to relate to new people in their life, especially when they don't see them every day, it can be a good idea to create your own 'passport' to leave with the class. This could include photos (especially ones of you 'off duty' such as on a day out) as they will find this far more interesting than your teacher 'persona'. Include short generic personal details and maybe some of the things you are hoping to do with them (pictures/photos if possible).

But most of all enjoy these visits! Immerse yourself as much as possible into the life of the school and learn as you go. Remember you are an asset to a busy teacher, and while it may be difficult for them to talk to you within a hectic school day, they will be more than happy to help their new 'apprentice' settle in.

PRACTICAL TASK   PRACTICAL TASK   **PRACTICAL TASK**   PRACTICAL TASK   **PRACTICAL TASK**

Can you gather information and timetables in order to track one pupil through the school day? How will the logistics of this impact on teaching and learning?

Extended placement

Introduction

If all your previous visits have gone to plan, then you should be ready and hopefully excited about your extended placement. By this point you should be acquainted with the general organisation and layout of the school, and have begun to get to know the teacher, staff and pupils in your class/group.

Classroom organisation

As you are now no doubt aware, a special needs classroom/area/provision is a very busy place with little or no 'down time'. It can be challenging both mentally and physically for all staff members, and no amount of planning or organisation can foresee some of the problems you may encounter, although along with team working, they can go a long way to making things much easier.

Morning routine

You will be familiar with the morning routine within mainstream schools which ensures that teaching and learning can begin immediately, but there is often more to consider within a special school setting. If you are in a class with pupils who have various needs, such as cognitive, physical, communication or sensory needs, you will need to consider the resources that are needed to overcome barriers to learning, participation and achievement. Many teachers will devise rotas so that all staff know exactly what and who they are responsible for. Communication with team members is vital within a setting such as this, but with time at a premium, effective and clear written instructions and rotas accessible to all staff are an excellent way of achieving this.

PRACTICAL TASK PRACTICAL TASK **PRACTICAL TASK** PRACTICAL TASK **PRACTICAL TASK**

Try to collect examples of written notes that teachers give to support staff to enable them to carry out their roles and responsibilities.

Some pupils may need large pieces of equipment prepared in advance of sessions, e.g. standers and hoists, and these should be checked to ensure they are in working order, have all the necessary parts and are clean and fit for purpose. Ensure that pupils using this equipment are still included as part of the group – this may involve some rearrangement of furniture.

Other pupils may need smaller more specific resources such as pencil grips, scissors attached to a block or prompt cards and these must also be in place to ensure that the child can participate fully in the learning experience. Ensuring that all resources are available and in place at the start of lessons will enable you to focus fully on the pupil during the lesson.

The physical layout of the classroom is very important and can vary from day to day or even lesson to lesson. As mentioned above inclusion is the key, and no matter the children's needs, abilities or behaviour, they must all be included within each lesson. However, this needs careful consideration and could involve something as simple as moving chairs to allow a wheelchair user the independence to bring themselves to the group or ensuring that a pupil who needs to be supported by two members of staff is positioned at a safe but acceptable distance from other pupils due to challenging behaviour. Also give careful consideration to the positioning of pupils with sensory impairments within a particular group.

When you are confident that the physical environment is appropriate you can then turn your attention to your first lesson and the preparation of appropriate resources. By this point in your training differentiation should be embedded in your practice. However, you may find that this placement takes it to a whole new level! You may have eight pupils in your group all with differing needs, abilities, learning styles and hugely different levels of achievement. The theory you will have covered before your placement should have addressed these issues. However, this now needs to be put into practice and the best people to help you are your class teachers/mentors. Also remember that TAs have a wealth of expertise and are very much part of your team. They are usually also very honest when it comes to giving a view on something you have planned. Take heed – often they have seen it all before and are very in tune with the pupils in their care.

Pupils with special needs often find it very difficult to cope with 'down time', often filling it with inappropriate behaviour, so it is imperative that all children irrespective of needs have an activity ready and waiting for them when they arrive in class.

REFLECTIVE TASK

Look back at a morning when you have prepared equipment, resources and activities. Were they effective? What could you have changed to make them more effective?

Pupils on the ASD spectrum

Most pupils who have autism as an identified need will be able to be fully or partly included within the usual classroom routine. However, some specific provisions may have to be considered for some pupils including the use of withdrawal/quiet areas, individual work stations and the resources and opportunities to adhere to a very fixed structure and routine.

Transport to school

As previously mentioned most, if not all pupils, will arrive by school transport dependent upon needs. Each form of transport will have at least one escort, who will be assigned to a particular route and this person is your link with the pupils' home. Staff must be assigned and ready to meet pupils from the transport, as a lengthy wait in a stationary bus can cause distress and often behaviour problems in some pupils.

Just as you would expect a parent in a mainstream school to come into class to inform you of any problems/illness/appointments, you will gain this information from the escort. They will also have been present when the pupil has left the house and can often provide you with an insight into the type of day you might expect!

Some pupils enjoy the journey to school (and will not always want to get off the bus!), while others find it a challenge. Pupils with emotional and social difficulties often feel more anxious at this point in the morning and at home time, while children with physical difficulties may experience stiffness or pain. However, whatever problems these pupils may pose at this time it is up to the team to transport them safely to the classroom, resolve any issues and begin the teaching and learning process.

Movement between lessons/areas

As mentioned previously, many pupils have to access a range of services and professionals throughout the school day. This of course involves movement and must be carried out in the safest and least disruptive way possible. Getting pupils to 'line up' and then follow you is not a good idea, as you may find that ten metres later you are missing quite a few! While we can all see the humorous side of this, it is imperative that all pupils are kept in the sight of at least one member of staff when moving in a group. On the other hand, some pupils are encouraged to move around the school independently, taking messages or delivering a resource, but this is a planned event and will have been risk assessed by the teacher.

Break/snack times

As previously mentioned in the section concerning pre-placement visits, break/snack times can be quite a social occasion and can reinforce many skills for the pupils. This is also a good time to sit with the pupils on a more 'informal' basis, in order to build on relationships and encourage communication.

Break times need to be very well organised in terms of staffing, pupil groupings and environment. Some pupils, as in mainstream schools, may want to play football, or run freely. However, for some pupils this may be impossible and the movement may actually be terrifying for them. Some pupils cannot tolerate loud noises, while others use this as their way of communicating. Some love the camaraderie of friends while others are only able to cope in solitary situations. Just like in mainstream schools, all children are different!

Makaton

This is a method of signing which supports communication and is now used widely in both special and mainstream settings. It is used by many pupils in order to communicate and is accepted as the norm in some classes or settings. Makaton gives you the ideal opportunity to learn alongside your pupils – many of whom will be more than eager to point out your mistakes! The speech and language therapists will be able to offer you training manuals to support Makaton, and by beginning to learn this technique you are addressing inclusive practice. Booking yourself into a sign language course prior to undertaking this placement will provide you with knowledge and skills that you will find invaluable throughout your placement.

Use of specific areas/professionals

Within your placement it is envisaged that you will experience all areas of special needs provision, which are vital contributions to a holistic approach for each pupil. If possible, and dependent on the type of provision, it would be beneficial for you to observe pupils accessing the following areas/services:

- hydrotherapy pool;
- physiotherapy;
- occupational therapy;
- speech and language therapy;
- medical facility;
- light and sound area;
- sensory area;
- soft play area;
- pupil advisor/counsellor;
- teacher/service for the hearing impaired;
- teacher/service for the visually impaired;
- teacher/service specific to the setting/needs of pupils e.g. autism;

- educational psychologist;
- other professional bodies who may work within school e.g. Barnardos, Sure Start, and behaviour support services.

This is not an exhaustive list, nor can it be guaranteed that you will be able to access opportunities to meet with all these services/professionals during your placement. However, access whatever is available as this will enhance your understanding of the holistic approach needed, in order to meet the needs of pupils with SEND. Some of these professionals may be based in school on a part- or full-time basis making access easier, both for the pupils and for you. Others may be based externally and may only give the school limited time, so it is worth finding out when these visits take place in order to facilitate discussion time.

CASE STUDY

Within a placement school, the placement manager ensured that all trainees had either a morning or an afternoon session with each of the professionals within the school. Although some of this time could be used for discussion, the main focus was for the trainee to shadow the professional to see first-hand their interaction with the pupils.

All trainees found this aspect of their placement extremely beneficial, as they were able to observe the professionals' expertise and how this could enhance the school experience for the pupils.

Medication within school

As you can imagine, within a setting such as this, there are a high proportion of pupils on regular medication. Many special school and provisions have at least one nurse, with some settings having access to a nursing team. As a trainee, you are not responsible for this area, and if you are in any doubt about the health or well-being of a pupil you must inform a member of staff immediately.

Behaviour management

Just as the behaviour in a special school can seem extreme, so can the strategies to control it. If a pupil is deemed as being a danger to themselves or others, and all other strategies have failed, the pupil may have to be restrained.

Under no circumstances should you be involved in this, as only staff members fully trained in the techniques of handling are allowed to use these. Most schools use the Team Teach method which ensures that all handling is carried out safely and for the shortest time possible. Staff undergo training in order to obtain a Team Teach qualification and this must be updated and renewed every year.

Home time routines

Because contact with parents/carers can be limited, it is essential that an effective form of communication is established. Many schools use a home–school diary which can be accessed by all professionals and staff in the school, and is sent home to parents/carers every day. It is envisaged that they too will record any points that may be helpful to school staff. As mentioned previously the transport escorts are an integral part of this communication, but it is also beneficial to record pertinent points in writing in the diary to save omissions.

Some schools use telephone conversations with parents each evening, and this is also the course of action that must be taken if the communication in question is of a sensitive nature, remembering of course that some pupils are very good readers despite their needs!

As with the morning routine some pupils find home time unsettling and this can be due to many different reasons. With this in mind, some pupils may need quiet, one-to-one time before departure on school transport. The home time routine is very much a reversal of the morning one, with staff taking the pupils to the escorts and the pupils being safely placed into the transport. You may now feel like collapsing in a heap! But you will find that staff now spend time assessing both the pupils and the day, putting together plans and resources for the next day's activities, and participating in staff training.

After school activities

Some schools offer after school clubs, where pupils can participate in a less formal setting, often with other pupils that they do not see during the normal school day. These clubs can offer a wide range of activities tailored to the needs of the pupils and are often run by TAs. It is useful to be involved with at least one of these, as you are able to see the pupils in a different environment in which you will have the opportunity to talk/communicate on a more social basis.

Special events

Just as in a mainstream setting, special schools and provisions have events such as coffee mornings, fairs, productions and presentations. These are the times when you can meet families, and often see your pupils in a new light. Becoming part of a team responsible for staging a production, or organising a sports day, can help develop your skills in relation to inclusion and can also give you the opportunity to identify and solve some of the logistical problems of giving access for all. It can also give you opportunities that you had never envisaged, such as directing a choir consisting of pupils unable to speak, or choreographing a dance routine for wheelchair users.

Suggested tasks to be undertaken

The previous sections have dealt very much with the actual logistics and organisation of your placement and we now need to consider the tasks that need to be undertaken during this placement.

As this is not a teaching experience alone, trainees also need to engage in

- study tasks;
- preparation of learning materials;
- discussions with a range of professionals;
- a visit to a setting providing a different area of need.

Teaching activities need to enable trainees to observe, assist and then teach small groups, so that by the end of the placement, it should be possible to gain whole class/ group teaching experiences, including the management of support staff/TAs. This can be undertaken through the following phases.

1. **Introductory phase** – Shadowing both the teacher and TA, assisting with lessons and participating in discussions about pupils' needs or the provision.
2. **Development phase** – Increased involvement with teaching and learning by taking increased responsibility for planning, assessing, recording and the teaching of small groups or participating in team-teaching opportunities.
3. **Consolidation phase** – Improving the quality of your teaching through feedback and self-reflection. Suggested activities include:

   - planning and leading a whole morning or afternoon session including breaks;
   - managing TAs – teacher to observe;
   - reflection and analysis by planning for a second lesson following feedback from an initial session.

It is envisaged that trainees working with pupils with severe and/or complex needs and/ or disabilities will require extra support and supervision. This does not detract from your abilities, but is to ensure the well-being and safety of both you and the pupils.

The above suggestions may provide you with a framework for your placement. However, you need to discuss these with your mentor as the structure, timing and nature of the tasks will be dependent upon the specific needs of the school/setting and the individual pupils.

Possible directed tasks

The following tasks will help to develop your knowledge and understanding of SEN provision.

1. **Acoustic experience of classrooms** – Explore how easy/difficult it is for pupils to hear the teacher in differing environments. Consider the physical environment, the teacher's delivery and the pupils' ability to hear. Concentrate on aspects that can be governed by the teacher.
2. **Physical accessibility and circulation of pupils in the school** – How easy/difficult is it for pupils to move around the school? Observe pupil movements in differing situations. Discuss with pupils some of the problems they encounter.
3. **Organisation of classroom for learning** – Make observations of how teachers adapt classrooms according to needs. How does classroom organisation relate to the learning objectives of the lesson, the individual learning goals of pupils, and fostering independence in learning?
4. **Production of learning materials and resources** – Consider the resources produced by the teacher and TAs. Discuss with them their roles in this process. Establish with class staff how the materials and resources are designed to foster learning, how the materials enable a diversity of learning needs to be met, and how staff decide on the content and form of the materials and resources.
5. **Planning of lessons and learning objectives** – Interview teachers and TAs both collectively and individually in order to understand the process of lesson planning and the setting of objectives. Find out how lesson content and strategies are decided upon and what parts do the teacher and TAs play in this, who decides on learning goals for individual pupils, how the pupils are involved in the setting and evaluation of their own individual goals if this is possible, and the role played by the teacher and TAs in evaluating teaching and objectives.
6. **Learning and development in informal situations** – Observe pupils in informal settings such as the playground or dining hall, focusing on pupils' speaking and listening skills. Consider the social and emotional skills that pupils require to interact effectively with one another. Consider whether pupils with different kinds of SEND

interact differently with their peers, whether they are able to take turns, whether there are gender differences in pupil behaviour, and whether pupils behave or speak differently from the way they interact in the classroom.

7. **Storytelling and retelling** – The aim of this task is to find effective ways of storytelling. This will be very dependent on the needs of the pupils, their age, and their experiences of stories/storytelling. It will give the opportunity to create a wide range of resources, props and materials, and will help trainees understand the wide range of communication methods that can be deployed.

(Tasks taken from TDA, 2008)

It must now be clear to the reader that the previous sections highlighting school routine and environment sit very well with these tasks, and rather than them being an 'add on' to your placement, they actually become an integral part of it.

Portfolio

All evidence from the placement should be collected and collated within a portfolio, which should be referenced to the Teachers' Standards.

Assessment

Assessment is a vital tool in the special needs setting, especially with pupils who do not 'fit' the normal assessment criteria. Pupils with SEN tend to learn in a very 'fragmented' way, often achieving a desired target one day, only not to be able to do so the next day. They may often complete only a small part of a learning target, but then show skills and abilities which match a lower or even higher target.

It is very important therefore, that the assessment 'fits' the pupil rather than the pupil 'fitting' the assessment. Many schools devise their own methods of assessment while some buy in commercially produced materials.

Many schools will use the 'P' levels in order to assess pupils. This aspect will have been covered during your theory sessions with your ITT provider. However, you now have an excellent opportunity to see how they are used in practice and how this can influence assessment.

A SUMMARY OF **KEY POINTS**

➤ **School-based training is essential in developing trainees' knowledge, skills and understanding of inclusive practice by providing exposure to a wide range of SEND that is not normally found in mainstream education.**

➤ **The skills which can be developed on this placement are not solely beneficial to pupils with SEND. Many trainees find that skills gained on this placement have been extremely successful when transferred to mainstream settings.**

➤ **Special needs provision is an excellent arena in which to try new approaches to teaching and learning. You have access to a vast amount of knowledge from a range of professionals, who are also constantly trying to devise and trial new approaches in order to facilitate each pupil achieving their full potential.**

> ➢ In no other setting will you get the opportunity to work with such a large and diverse range of staff. Partnership working is the norm, and as such this is the ideal setting for you to examine the benefits and challenges associated with this.

RESEARCH SUMMARY RESEARCH SUMMARY **RESEARCH SUMMARY** RESEARCH SUMMARY

Golder, Jones and Eaton Quinn (2009) researched the impact of special school placements on trainee teachers following a course of initial teacher training. They found that experiences in special schools enhanced trainee teachers' knowledge and understanding of SEN and increased their confidence. After completing the placement trainees had improved their knowledge of the range of inclusive teaching and learning strategies. Research of this nature illustrates the important role that special school placements can serve within courses of initial teacher training.

MOVING *ON* > > > > > > MOVING *ON* > > > > > > MOVING *ON*

While this chapter set out to give you an insight into school-based training and the practicalities of your extended placement, it is hoped that you have also come to realise what an exciting and enlightening time this can be. You may never have considered special needs education as an option before, but after this placement, many trainees revise their thinking, and begin to consider a future career in various types of special needs provision.

Most of all, enjoy this placement, and reap the benefits which it can offer to you, both as a teacher and a member of society.

REFERENCES REFERENCES **REFERENCES** REFERENCES REFERENCES REFERENCES

Booth, T. (2011) *Index for Inclusion: Developing Learning and Participation in Schools*, Bristol: CSIE. http://www.csie.org.uk/resources/inclusion-index-explained.shtml (accessed 25 August 2014).

Department for Education (DfE) (2014) *Special Educational Needs and Disability Code of Practice: 0 to 25 Years: Statutory Guidance for Organisations Who Work With and Support Children and Young People with Special Educational Needs and Disabilities*, London: DfE.

Golder, G., Jones, N. and Eaton Quinn, E. (2009) 'Strengthening the special educational needs element of initial teacher training and education', *British Journal of Special Education*, 36(4), 183–90.

Training and Development Agency for Schools (TDA) (2008) *Special Educational Needs and/or Disabilities: A Training Resource for Initial Teacher Training Providers: Primary Undergraduate Courses*, TDA.

FURTHER READING FURTHER READING **FURTHER READING** FURTHER READING

Goepel, J. and Sharpe, S. (2014) *Inclusive Primary Teaching: A Critical Approach to Equality and Special Educational Needs*, Northwich: Critical Publishing.

USEFUL WEBSITES USEFUL WEBSITES **USEFUL WEBSITES** USEFUL WEBSITES

www.makaton.org

www.communicationmatters.org.uk

www.nasen.co.uk

13
The role of the SENCO

Chapter objectives

By the end of this chapter you should be aware of:

- the management roles and responsibilities of the special educational needs co-ordinator (SENCO);
- the strategic leadership roles and responsibilities of the SENCO;
- the challenges associated with being a SENCO.

Teachers' Standards

TS8: develop effective professional relationships with colleagues, knowing how and when to draw on advice and specialist support

Introduction

This chapter will introduce you to the roles and responsibilities of the SENCO within primary schools. It will address the historical development of SENCOs but will focus more sharply on the role of the SENCO within the new Code of Practice (DfE, 2014). The chapter will introduce you to some of the challenges associated with being a SENCO and consider ways in which these might be overcome. An account from a serving SENCO has been included to provide a voice from the field.

Historical development of the SENCO role

The 1994 Code of Practice (DfE, 1994) placed a statutory obligation on all schools to appoint a teacher with responsibility for the co-ordination of educational provision for pupils with SEN. The Teacher Training Agency (TTA) produced a set of national standards for SENCOs in 1998, enabling SENCOs to audit their knowledge and skills and identify their professional development needs. These were offered as guidance. At this time professional development courses for SEN co-ordination were introduced by local authorities and higher education institutions to provide SENCOs with professional training and accreditation, although there was no mandatory requirement for SENCOs to participate in the training (Layton, 2005).

The TTA stated that:

> The SENCO, with the support of the headteacher and governing body, takes responsibility for the day-to-day operation of provision made by the school for pupils with

SEN and provides professional guidance ... in order to secure high quality teaching and the effective use of resources to bring about improved standards of achievement for all pupils.

(TTA, 1998: 5)

The focus for SENCOs was to co-ordinate four main areas of SEN provision:

- strategic direction and development of SEN provision;
- teaching and learning;
- leading and managing staff;
- efficient and effective deployment of staff and resources. (Layton, 2005)

The SENCO was responsible for developing a whole school approach to the co-ordination of SEN but there was never an expectation that the SENCO 'would have exclusive responsibility for pupils whose learning needs threatened to challenge the teaching approaches or classroom organisations with which teaching colleagues were more familiar' (Layton, 2005: 54).

When the 1994 Code of Practice was revised in 2001 (DfES, 2001) the new Code explicitly made reference to the fact that many mainstream primary and secondary schools 'find it effective for the SENCO to be a member of the senior leadership team' (DfES, 2001: 51, 66). This was later reinforced in the Labour government's SEN strategy *Removing Barriers to Achievement*, which stated that:

We want schools to see the SENCO as a key member of the senior leadership team, able to influence the development of policies for whole school improvement.

(DfES, 2004: 58, para 3.14)

The House of Commons' Education and Skills Select Committee (2006) recommended that the SENCO should be a member of the school leadership team but this was not made a statutory requirement (Pearson *et al.*, 2014). However, subsequent legislation (DCSF, 2008) stated that all newly appointed SENCOs would be required to undertake the National Award for SEN Co-ordination in which they would be required to demonstrate their ability to influence strategically the development of an inclusive culture, policies and practices across the whole school.

The role of the SENCO in promoting whole school inclusion over their specialist knowledge of SEN-related issues has to some extent led to ambiguity in relation to the requirements of the role (Rosen-Webb, 2011). The debate focuses on whether the SENCO is a 'change agent' for whole school inclusion (Hallett and Hallett, 2010) or whether the role should be more focused on strategies to support individual students with highly specific needs. Additionally, the notion of the SEN 'expert' has been subjected to critical debate. It has been emphasised that all teachers are teachers of pupils with SEN (Norwich, 1990) and that the introduction of a specialist role may make it easier for teachers to effectively abdicate their responsibilities for the education of pupils with SEN to those with more experience, knowledge and higher qualifications.

Current developments

It certainly seems that the SENCO role has been given a higher profile in recent years (Robertson, 2012). The Green Paper (DfE, 2011) emphasised the failings of the education system for pupils with SEND and the need to reduce bureaucracy, increase parental confidence and improve outcomes for children and young people with SEND (Pearson *et al.*, 2014). The key concepts underpinning educational reform are performativity, marketisation and decentralisation (Pearson *et al.*, 2014) and the reforms have significant implications for SENCOs who will be responsible for managing the transition to the new Code of Practice (DfE, 2014).

The fundamental changes which have implications for SENCOs include:

- replacing Statements with Education, Health and Care Plans;
- reducing the proportion of students with SEND;
- removing School Action and School Action Plus and replacing them with one phase of school-based support;
- accelerating achievement and attainment of pupils with SEND;
- giving parents and carers more control;
- increasing the participation of pupils in decision making;
- increasing collaboration between different services;
- managing financial restraints.

SENCOs are operating currently in a climate of 'service rationing' (Robertson, 2012: 81) and they will increasingly need to look outwards 'by using professional networks to build their own expertise' (Pearson *et al.*, 2014: 8). Schools are now increasingly working collaboratively through the formation of academy trusts and teaching school alliances as LA services are shrinking. This provides school leaders with exciting opportunities to make decisions about how best to deploy resources to meet the needs of all pupils. Developments are already taking place in relation to staff deployment in some networks, for example through schools sharing staff. Within this policy context the role of the SENCO is no longer restricted to one school and there are examples of SENCOs working across schools within networks.

Under the new system SENCOs will take increasing responsibility for financial management. They will be required to make decisions about how to spend delegated budgets including where to purchase external expertise and resources as services become increasingly decentralised. SENCOs will be required to make decisions about the purchasing of educational psychology time and advisory teachers' expertise and whether to purchase services from voluntary and community sectors (Robertson, 2012). SENCOs will need to make decisions about whether to purchase expertise from special schools and they will be required to account for expenditure. They will also be required to take increasing responsibility for staff development to ensure that all teachers are using inclusive pedagogies (Pearson *et al.*, 2014) in order to maximise learners' achievements. Additionally, SENCOs will be required to take increasing responsibility for the training of future teachers as schools move towards a system of school-led initial teacher training, thus enabling them to fulfil the role of teacher educator (Robertson, 2012).

The focus on closing the achievement gap will inevitably mean that SENCOs will have to spend a significant proportion of their time analysing pupil achievement data. All of the roles and responsibilities outlined in this section indicate that the role of SENCO is increasingly likely to be assumed by a teacher in a leadership position rather than in a teaching role. The role is a strategic whole school role and teaching responsibilities may impede the quality of the leadership that the SENCO is able to provide. However, a non-teaching role can also be contentious, particularly with colleagues who have to balance the responsibilities of individual pupils with SEND alongside their responsibilities for all pupils. The role of the SENCO in supporting colleagues to understand the links between inclusive pedagogy and high achievement for all pupils is therefore critical and fundamental to closing the achievement gap.

Challenges of the SENCO role

Research (Cole and Johnson, 2004) has indicated that the role of the SENCO is challenging, stressful and demanding on many levels due to limited time, resources, funding and fear of parental litigation. Very often SENCOs appear to be overworked but remain 'completely committed to their struggle on behalf of children with special educational needs' (Cole, 2005b: 298).

Education operates within a quasi-market which privileges school performance, parental choice and engenders a culture of competition. According to Cole 'within this contentious context, the role of the SENCO was never going to be an easy one' (2005b: 296). While SENCOs tend to be advocates of inclusion and agents of change, they are also accountable for the achievement of pupils with SEN and/or disabilities. Their practice is often underpinned by the principles of equity and social justice and an unquestionable commitment to care (Cole, 2005b). However, these values need to be balanced against market principles and it is possible that SENCOs might increasingly have to sacrifice their deep-rooted professional values in order to focus on maximising the performances of pupils with SEND with respect to school performance indicators.

PRACTICAL TASK PRACTICAL TASK PRACTICAL TASK PRACTICAL TASK PRACTICAL TASK

When you are in school obtain a copy of the school's SEND policy and read it carefully to find out about the roles and responsibilities of teachers in relation to SEND.

The role of the SENCO in the new Code of Practice

The Code of Practice (DfE, 2014) includes a number of statements about the roles and responsibilities of the SENCO. These include:

- overseeing the day-to-day operation of the school's SEND policy;
- co-ordinating provision for pupils with SEND;
- liaising with the designated safeguarding teacher where a looked after child has SEND;
- advising colleagues on a graduated approach to SEN support;
- advising on the use of the delegated budget or other resources which have been allocated;
- liaising with parents of pupils with SEND;
- establishing links with other education settings and outside agencies;
- liaising with potential future providers of education;
- ensuring that the school is fully compliant with the statutory obligations of the Equality Act 2010;
- ensuring that SEN records are kept up to date.

Specific statements relating to the roles and responsibilities of SENCOs taken directly from the Code of Practice are listed below:

6.84 Governing bodies of maintained mainstream schools and the proprietors of mainstream academy schools (including free schools) **must** *ensure that there is a qualified teacher designated as SENCO for the school.*

6.85 The SENCO **must** *be a qualified teacher working at the school. A newly appointed SENCO* **must** *be a qualified teacher and, where they have not previously been the SENCO at that or any other relevant school for a total period of more than twelve months, they* **must** *achieve a National Award in Special Educational Needs Co-ordination within three years of appointment.*

6.86 A National Award **must** *be a postgraduate course accredited by a recognised higher education provider. The National College for Teaching and Leadership has worked with providers to develop a set of learning outcomes … When appointing staff or arranging for them to study for a National Award schools should satisfy themselves that the chosen course will meet these outcomes and equip the SENCO to fulfil the duties outlined in this Code. Any selected course should be at least equivalent to 60 credits at postgraduate study.*

6.87 The SENCO has an important role to play with the headteacher and governing body, in determining the strategic development of SEN policy and provision in the school. They will be most effective in that role if they are part of the school leadership team.

6.88 The SENCO has day-to-day responsibility for the operation of SEN policy and co-ordination of specific provision made to support individual pupils with SEN, including those who have EHC plans.

6.89 The SENCO provides professional guidance to colleagues and will work closely with staff, parents and other agencies. The SENCO should be aware of the provision in the Local Offer and be able to work with professionals providing a support role to families to ensure that pupils with SEN receive appropriate support and high quality teaching.

6.90 The key responsibilities of the SENCO may include:

- overseeing the day-to-day operation of the school's SEN policy
- co-ordinating provision for children with SEN
- liaising with the relevant Designated Teacher where a looked after pupil has SEN
- advising on the graduated approach to providing SEN support
- advising on the deployment of the school's delegated budget and other resources to meet pupils' needs effectively
- liaising with parents of pupils with SEN
- liaising with early years providers, other schools, educational psychologists, health and social care professionals, and independent or voluntary bodies
- being a key point of contact with external agencies, especially the local authority and its support services
- liaising with potential next providers of education to ensure a pupil and their parents are informed about options and a smooth transition is planned
- working with the headteacher and school governors to ensure that the school meets its responsibilities under the Equality Act 2010 with regard to reasonable adjustments and access arrangements
- ensuring that the school keeps the records of all pupils with SEN up to date

6.91 The school should ensure that the SENCO has sufficient time and resources to carry out these functions. This should include providing the SENCO with sufficient administrative support and time away from teaching to enable them to fulfil their responsibilities in a similar way to other important strategic roles within a school.

6.92 It may be appropriate for a number of smaller primary schools to share a SENCO employed to work across the individual schools, where they meet the other requirements set out in this chapter of the Code. Schools can consider this arrangement where it secures sufficient time away from teaching and sufficient administrative support to enable the SENCO to fulfil the role effectively for the total registered pupil population across all of the schools involved.

6.93 Where such a shared approach is taken the SENCO should not normally have a significant class teaching commitment. Such a shared SENCO role should not be carried out by a headteacher at one of the schools.

6.94 Schools should review the effectiveness of such a shared SENCO role regularly and should not persist with it where there is evidence of a negative impact on the quality of SEN provision, or the progress of pupils with SEN.

(DfE, 2014: 97–8)

Leadership role

It is particularly refreshing to note that paragraph 6.87 emphasises that the SENCO fulfils a leadership role in the school. In this respect the role is not just a management or operational role in which the SENCO assumes responsibility for the smooth running of day-to-day SEND provision. The role is strategic and sits squarely within whole school improvement systems and processes. School leadership teams will need to make decisions about whether to draw up separate annual improvement plans and short-term action plans for SEND provision. Some schools embed targets for raising progress and attainment of pupils with SEND within plans for raising achievement for all pupils rather than drawing up separate improvement plans.

Ensuring high expectations

Within the new Code of Practice the SENCO will play a pivotal role in ensuring that all teachers across a school or within a federation of schools have sufficiently high expectations of pupils with SEND. SENCOs will need to check that targets in relation to pupils' achievements are sufficiently challenging and they will need to review pupils' progress against these targets with their colleagues on a regular basis. Progress meetings often take place every half term in schools and SENCOs will need to hold colleagues to account if pupils with SEND are making insufficient progress. The SENCO plays an important role in checking that the provision offered to pupils with SEND is high quality. In situations where the quality falls short, the SENCO will need to ensure that colleagues are set clear targets for improvement and they will need to monitor that colleagues have addressed these targets within a given timescale. Holding colleagues to account in this way is not easy and should not be underestimated. Although the SENCO should aim to start from a position of being supportive the achievement of pupils with SEND must always be their first concern. Where pupils' achievements are too low as a result of poor teaching or poor quality provision, the SENCO has a duty to hold colleagues to account and to ensure that improvements are made.

The SENCO needs to ensure that teachers and other colleagues implement the agreed interventions for pupils and that these take place at the agreed times. Often the SENCO will not be responsible for delivering specific interventions but they are responsible for ensuring that the agreed provision is evident in day-to-day practice. Teachers and other colleagues need to take responsibility for monitoring the impact of interventions on specific groups of pupils or individuals. In cases where interventions are not having the desired impact on pupils' achievements the SENCO may suggest additional interventions or strategies to accelerate achievement. The SENCO plays an important role in ensuring that interventions are monitored and evaluated and they should support colleagues in this process.

Securing high quality teaching for pupils with SEND

The SENCO plays a pivotal role in monitoring the quality of teaching and learning for pupils with SEND. This is most effective when the SENCO is a member of the school leadership team so that monitoring provision for pupils with SEND is part of processes and systems for monitoring the teaching and learning of all pupils. Monitoring might include:

- lesson observations;
- learning walks;
- scrutiny of pupils' work;
- scrutiny of pupils' achievement data each half term;
- discussions with pupils with SEND to collect their perspectives about the provision being offered to them;
- discussions with parents of pupils with SEND to collect their perspectives about the provision being offered to their child;
- discussions with teachers and TAs.

Although this is not an exhaustive list many of these monitoring processes are already embedded in schools and they tend to be repeated at fixed points in the year, often each half term, to collect a view about the quality of teaching and learning.

Learning walks (or enquiry walks) enable senior leaders in schools to research the quality of provision across the school. Leaders typically spend a few minutes in each classroom to enable them to form a view about what is happening. The SENCO might choose to focus on:

- The learning environment – Is it inclusive? Are resources available to support pupils with SEND?
- Differentiation – Are the tasks matched appropriately to the abilities of pupils with SEND?
- Deployment of TAs – Are TAs appropriately deployed to support the learning of pupils with SEND?
- Behaviour management – How are pupils with challenging behaviour supported in lessons?
- Engagement in lessons – What is the engagement of pupils with SEND like in lessons? Do they participate in lessons? What attitudes to learning do pupils with SEND demonstrate?
- Independence – Do pupils with SEND have opportunities in lessons to work independently? Do they know what to do when they become 'stuck' in their learning?
- Progress in lessons – Do pupils with SEND make sufficient progress in lessons? What factors facilitate progress or impede progress?

Again, this is not an exhaustive list but it is sufficient to get you thinking about the kinds of things SENCOs might choose to focus on during a learning walk. The learning walk may have a very specific focus (e.g. what does the deployment of TAs look like across the school?) where leaders dip in and out of lessons to look at one particular element of practice. Alternatively, the learning walk could be open ended where there is no specific focus. In open-ended learning walks senior leaders tend to walk into lessons and make notes about things that they observe taking place. After visiting several lessons leaders then collaborate to identify emerging themes in relation to teaching and learning across the school.

If the SENCO is a member of the leadership team they can participate in cycles of monitoring that are taking place as part of whole school monitoring. However, they can focus solely on monitoring the quality of teaching and learning for pupils with SEND. Qualitative evidence collected through learning walks, lesson observations and scrutiny of pupils' work can then be analysed against pupil progress data each half term. This will enable the SENCO to form a perspective about whether the quality of teaching and learning that they have observed in lessons is typical over time. A SENCO may go into a lesson and observe very effective differentiation but work scrutiny could reveal that this is not evident in every lesson. Additionally, a SENCO may observe that pupils with SEND make very good progress in a lesson but analysis of the pupils' progress data over the period of a half term could indicate that the teaching is not having an impact on their progress over time. This would then warrant further investigation from the SENCO who would need to ascertain why those pupils were not making progress. The SENCO, in collaboration with other colleagues on the leadership team, needs to triangulate the evidence collected from the various forms of monitoring to formulate a view about the quality of SEND provision across the school.

Whole school pupil achievement data for pupils with SEND will also be used to hold SENCOs to account. If pupils with SEND are not making good progress from their starting points across a year the SENCO will be held to account. There may be very specific cases where pupils have highly complex needs and there are genuine reasons for why these pupils have not made good progress. In these situations the SENCO will need to write up various case studies to explain the factors which have impacted detrimentally on the progress of these learners. However, it is important to emphasise that these cases should be the exception rather than the norm if the quality of teaching and learning for pupils with SEND is good. If large numbers of SEND pupils are underachieving the SENCO needs to analyse this in more depth in order to find out what aspects of the SEND provision need to be changed to make the provision more effective.

There may be cases of schools where the presence of pupils with highly complex needs has a detrimental impact on whole school achievement and attainment data. This might include small mainstream schools with provision for pupils with communication and interaction difficulties, including autistic spectrum disorder. In schools such as these the presence of even one or two pupils with highly specific and complex needs can have a detrimental impact on overall achievement data. In these cases leadership teams often 'double book-keep' the data. This means that achievement and progress data is presented and analysed for all pupils. It is then analysed separately with specific pupils being removed from the analysis. This process of double book-keeping helps school leaders to demonstrate the impact, for example, of resource provision on school data, thus enabling them to defend their position in school inspections.

A significant role of the SENCO is to be a moral advocate for pupils with SEND. The SENCO is employed to champion the rights of pupils with SEND and to ensure that the pupils and their families have a point of contact. These rights include but are not restricted to:

- the right to voice their opinions about all matters which affect them;
- the right to participate in decision making;
- the right to belong and to be accepted;
- the right to learn alongside their peers;

- the right to achieve and succeed through a personalised curriculum which meets their needs;
- the right to reasonable adjustments.

Promoting an inclusive culture

The SENCO plays a pivotal role in shaping and embedding the inclusive culture of the school. This partly involves helping to shape positive attitudes and values in relation to SEND across staff, pupils, parents and the wider community. The SENCO needs to challenge attitudes which reflect a medical model of disability in which people view the 'problem' as being within the child. They should help others to understand that although pupils may have specific impairments, these impairments should not be disabling. They need to advance the message that pupils with SEND can achieve highly if colleagues have the knowledge and skills to teach them correctly. They need to ensure that colleagues have sufficiently high expectations of pupils with SEND and they should help them to reflect on how aspects of their own practice might be the source of the problem rather than locating the problem within the child. The SENCO needs to ensure special educational needs and disabilities are not viewed in ways which suggest a deficiency in the child. Their role is to help colleagues interrogate how the deficiency might be situated within their own practices, attitudes, skills and knowledge and provide them with appropriate continuing professional development to enable them to improve.

Effective SENCOs underpin their daily practices with a deep commitment to both the social and affirmative models of disability. They play a critical role in helping others to understand that disability is not something to be feared. It is not tragic and should not be pitied; rather, it can be a positive, energising and enriching force within the life of an individual or within a school. They play a fundamental role in helping colleagues to understand that people are differently abled rather than disabled and in helping to foster the development of socially inclusive attitudes across a school.

SENCOs need to ensure that positive images of disability are reflected in the school environment through books and displays which depict positive images of people with impairments. They also play a pivotal role in raising awareness and understanding of impairments across the school community. This might include setting up events which raise awareness of impairments such as communication and language impairment, physical, cognitive or sensory disabilities.

Developing positive relationships with pupils and parents

The SENCO will inevitably be the point of contact for pupils with SEND and their parents. They need to establish highly effective relationships with parents and carers and refer them to appropriate external services where this is appropriate. They need to have excellent interpersonal skills to support parents and pupils and they need to demonstrate empathy, patience and respect. The ethic of care should underpin their practice. Additionally, they need to liaise with and be the point of contact for numerous multidisciplinary teams, including but not restricted to educational psychology, behaviour support teams, communication and interaction teams, medical and health care professionals, social workers and speech and language therapy services. In order to communicate with this diverse range of professionals the SENCO needs to have excellent communication and organisational skills.

REFLECTIVE TASK

What are your views on pupils with SEND receiving specific individual or group support outside of the classroom during lesson time? Discuss the pros and cons of this with your colleagues.

PRACTICAL TASK   PRACTICAL TASK   PRACTICAL TASK   PRACTICAL TASK   PRACTICAL TASK

During your time in school plan an opportunity to meet with the SENCO to discuss his/her responsibilities in relation to SEN co-ordination. Ask them to explain their leadership and day-to-day management responsibilities.

AN ACCOUNT FROM A SENCO

I have been a SENCO for the past five years. This is a role towards which I had always been drawn. Working with the most vulnerable of children had been a passion throughout my career which at this point in time had spanned 39 years. Each and every cohort of children I had encountered had always presented me with at least a few children whose needs could not be effectively met by means of simply differentiating classroom tasks. Over my teaching career I had been charged with the daily responsibility of supporting children with diverse needs including those with autistic spectrum disorder, behaviour, emotional and social difficulties, learning and cognition difficulties, and speech and language difficulties. In the earliest years of my career there was no Code of Practice and little identified support for children with SEN. I seemed to possess an innate need to overcome barriers to learning for these children and thrived on overcoming any obstacle that stood in my way. When an opportunity to apply for the role of a school SENCO presented itself I did not hesitate to apply for the position.

It was September 2009 and, as I embarked on my new role, I was amongst the first newly appointed SENCOs to be required to complete the National Award for SEN Co-ordination. The National Award for SEN Co-ordination is a DfE-approved postgraduate qualification which must be achieved by teachers new to the role of SENCO. Experienced SENCOs can also gain the qualification.

It is estimated that one in five pupils is identified with a special or additional educational need. I work in a small primary school in an area of social, economic and cultural deprivation. In this school over 40% of the pupils have been identified as having a special educational need or disability. The role of the SENCO is vital in its contribution to whole school development and improvement. Both the new Ofsted framework and the current Teachers' Standards focus on teachers supporting all children, including the most vulnerable pupils, to ensure that they are making significant progress. The current Teachers' Standards place emphasis on supporting pupils with SEN. Professionals are required to adapt teaching to respond to the strengths and needs of all pupils. There is an expectation that teachers must use and evaluate distinctive approaches to engage and support learners. The expectations of both the Teachers' Standards and Ofsted impact directly on the role of the SENCO. The responsibilities of a twenty-first century SENCO are diverse.

(Continued)

(Continued)

The responsibility for pupils with SEND does not lie solely with the SENCO. It is the responsibility of each and every adult who comes into daily contact with a child. It is the role of the school SENCO to ensure that all teachers and staff in school who support and teach children are familiar with age-related expectations as well as the current learning needs of individual children. It is only by having an understanding of this information that they will be able to identify the specific needs of individual pupils. SEND is a shared responsibility which must be embraced by all staff members. It is led, managed and monitored by the school SENCO. The role, in more recent times, encompasses the line management of a far greater number of support staff. Clear and timed systems must be developed and understood by all. These must be meaningful and manageable and they should be adhered to by all adults working with children. As in all areas of education, change is inevitable and necessary and the school SENCO must ensure that they are familiar with current political change which must in turn be disseminated clearly to colleagues. School systems will require evaluation and adaptation in the light of change and such systems must in turn be clearly communicated through ongoing professional development delivered by the LA, multi-agency training and the school SENCO. 'No man is an island' and there was never a truer word spoken when considering the roles and responsibilities of the SENCO. Supporting children with SEND necessitates a well co-ordinated approach and it should be effectively planned and led by the SENCO.

Every school is required to meet the specific needs of children with SEND. It is the responsibility of the school SENCO to ensure that provision is made for all pupils who have SEND. Children and young people should engage in activities alongside their peers. The role of the SENCO must be undertaken by a qualified teacher and parents must be informed whenever a school is required to make special educational provision for their child. The quality of teaching for children with SEN will be central to each school's performance management systems and the identification of professional development for both teaching and support staff will be fundamental in improving outcomes for all children, including those with SEN. Training must go beyond a differentiated approach to teaching and must consider approaches that are different to or additional to those which are usually effective in supporting children of the same age.

Every teacher is responsible for the progress and development of every pupil in their class – they will be held to account for the progress of all learners they teach. Children may access support from either specialist staff or TAs. However, the responsibility for progress and development remains that of the class teacher. In consultation with the school SENCO children may be identified as having SEN. Some children may have been identified before coming into full-time education. Those that have not been identified before coming to school but are causing a concern should be carefully monitored and identified at the earliest opportunity. The first response must be for the SENCO to ensure that every child has access to high quality, differentiated teaching. All children are entitled to receive this as a bare minimum. The SENCO will be required to work alongside the class teacher and must develop systems that frequently monitor the progress and development of all pupils to ensure that there is early identification of pupils with SEN and that there is then a quick response to meet individual needs and development. Additional support must be made available to any pupils making less than expected progress. Special educational provision must be put in place and barriers to learning should be addressed. There will be occasions when a child continues to make little or no progress, despite well considered and effectively implemented support being matched to the child's area of need. Under such circumstance the school SENCO will consider involving specialists, including those from outside agencies in consultation with the parents and the pupils.

Whenever a pupil is receiving SEN support, parents should engage termly with the school to review current progress and outcomes, to identify new clear and measurable outcomes, discuss the activities and support that will help achieve them, and identify the role of the parent, the pupil and the school. Class teachers may conduct these meetings, especially when there are several children in a school with SEN. However, the school SENCO must ensure that they are available to support teachers, parents and pupils and must have clear knowledge and understanding of what, why and how the individual needs of every pupil with SEN will be supported and achieved. It is essential that a SENCO establishes a cycle of assessing a child's need, plans, in collaboration with the class teacher how such needs can be supported, ensures that agreed interventions are systematically delivered and finally reviews the impact of such intervention. This cycle will then be repeated.

Record keeping is also essential and must be devised, developed and shared, by the SENCO with colleagues. It is for schools to determine their own approach to record keeping. However, all provision made for pupils with SEN should be accurately recorded and must be kept up to date. Ofsted will expect to see evidence of pupil progress, a focus on outcomes and a rigorous approach to the monitoring and evaluation of all SEN support provided to every child in your school. Every school must publish information on their websites about the policy for pupils with SEN. This information must be updated annually by the SENCO and any changes to the information must be updated. The Local Offer for children with SEND must also be available on the school website. The SENCO has an essential role to play with the head teacher and governing body and must determine the strategic development of SEN policy and provision across the school. Schools should ensure that the SENCO has sufficient time and resources to complete their role. This would ideally include providing the SENCO with sufficient administrative support. Some time away from teaching responsibilities is essential to enable them to fulfil their SEND responsibilities. The role of SENCO is an important strategic role within a school.

Mainstream schools are provided with resources that they can use in supporting those with additional needs, including pupils with SEND. Within the overall budget schools have an amount, called the notional SEN budget. This is not a ring-fenced amount, and is used by a school to provide appropriate and quality support from the whole of its budget. All schools should decide how they will approach accessing and purchasing resources to effectively support the progress of pupils with SEND. This may well be the responsibility of the SENCO who will work in collaboration with teachers as well as the leadership team. More expensive support will not be expected to come from their core funding. Schools are expected to provide additional support which costs up to a nationally prescribed threshold. The LA, where the child or young person resides, should provide additional top-up funding where the cost of the special educational provision is in excess of the nationally prescribed threshold. However, to access additional funding it will be necessary for the SENCO to provide clear evidence of the expenditure to date and to account for the ways in which it has been used to support an individual child with SEN.

The Code of Practice (DfE, 2014) covers the 0–25 age range and includes guidance relating to disabled children and young people as well as those with SEN. The Code of Practice became statutory in September 2014. There are several key principles in the Code which all SENCOs should be familiar with and should endeavour to adhere to in their role:

- There is a clearer focus on the participation of children and young people and parents in decision making at individual and strategic levels.

(Continued)

(Continued)

- There is a stronger focus on high aspirations and on improving outcomes for children and young people.
- It includes guidance on the joint planning and commissioning of services to ensure close co-operation between education, health and social care.
- It includes guidance on publishing a Local Offer of support for children and young people with SEND.
- There is new guidance for education and training settings on taking a graduated approach to identifying and supporting pupils and students with SEN (to replace School Action and School Action Plus).
- For children and young people with more complex needs a co-ordinated assessment process and the new 0–25 Education, Health and Care plan (EHC plan) replace statements and Learning Difficulty Assessments (LDAs).
- There is a greater focus on support that enables those with SEN to succeed in their education and make a successful transition to adulthood.

I remain committed to my roles and responsibilities. I view myself as an advocate for children with SEND. I feel that through my role I am making a positive difference to the education of our most vulnerable learners. In helping to improve provision in school for these learners I have also helped to embed a culture of inclusion throughout our school. The development of more inclusive teaching strategies has helped to improve teaching and learning for all pupils because inclusive approaches to learning and teaching benefit all learners. I have, in a small way, helped to transform the attitudes of colleagues towards pupils with SEND. Positive attitudes are evident throughout the school and colleagues have become more reflective and analytical about their own teaching. They are now able to identify how barriers to learning are often rooted in their own practice rather than within the child. Through organising continuing professional development for staff I have enabled my colleagues to become more knowledgeable and confident in supporting learners with SEND. I have empowered them to believe in themselves and I have enabled them to recognise that good teaching, rather than specialist teaching, benefits all pupils.

Case Study

A SENCO in a primary school had become frustrated about the various ways in which different practitioners had interpreted the school's inclusion policy. Practices varied across the school. In some classrooms pupils with SEND were supported by TAs in the classroom during lessons but in other classrooms pupils with SEND were supported in groups outside of classrooms. In some classrooms there was evidence that visual prompts (including visual timetables, signs and symbols) were being used to support practice but this practice was not consistent across the school.

The SENCO set about developing a shared understanding of inclusion. She carried out focus groups with pupils with SEND and separate focus groups were held with their parents. Discussions focused on what would help pupils to learn more effectively in the classroom. Ideas were generated and then each group agreed on the best ten ideas. These were then recorded and stored. A staff meeting was then held as a mechanism through which the SENCO could consult staff. During the meeting the staff discussed their understandings of inclusion and agreed on a list of practices which needed to be visibly present in each classroom in order to demonstrate a school-wide commitment to inclusion. Parents' and pupils' ideas were incorporated into this list. It was agreed that every classroom needed to include the following:

- a whole class visual timetable;
- personalised visual timetables for pupils with SEND;
- specific visual cues to support adult commands – consistent in each classroom;
- texts which include images of people with disabilities;
- an agreed set of children's rights on display;
- a notice board for parents to signpost them to services in the community;
- sign language symbols on display and used by adults to support verbal communication.

This list only represents a partial selection of the practices which were agreed but it demonstrates how one SENCO set about developing a more consistent approach to practice across the school.

REFLECTIVE TASK

What are your views on pupils with SEND being removed from lessons on the wider curriculum to focus on interventions in English and mathematics? Discuss this with your colleagues and debate the pros and cons.

PRACTICAL TASK   PRACTICAL TASK   PRACTICAL TASK   PRACTICAL TASK   PRACTICAL TASK

During your time in school research the interventions that are in place to support pupils with SEND. Find out how pupils are selected for these interventions and how their progress on the interventions is measured. Also research who delivers the interventions and at what times they take place.

CASE STUDY

A SENCO worked in a mainstream school with resource provision for pupils with autism. When she assumed the SENCO role the resource provision operated like a mini special school and pupils enrolled spent the majority of each day in the provision rather than being included in mainstream classes. The SENCO was keen to develop more inclusive practices. She discussed her concerns with the teacher in charge of the provision and together they developed a flexible model which allowed children to spend most of each day in mainstream lessons. Children were only taught in the provision when they needed to work on very specific, focused skills.

A SUMMARY OF **KEY POINTS**

➢ The SENCO role is a strategic role within a school.

➢ The role includes elements of strategic leadership and day-to-day management of SEND provision.

➢ The role must be assumed by a qualified teacher.

➢ Effective SENCOs are moral activists for pupils with SEND: they support them and their families and believe that they can all achieve highly.

➢ SENCOs play a pivotal role in shaping the development of positive attitudes amongst colleagues towards pupils with SEND as well as helping to shape and embed the development of a culture of inclusion across the school.

➢ The role is demanding, time-consuming and at times frustrating, but always extremely rewarding.

RESEARCH SUMMARY RESEARCH SUMMARY **RESEARCH SUMMARY** RESEARCH SUMMARY

Barbara Cole's (2005a) research with parents (who are also teachers) of pupils with SEND demonstrates how parents often value the small and caring things that professionals do to ensure that their children feel safe and have a sense of belonging. They valued teachers who tried to ensure that their children felt part of a community. Issues around the achievements of their children were considered to be less important.

MOVING *ON* > > > > > > MOVING *ON* > > > > > > MOVING *ON*

Now that you have an understanding about the roles and responsibilities of the SENCO you need to consider whether you would be interested in undertaking this leadership position in schools during your future career. Take a look at some of the job descriptions for SENCOs and look at the criteria that candidates have to be able to demonstrate to be successfully appointed. If you are interested in a career as a SENCO start planning the journey now to enable you to evidence the criteria. Job advertisements can be found on www.tes.co.uk

REFERENCES REFERENCES **REFERENCES** REFERENCES **REFERENCES** REFERENCES

Cole, B. (2005a) 'Good faith and effort? Perspectives on educational inclusion', *Disability and Society*, 20(3), 331–44.

Cole, B.A. (2005b) 'Mission impossible? Special educational needs, inclusion and the re-conceptualization of the role of the SENCO in England and Wales', *European Journal of Special Needs Education*, 20(3), 287–307.

Cole, B.A. and Johnson, M. (2004) 'SENCOs and the revised Code of Practice', unpublished survey, University of Sheffield and Keele University.

Department for Children, Schools and Families (DCSF) (2008) *Quality Standards for Special Educational Needs (SEN) Support and Outreach Services*, Nottingham: DCSF Publications.

Department for Education (DfE) (2011) *Support and Aspiration: A New Approach to Special Educational Needs and Disability – Progress and Next Steps*, London and Norwich: DfE. https://www.gov.uk/government/publications/support-and-aspiration-a-new-approach-to-special-educational-needs-and-disability-progress-and-next-steps (accessed 25 August 2014).

Department for Education (DfE) (1994) *Code of Practice for the Identification and Assessment of Special Educational Needs*, London: HMSO.

Department for Education (DfE) (2014) *Special Educational Needs and Disability Code of Practice: 0 to 25 Years: Statutory Guidance for Organisations Who Work With and Support Children and Young People with Special Educational Needs and Disabilities*, London: DfE.

Department for Education and Skills (DfES) (2001) *Special Educational Needs Code of Practice*, Nottingham: DfES.

Department for Education and Skills (DfES) (2004) *Removing Barriers to Achievement: The Government Strategy for SEN*, Nottingham: DfES.

Hallett, F. and Hallett, G. (2010) *Transforming the Role of the SENCO*, Maidenhead: Open University Press.

House of Commons Education and Skills Committee (2006) *Special Educational Needs: Third Report of the Session 2005–06*, Vol. 1, HC478-1, London: The Stationery Office.

Layton, L. (2005) 'Special educational needs coordinators and leadership: a role too far?', *Support for Learning*, 20(2), 53–60.

Norwich, B. (1990) *Reappraising Special Needs Education*, London: Cassell Educational Ltd.

Pearson, S., Mitchell, R. and Rapti, M. (2014) 'I will be "fighting" even more for pupils with SEN: SENCOs' role predictions in the changing English policy context', *Journal of Research in Special Educational Needs*. Early view. http://onlinelibrary.wiley.com/doi/10.1111/1471-3802.12062/abstract (date accessed 5 December 2014).

Robertson, C. (2012) 'Special educational needs and disability co-ordination in a changing policy landscape: making sense of policy from a SENCO's perspective', *Support for Learning*, 27(2), 77–83.

Rosen-Webb, S.M. (2011) 'Nobody tells you how to be a SENCO', *British Journal of Special Education*, 38, 159–68.

Teacher Training Agency (TTA) (1998) *National Standards for Special Educational Needs Coordinators*, London: TTA.

FURTHER READING FURTHER READING FURTHER READING FURTHER READING

Pearson, S. (2008) *The Working Lives of SENCOs*, Tamworth: NASEN.

USEFUL WEBSITES USEFUL WEBSITES USEFUL WEBSITES USEFUL WEBSITES

www.nasen.org.uk/sen-research/

Concluding comments

The Code of Practice for SEN (DfE, 2014) aims to improve outcomes for children and young people with special educational needs and/or disabilities. The Code is outcome focused and it projects a clear message that with high expectation, high quality teaching and support, children and young people with SEND can achieve their aspirations, thus enabling them to lead fulfilling lives. No child or young person deserves to be failed by an education system which does not respond to the specific needs of individuals. The Code communicates a clear message that schools, teachers, parents and other agencies must work collaboratively to enable children and young people with SEND to achieve the best possible outcomes. The messages in the Code are both powerful and refreshing. It is clear from the evidence available that too many pupils with SEND are being let down by an education system which is not doing enough to meet their needs. Schools, teachers and other professionals need to work proactively to ensure that the education pupils with SEND receive is of high quality and targets areas of need precisely.

We do not underestimate the challenges ahead. Developing effective collaboration is not unproblematic and the new National Curriculum has increased expectations even further. Learners with SEND will only achieve their potential if they have teachers who believe in them and have faith that they can achieve. These teachers will engender the same belief in the child or young person and it is this 'can-do' culture which will help to eradicate notions of learned helplessness. As you go forward into your teaching career continue to believe in all of your learners. Good teachers never give up on a child. Continue to have high expectations of all those that you teach. Continue to deeply and rigorously reflect on your practice and be willing to make adaptations to your teaching so that you can respond effectively to the diverse needs of learners.

Finally, view diversity as an enriching, energising force which makes the world a more interesting place. View 'needs' within learners as your problem rather than as problems within the child. When learners make less than expected progress or are disengaged use this as an opportunity to consider how you might improve your teaching to enable them to make better progress or to re-engage them. Keep reflecting on your practice, keep thinking and keep talking to others. No one has all the solutions. There is no magic pill which will suddenly make a child learn more effectively. You are not expected to know all the answers to all the challenges you will face but collaborating with colleagues and parents will take you one step closer to meeting children's diverse needs. Enjoy learning about the learners that you teach as much as they enjoy learning from you.

REFERENCES REFERENCES **REFERENCES** REFERENCES **REFERENCES** REFERENCES

Department for Education (DfE) (2014) *Special Educational Needs and Disability Code of Practice: 0 to 25 Years: Statutory Guidance for Organisations Who Work With and Support Children and Young People with Special Educational Needs and Disabilities*, London: DfE.

Glossary

The definitions below have been taken directly from the *Special Educational Needs and Disability Code of Practice: 0 to 25 Years: Statutory Guidance for Organisations Who Work With and Support Children and Young People with Special Educational Needs and Disabilities* (London: DfE).

Child and Adolescent Mental Health Services (CAMHS)

These services assess and treat children and young people with emotional, behavioural or mental health difficulties. They range from basic pastoral care, such as identifying mental health problems, to specialist 'Tier 4' CAMHS, which provide in-patient care for those who are severely mentally ill.

Education, Health and Care plan (EHC plan)

An EHC plan details the education, health and social care support that is to be provided to a child or young person who has SEN or a disability. It is drawn up by the local authority after an EHC needs assessment of the child or young person has determined that an EHC plan is necessary, and after consultation with relevant partner agencies.

Equality Act

The Equality Act 2010 sets out the legal obligations that schools, early years providers, post-16 institutions, local authorities and others have towards disabled children and young people:

- They must not directly or indirectly discriminate against, harass or victimise disabled children and young people.
- They must make reasonable adjustments, including the provision of auxiliary aids and services, to ensure that disabled children and young people are not at a substantial disadvantage compared with their peers.

This duty is anticipatory – it requires thought to be given in advance to what disabled children and young people might require and what adjustments might need to be made to prevent that disadvantage.

The Equality Act 2010 prohibits schools from discriminating against disabled children and young people in respect of admissions for a reason related to their disability.

Graduated approach

This is a model of action and intervention in early education settings, schools and colleges to help children and young people who have special educational needs. The approach recognises that there is a continuum of special educational needs and that, where necessary, increasing specialist expertise should be brought to bear on the difficulties that a child or young person may be experiencing.

Local Offer

Local authorities in England are required to set out in their Local Offer information about provision they expect to be available across education, health and social care for children and young people in their area who have SEN or are disabled, including those who do not have Education, Health and Care (EHC) plans. Local authorities must consult locally on what provision the Local Offer should contain.

Personal Budget

A Personal Budget is an amount of money identified by the local authority to deliver provision set out in an EHC plan where the parent or young person is involved in securing that provision. The funds can be held directly by the parent or young person, or may be held and managed on their behalf by the local authority, school, college or other organisation or individual and used to commission the support specified in the EHC plan.

Special Educational Needs (SEN)

A child or young person has SEN if they have a learning difficulty or disability which calls for special educational provision to be made for him or her. A child of compulsory school age or a young person has a learning difficulty or disability if he or she has a significantly greater difficulty in learning than the majority of others of the same age, or has a disability which prevents or hinders him or her from making use of educational facilities of a kind generally provided for others of the same age in mainstream schools or mainstream post-16 institutions.

Special Educational Needs Co-ordinator (SENCO)

The SENCO is a qualified teacher in a school or maintained nursery school who has responsibility for co-ordinating SEN provision. In a small school, the head teacher or deputy may take on this role. In larger schools there may be a team of SENCOs.

SEN Support

Where a pupil is identified as having SEN, schools should take action to remove barriers to learning and put effective special educational provision in place. This SEN support should take the form of a four-part cycle through which earlier decisions and actions are revisited, refined and revised with a growing understanding of the pupil's needs and of what supports the pupil in making good progress and securing good outcomes. This is known as the graduated approach.

Index

Added to a page number 'g' denotes glossary.